Nº 03

Happy Cooking

Nigel
/x

NB.
HOW TO COOK

NIGEL BROWN

First published in 2015 in Great Britain by Nigel Brown.

Copyright © Nigel Brown

Photography by Tim Green,
copyright © 2015 Tim Green
www.timgreenphotographer.co.uk

Nigel Brown has asserted his right to be identified as the author of this work in accordance with the Copyright, Designs and Patents act 1998. All rights reserved.

No part of this publication may be reproduced, stored in a retrieval system, or transmitted in any form or by any means, electronic or mechanical, photocopying, recording or otherwise, without the prior permission of the copyright owners.

A catalogue record of this book is available from the British Library.

ISBN 9780993342707

Written by Nigel Brown
Photography by Tim Green
Designed by Anthony Hodgson
Edited by Jeannie Swales

Produced in association with Face Publications
www.facepublications.com

Printed and bound in China.

www.nigelbrownchef.co.uk

For my soulmate and best friend, Lisa

FOREWORD
JEAN-CHRISTOPHE NOVELLI.8

INTRODUCTION
NIGEL BROWN.12

PÂTÉS & TERRINES
CHAPTER 1.24

FISH & SHELLFISH
CHAPTER 2.38

MEAT, POULTRY & GAME
CHAPTER 3.60

SAVOURY PUDDINGS, PIES & CASSEROLES
CHAPTER 4.82

NICELY SPICY
CHAPTER 5.96

PIZZA & PASTA
CHAPTER 6.108

JUST DESSERTS
CHAPTER 7.120

CHOCOLATE & SUGAR WORK
CHAPTER 8.132

BREADS & SWEET DOUGHS
CHAPTER 9.146

SOMETHING FOR THE WEEKEND
CHAPTER 10.158

SEASONAL FAVOURITES
CHAPTER 11.170

AFTERNOON TEA
CHAPTER 12.188

ULTIMATE DINNER
CHAPTER 13.202

THE BASICS
CHAPTER 14.214

KITCHEN NOTES
254

SEASONAL INGREDIENTS
258

RECIPE INDEX
262

CREDITS
270

NB.
CONTENTS
HOW TO COOK

In the words of my dear, sadly departed, friend Keith Floyd, 'cooking is an art and patience is a virtue'. These words sprang to mind when I heard that Nigel had finally bitten the bullet and decided to share his much loved recipes.
He's been promising me for years that he would write his book and finally, like waiting for a fine wine to mature, it's ready to be savoured and enjoyed by all those who enjoy outstanding food.

From the first time I watched Nigel demonstrate on stage at a food festival I instinctively knew that this was a chef with a perfect combination of talent, integrity and sense of humour; all essential ingredients for a great ambassador of the culinary world. His gentle manner and quick-witted humour makes his teaching style relaxed and fun, which was why, that very first day I met him, I asked him to come and teach at my cookery school. The cheeky devil then opened his own academy and now only graces my kitchen with his presence to drink my coffee and eat my Hobnobs.

We've worked together ever since at festivals and events and I really look forward to our double-act demonstrations where we can cook, laugh and chat together – Nigel keeps me on my toes. He's a great practical joker and once swapped the water in the on-stage tap for red wine and wafted plumes of dry ice smoke from behind my oven, but it's all done with affection and makes great entertainment.

To some people food is an all-consuming passion. Some love scouring the country, or indeed the world, looking for the latest fashionable ingredients, or spend hours in the kitchen creating a masterpiece worthy of a Michelin star or two. Others just love to eat; it doesn't matter whether it's a seven-course taster menu or simply a chip butty, it's the sight and taste that hits the spot.

But if you ask Nigel whether it's the cooking or the eating that excites him, he'll tell you it's neither: it's the company that's the vital ingredient. To create, cook and present a dish, made and eaten with love: that's what makes a good meal into a great meal. It doesn't matter to Nigel whether he's eating alone or with family and friends. What does matter is the pleasure it creates.

This is more than just a book of recipes.
This is a book full of Nigel's heart and soul, his passion, the very essence of his being. He's a Yorkshireman and when he says he's going to do something he does it with quiet determination and his trademark charm and grace.

This may be the first cookery book in your collection or you may have 1001 stashed away in cabinets, on shelves, or under the bed: but this is the book you need in your kitchen and close at hand. It brings you all the information you will need to create basic recipes through to sophisticated dining, and will inspire you to create your own food heaven to share with those you love.

Nigel is an amazing chef who sticks closely to his traditional roots and classical training, and I'm proud to say he and Lisa, his wife, are very dear, long-standing friends of mine.

Now with Nigel's recipes firmly in my grip my patience has been rewarded.

NB.
FOREWORD

JEAN-CHRISTOPHE NOVELLI

AFTER MUCH DELIBERATION, I'VE FINALLY PERSUADED MYSELF TO DO WHAT SO MANY OTHERS HAVE DONE BEFORE: WRITE A COOKBOOK. WILL IT BE THE FIRST OF MANY? WHO KNOWS… MANY HAVE TRIED SOME HAVE FAILED; SOME HAVE MANAGED TO GET THEIR ACHIEVEMENTS IN THE KITCHEN INTO THE BOOKSHOPS. SOME BOOKS HAVE BEEN CAREFULLY SELECTED AND BOUGHT, AND SOMETIMES LOVINGLY GIFT-WRAPPED. THEN, JUST A MATTER OF MONTHS LATER, THEY'VE ENDED UP BACK IN THE CAR BOOT TO BE SOLD ON A COLD AND MISERABLE SUNDAY MORNING BECAUSE THEY JUST DIDN'T CUT THE MUSTARD.

I've either created or reconstructed all of these recipes over the years, and they've been enjoyed by many. Some are true culinary classics; some are the result of experimentation or just pure indulgence on my part. However they came about though, I love them all and wanted to share them with you. I hope that you'll enjoy this book enough to keep it in your collection and use it again and again.

Throughout the book, you'll find everything from asparagus to zabaglione, with some really great classic recipes that have almost become extinct these days, such as salmon coulibiac: a great classic and a fabulous recipe to revive.

You'll be able to recreate all the recipes at home for your family and friends. You won't need to go and buy a special temperature-controlled water bath or get yourself certified to use liquid nitrogen for making ice cream. It's all just good quality ingredients, cooked traditionally and presented well – just how they should be.

You'll find stories from my life in food, hopefully making each chapter a little more colourful, from my early days as a young child, through the journey that brought me to what I've become today. Hopefully, some of these stories will unlock your own recollections.

And finally… all the recipes in this book have been written and cooked by me and tried and tested by all who worked tirelessly during the photography and production of this book. Now it's your turn!

Happy cooking.

NB.
INTRO-
DUCTION

NIGEL BROWN

HARD WORK PAYS, OR SO THEY SAY! WHEN I WAS ABOUT 13 THAT WAS ONE OF THE LAST PHRASES ON MY MIND. BUT, HARD WORK WAS SOMETHING I WAS ALREADY FAMILIAR WITH. FROM AN EARLY AGE I WORKED IN THE FAMILY BUSINESS ALONG WITH MY TWO OLDER BROTHERS AND YOUNGER SISTER. IT WAS A FABULOUS AND WELL-RESPECTED ESTABLISHMENT CALLED THE FOUR WINDS RESTAURANT, JUST OUTSIDE DRIFFIELD IN EAST YORKSHIRE.

Brown Crab on Toast

INGREDIENTS:
Serves 4

250g freshly picked crabmeat
50g mayonnaise
juice of 1 lemon
10ml Worcestershire sauce
pinch of cayenne
pinch of salt and ground black pepper
4 slices of tomato bread (or similar)
100g parmesan
small bunch of chopped tarragon

METHOD:

Place the crabmeat, mayonnaise, lemon juice, Worcestershire sauce, cayenne pepper and seasoning in a bowl and bind together.

Toast the bread slices and divide the crab between the slices, spreading thickly and evenly.

Sprinkle generously with parmesan and place under the grill for 3 minutes or until browned.

Sprinkle with chopped tarragon and serve.

During my school years I remember having a meeting with the careers officer at school as I was nearing my final days there. She didn't ask: "What would you like to be?" Instead, she said: "Your parents have a restaurant, so you'd like to be a chef?" "Er, yes, miss!" I replied, and so catering college it was.

I followed my two brothers' footsteps to Hull College to do my two years' full-time catering training. The years passed by in Hull and out popped another trained chef into the family workforce, with high aspirations but little confidence to face the larger world of catering beyond the family business.

Not content with just the basic training that I'd received at Hull College, I also attended Grimsby College to enrich my skills in the patisserie section and Scarborough Technical College to enhance my kitchen and larder skills. These two courses, better known then as the City and Guilds 706-3, were in the culinary world the equivalent to Her Majesty's elite SAS training.

Another three years' training under my belt; just one more to go. Not catering this time though: teacher training at Beverley College. That should sort out my self-confidence issues! What an eye-opener that was…

I'd realised by this time that I had just spent seven years at college: I could have studied to be a doctor in the same time. Oh well, never mind: we all need to eat!

In 1988 I broke free, left home and headed off in the direction of London, ending up amid the bright lights of Middlesex and Heathrow. Believe me, it was no holiday. I was interviewed and shown the kitchens of an 800-bed hotel with conference catering for 1,000. One of the bedrooms was to be my home; I literally started work there the next day. Reality had kicked in!

The executive chef must have seen something promising in me as my entry into his kitchen was as junior sauce chef – sixth in line for his job in the à la carte restaurant kitchen. Talk about pressure! It was all there and I couldn't afford to get myself into a pickle.

The restaurant's à la carte dining room overlooked the runway at Heathrow. This was in the days when Concorde was flying from Heathrow – what a sight that was. I was very lucky to experience it every day.

I survived my first week at the hotel. Even sharing a bedroom with the night porter didn't put me off. After six months, and hungry for change and more cash – I looked for a new challenge. I'd impressed the executive chef in the six months, so I asked for a promotion and pay rise.

That paid off: a pay rise and a title upgrade to senior sauce chef. Chef was so impressed with my skills that he wrote me a glowing reference for my next challenge as pastry chef de partie in another top Heathrow hotel, The Excelsior, one of Trust House Forte's 'grand' hotels.

I found myself working in a fantastic pastry kitchen alongside a great Italian head pastry chef called Marcello Pocaterra.

It was a struggle to understand Marcello at first, but in time it got easier. We worked well together and he too liked my style and commitment to the job. He had a cupboard in the pastry kitchen that he kept locked at all times, even when he was working! On his days off he would only let Manfred Ingenhurst, the executive chef, and me have the key. He kept his hand-made chocolates and petit fours in there. I felt honoured that I was allowed to be a key holder in his absence.

A one-month secondment at Lenôtre, a highly-acclaimed patisserie school in Paris, was next on the cards – and all thanks to Marcello, who pushed my boundaries even further.

When Marcello retired to move back to Italy, I took over the reins as head pastry chef: not bad for a quiet, shy lad from East Yorkshire.

Twenty-three years on and I'm still donning the chef's jacket. There've been lots of ups and downs along the way, from teaching in colleges to running my own fine dining catering business and now a rather successful cookery school with more than the occasional cookery demonstration.

I've been extremely fortunate too: over the years I've been offered many things to promote during my appearances, from superfoods to supercars!

Requests for a cookbook have been frequent and I've got a television series under my belt too that was screened to 136 countries around the world. I've worked with most of the nation's favourite chefs – or maybe they've worked with me!

Along the way I've also been lucky enough to enjoy a friendship spanning more years than I care to remember with an overwhelmingly kind and generous man who also happens to be a great chef: Jean-Christophe Novelli.

My life so far has been amazing. I've gone from being the shyest boy in school to producing a set of cookery DVDs and screen testing for BBC2's Ready Steady Cook. I've catered for the legendary Nelson Mandela and for royalty, opened a cookery school, been the anchorman of a global TV cookery series, and now I'm the author of a cook book.

It's true what they say about life in the kitchen: long unsocial hours, split shifts, low pay, hot environments, fiery temperaments, growling chefs and managers with scary budget demands. A life in catering can be hard work and can seem relentless and unrewarding. But like any profession, hard work does pay rewards. You just have to stick at it, push yourself into the unknown and believe in yourself. I'm the proof of the pudding!

IT WAS LIKE THE SAS OF CATERING TRAINING BUT TO BE ONE OF KEN ALLINSON'S MEN AT COLLEGE IS AN HONOUR IN MY BOOK! MY COLLEGE DAYS ARE WAY BEHIND ME, BUT KEN'S COURSE IS IN MY THOUGHTS EVERY TIME I COOK. WITH MY TWO YEARS' BASIC CATERING TRAINING COMPLETED, IT WAS ONWARDS, UPWARDS AND BACK TO COLLEGE AGAIN FOR A FEW MORE YEARS; THIS TIME, ALL PART-TIME COURSES WHILST I WAS CHEFFING AT THE FAMILY BUSINESS, THE FOUR WINDS RESTAURANT.

Pâtés

CHICKEN LIVER PÂTÉ.26
DUCK LIVER PÂTÉ.28
MUSHROOM PÂTÉ.30

Terrines

CHICKEN AND HAM TERRINE.32
GAME TERRINE.34
SMOKED SALMON, CRAB AND WATERCRESS TERRINE.36

With a little persuasion I enrolled on the City and Guilds Advance Kitchen and Larder course at Scarborough Technical College. Both my two older brothers had completed and passed this course, so I knew failure wasn't an option.

It didn't help my nerves when my brothers came home from a gruelling day at college telling me that Ken, the senior course tutor, was an ex-forces chap who was extremely keen on discipline and good timing. Perfection was his middle name!

The course was tough: the SAS of catering training. Staying power and real determination to succeed were needed to become one of Ken's men. Not many had what it took and numbers dwindled each week until just an elite handful of us remained.

With the written exam paper done, the last hurdle was a simple matter of a six-hour practical cookery exam with Ken and the City and Guilds examiner. They hovered over the four or five of us like Chinook helicopters in a war zone, armed and with twitchy fingers over the firing button.

After what seemed like a lifetime the results were in; I'd earned my place as one of 'Ken's men'. Just how proud was I? I'd done it at last! Ken, now retired, still tells the story of how all three of the Brown brothers passed with him, an achievement in itself.

Ken instilled discipline and a drive for perfection in me. It still makes the hairs on the back of my neck prickle at the mere thought of doing it all again. Would I do it again? I do, every day when I'm cooking!

Thanks Ken.

Ken was definitely a savoury man at heart, so this chapter is dedicated to him and would be right up his street!

NB.
PÂTÉS & TERRINES

CHAPTER 1

Chicken Liver Pâté

INGREDIENTS:
Serves 4

10g salted butter, for frying
2 large shallots, peeled and finely chopped
2 cloves of garlic, peeled and crushed
60ml brandy
200g chicken livers
pinch of salt and ground black pepper
150ml double cream
100g salted butter, diced
20g melted butter

METHOD:

Place the 10g of salted butter in a thick-bottomed pan and melt it on a medium heat. Add the shallots and garlic and cook for 3 minutes until golden brown.

Add the brandy and ignite it with a naked flame to burn off the alcohol. Add the chicken livers and cook through thoroughly.

Remove the mixture from the pan, cool slightly, then place in a food processor. Season with salt and pepper, add the double cream and blitz. Gradually add the diced butter to the pâté in the food processor until it's blended through.

Spoon the pâté into suitable pots and level the surface. Pour the melted butter over to seal the pots.

Duck Liver Pâté

INGREDIENTS:
Serves 4

10g salted butter, for frying
2 large shallots, peeled and finely chopped
2 cloves of garlic, peeled and crushed
50ml port
50ml red wine
50ml medium sherry
200g duck livers
pinch of salt and ground black pepper
150ml double cream
100g butter, diced
4 slices of fresh orange
4 fresh bay leaves
20g melted butter

METHOD:

Place the 10g of salted butter in a thick-bottomed pan and melt on a medium heat. Add the shallots and garlic and cook for 3 minutes until golden brown.

Add the port, red wine and sherry and ignite with a naked flame to burn off the alcohol, then add the duck livers and cook through thoroughly.

Remove the mixture from the pan, cool slightly then place into a food processor. Season with salt and pepper, add the double cream and blitz. Gradually add the diced butter to the pâté in the food processor until it's blended through.

Spoon the pâté into suitable pots and level the surface. Place a thin slice of fresh orange and a bay leaf on each pot of pâté before pouring on the melted butter to seal the pots.

Mushroom Pâté

INGREDIENTS:
Serves 4

10g salted butter, for frying
1 onion, finely chopped
500g portobello mushrooms, finely chopped
pinch of cayenne pepper
pinch of grated nutmeg
60ml port
60ml brandy
150g mascarpone cheese
100g salted butter, diced
20g melted butter

METHOD:

Place the 10g of salted butter in a thick-bottomed pan and melt it on a medium heat. Add the onion and fry until golden brown.

Add the portobello mushrooms, cayenne pepper and nutmeg and cook until all the moisture has evaporated. Add the port and brandy and ignite with a naked flame to remove the alcohol, then add the mascarpone cheese and the diced salted butter. Stir until the cheese and butter have melted.

Cool, stirring occasionally. When the pâté is cold, spoon into suitable pots and seal the tops with melted butter.

Chicken and Ham Terrine

INGREDIENTS:
Serves 4

200ml chicken stock, see page 218
25g leeks, diced
25g carrots, diced
25g celery, diced
pinch of ground black pepper
3g leaf gelatine
150g chicken breast, cooked and diced
150g gammon, cooked and diced
20g leaves of tarragon

METHOD:

Place the chicken stock in a pan with the leeks, carrots, celery and pepper. Bring to the boil and simmer until the vegetables are cooked to a soft crunch.

Soak the gelatine leaves in a dish of cold water for 5 minutes.

Line a small terrine dish with cling film.

When the vegetables are cooked, remove from the pan and set to one side. Take the pan off the heat and stir in the softened gelatine leaves.

Randomly assemble the chicken, gammon and vegetables into the terrine dish with the tarragon leaves. Flood the terrine with the warm cooking liquid to cover the ingredients. Cool, cover, and refrigerate for 24 hours.

Serve sliced with a little fresh mustard.

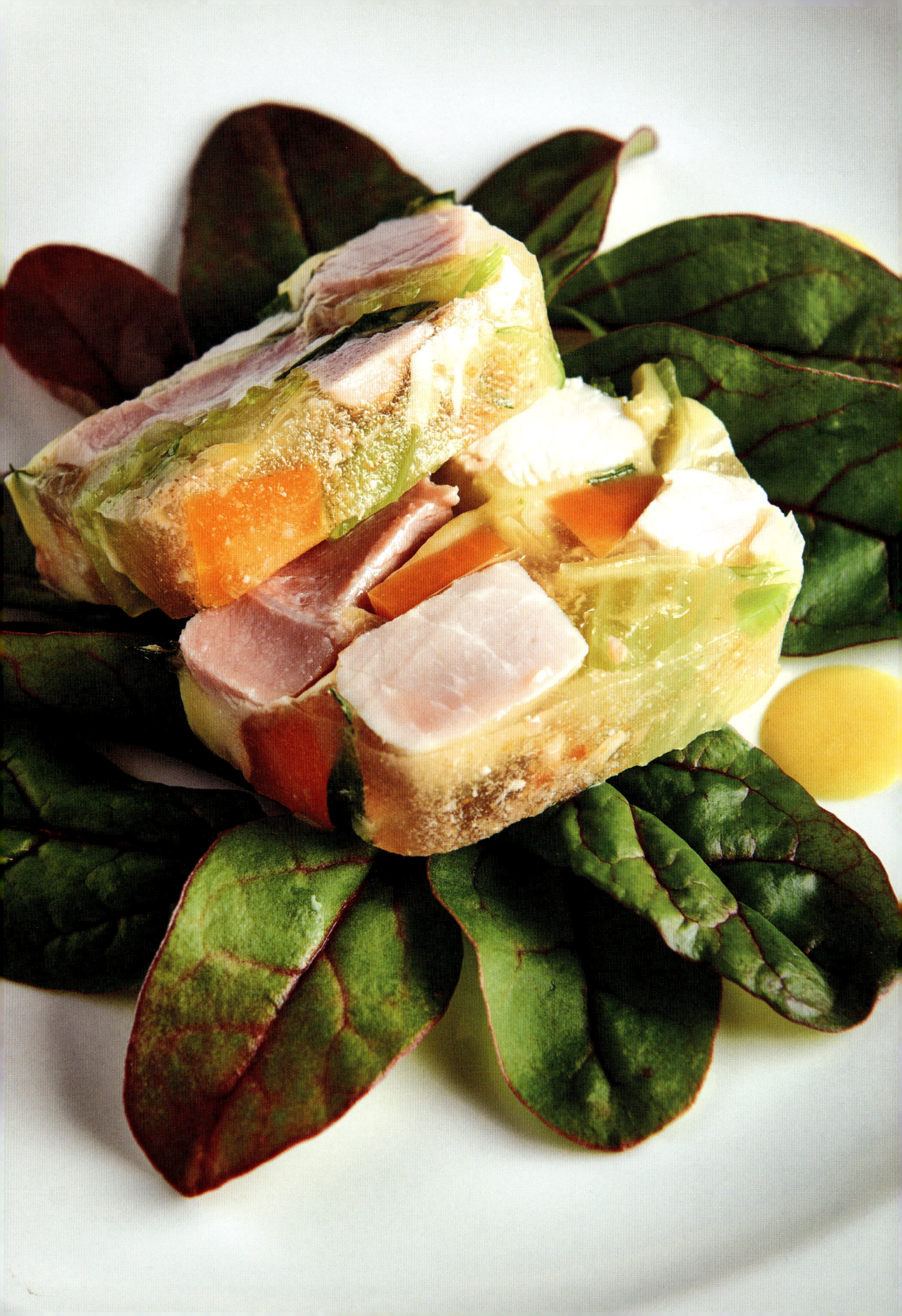

Game Terrine

INGREDIENTS:
Serves 4

1 breast of pheasant
2 breasts of pigeon
1 breast of duck
1 saddle of rabbit
100g venison fillet
8 quail's eggs, hard-boiled for 4 minutes and shelled

For the forcemeat
100g sausagemeat
10g parsley, finely chopped
leaves from 2 sprigs of thyme, chopped
5-6 juniper berries, crushed
2 cloves garlic, finely chopped
pinch of salt and ground black pepper

To line the dish
300g pancetta

METHOD:

Slice the pheasant, pigeon, duck, rabbit and venison into thin strips and set to one side.

For the forcemeat, mix the sausagemeat with the parsley, thyme, crushed juniper berries and chopped garlic and season with salt and pepper. Line a suitable terrine dish, or small loaf tin, with the pancetta, slightly overlapping each slice and leave an overhang around the edges and ends of the dish to fold over the terrine at the end. Fill the terrine by layering the game meat, quail's eggs and sausagemeat in a random fashion until you have a domed effect on top of the dish.

Fold over the excess pancetta strips to seal the dish. Cover with foil and bake in the oven at 180°C for approximately 1 hour or until the juices run clear.

Allow to cool before slicing the terrine into 8 portions and serve with pickles or chutney.

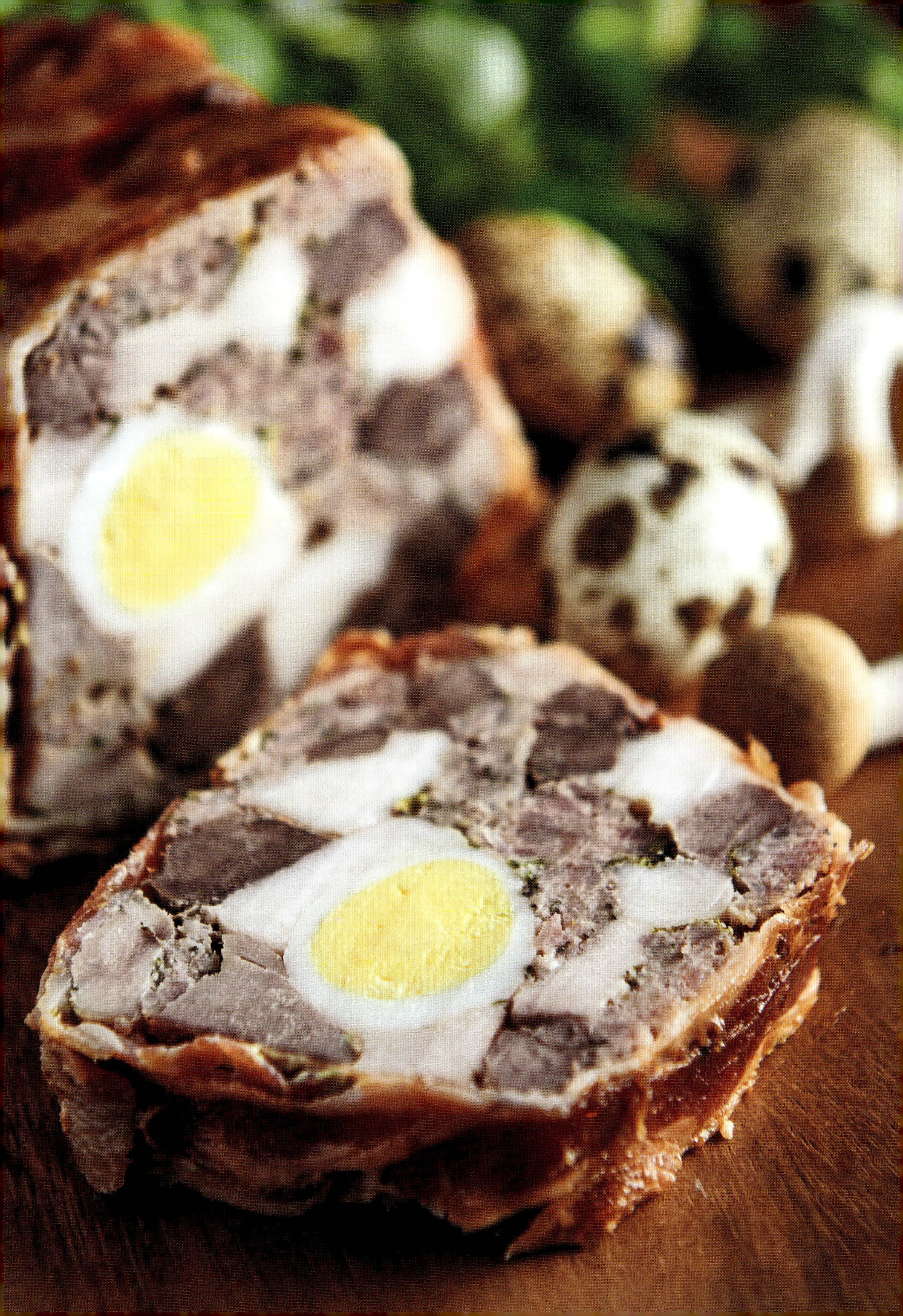

Smoked Salmon, Crab and Watercress Terrine

INGREDIENTS:
Serves 4

150g smoked salmon slices
100g watercress, stems removed, chopped
20g fresh dill, finely chopped
100g cream cheese
1 lemon, finely grated, zest only
pinch of salt and ground black pepper
100g brown crabmeat

METHOD:

Line a small terrine dish, or small loaf tin, with cling film.

Finely chop the smoked salmon slices and lay neatly at the bottom of the terrine dish.

Combine the watercress, cream cheese, dill, lemon zest and then season. Layer this on top of the salmon.

Cut the lemon in half, squeeze the juice into the brown crabmeat and pack this on top of the watercress mousse in the terrine.

Fold over the cling film and firmly compress all the ingredients by hand. Refrigerate for 24 hours before serving.

Serve sliced with either cooked samphire or salad leaves.

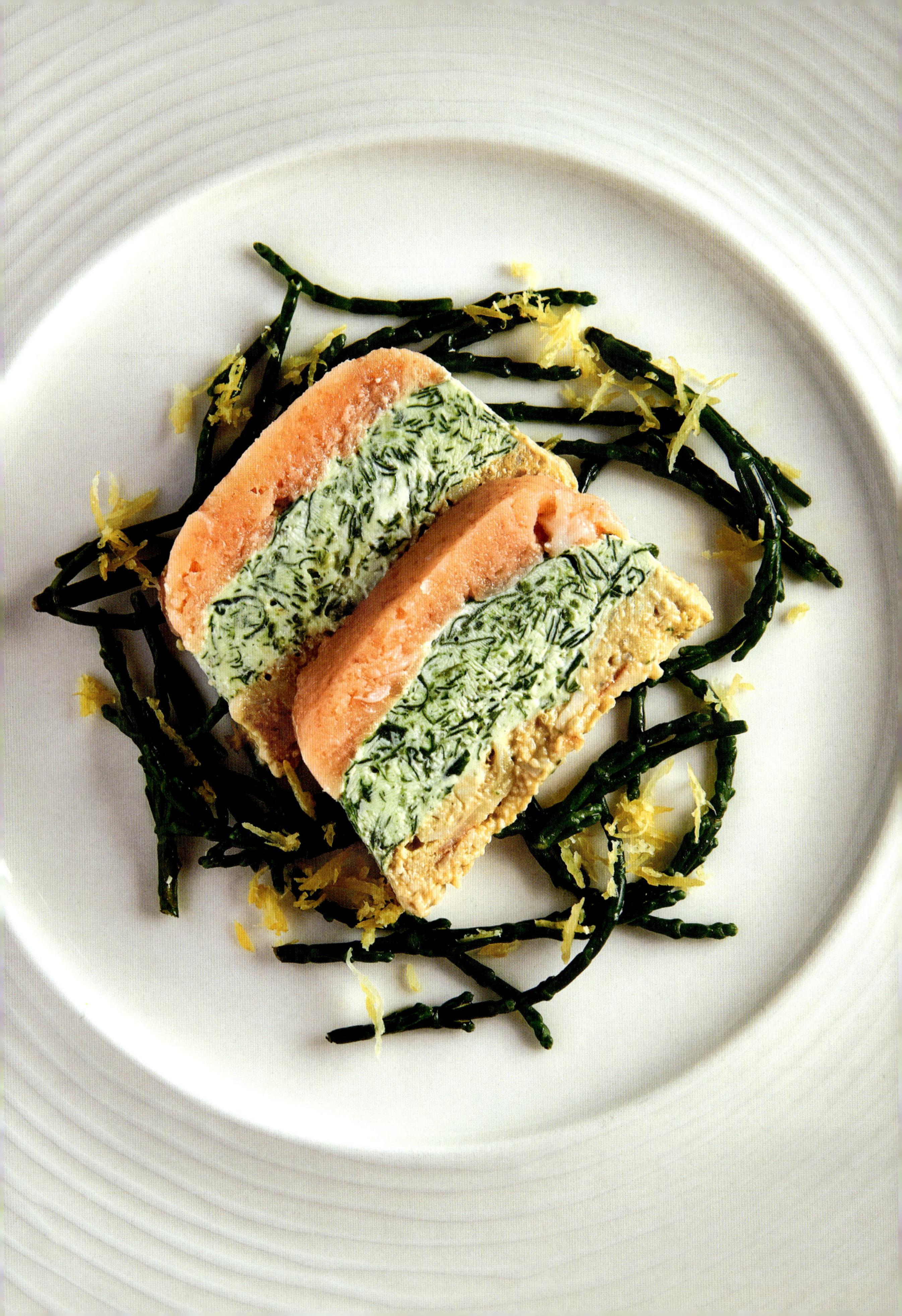

I LOVE FISH. BUT THERE'S A HUGE DIFFERENCE BETWEEN COOKING IT, AND CATCHING IT – AND I'M TALKING FROM EXPERIENCE HERE. MANY YEARS AGO MY TWO BROTHERS AND I GOT THE CHANCE TO GO SEA FISHING: A MORNING'S SAILING FROM BRIDLINGTON.

Fish

OMELETTE ARNOLD BENNETT.40
PAN-FRIED SEA BASS WITH BEURRE NOISETTE.42
POACHED FILLET OF PLAICE VERONIQUE.44
POACHED FILLET OF SALMON WITH MUSHROOM REDUCTION SAUCE.46
SMOKED MACKEREL FISHCAKES.48

Shellfish

BROWN CRAB ON TOAST.50
BRIDLINGTON BAY DRESSED BROWN CRAB.52
HOT LOBSTER SALAD.54
LOBSTER THERMIDOR.56
SEARED SCALLOPS WITH ASPARAGUS SPEARS AND SAFFRON SAUCE.58

The anticipation of catching our own cod, haddock, plaice, lemon sole and mackerel to take back to our family restaurant and cook was great. The competition was set between the three of us with the agreement that the day's loser would pay for our well-earned fish and chips at the end.

We arrived bright and early for the morning sailing in a small fishing coble out of Bridlington harbour. We were due to drop anchor just off Flamborough Head at around 9am. Three teenage brothers suitably kitted out in wellies and woolies, having a day out together, and for once, fishing, not fighting. Sounds great so far, doesn't it?

But not only was our anchor due to sink; so were our hearts. The skipper was all set, as were we; however, he was just waiting for nine keen fishermen from West Yorkshire to arrive.

They turned up eventually with enough fishing kit to stock a shop and potentially sink our coble. That was the least of our worries; if we capsized we could swim to shore from Flamborough Head.

All aboard, and off we sailed out of the harbour and into the open sea, bobbing up and down. It was getting choppy and the swell was starting to kick in for me. But that feeling of queasiness was surely bearable for a three-hour trip?

Being the shyest and youngest lad on the coble, I kept myself to myself, and my two brothers and I prepared our rods and lines with bait.

This was our first sea fishing trip, so you can imagine our delight when we heard the skipper chatting to the nine burly fishermen and saying that by the time we got back to harbour at 4 in the afternoon, we should have buckets full of fish to land. My maths wasn't great, but even I could work out that that was no three-hour fishing trip. It meant a full day at sea. With a churning stomach just 20 minutes in, I was having visions of the skipper having to call out the lifeboat to rescue me. If there's a world record for lying on a fishing coble's deck, I think I hold that title. Suffice to say, I experienced every shade of green, I caught no fish at all and I had to pay for our fish and chips.

NB.
FISH & SHELLFISH

CHAPTER 2

Omelette Arnold Bennett

INGREDIENTS:
Serves 4

20g unsalted butter
100g smoked haddock, diced
100ml whole milk
100ml double cream
2 fresh bay leaves
1 lemon, zested and juiced
55g parmesan, finely grated
pinch of salt and ground black pepper
20g salted butter
30ml rapeseed oil
3 large free-range eggs, beaten
a small bunch fresh chives, finely chopped
small bunch of fresh watercress

METHOD:

In a pan, melt the unsalted butter and add the smoked haddock, milk, double cream, bay leaves, lemon zest and juice and parmesan. Season with salt and pepper and cook on a medium heat until the haddock flakes and separates.

In a separate pan, heat the salted butter and rapeseed oil together until sizzling. Beat the eggs with the chopped chives and add to the pan, stirring continuously, until the mixture starts to cook and form an omelette.

Once the omelette is cooked remove it from the pan and fill with the smoked haddock mixture.

Serve with a small bunch of watercress and a drizzle of rapeseed oil.

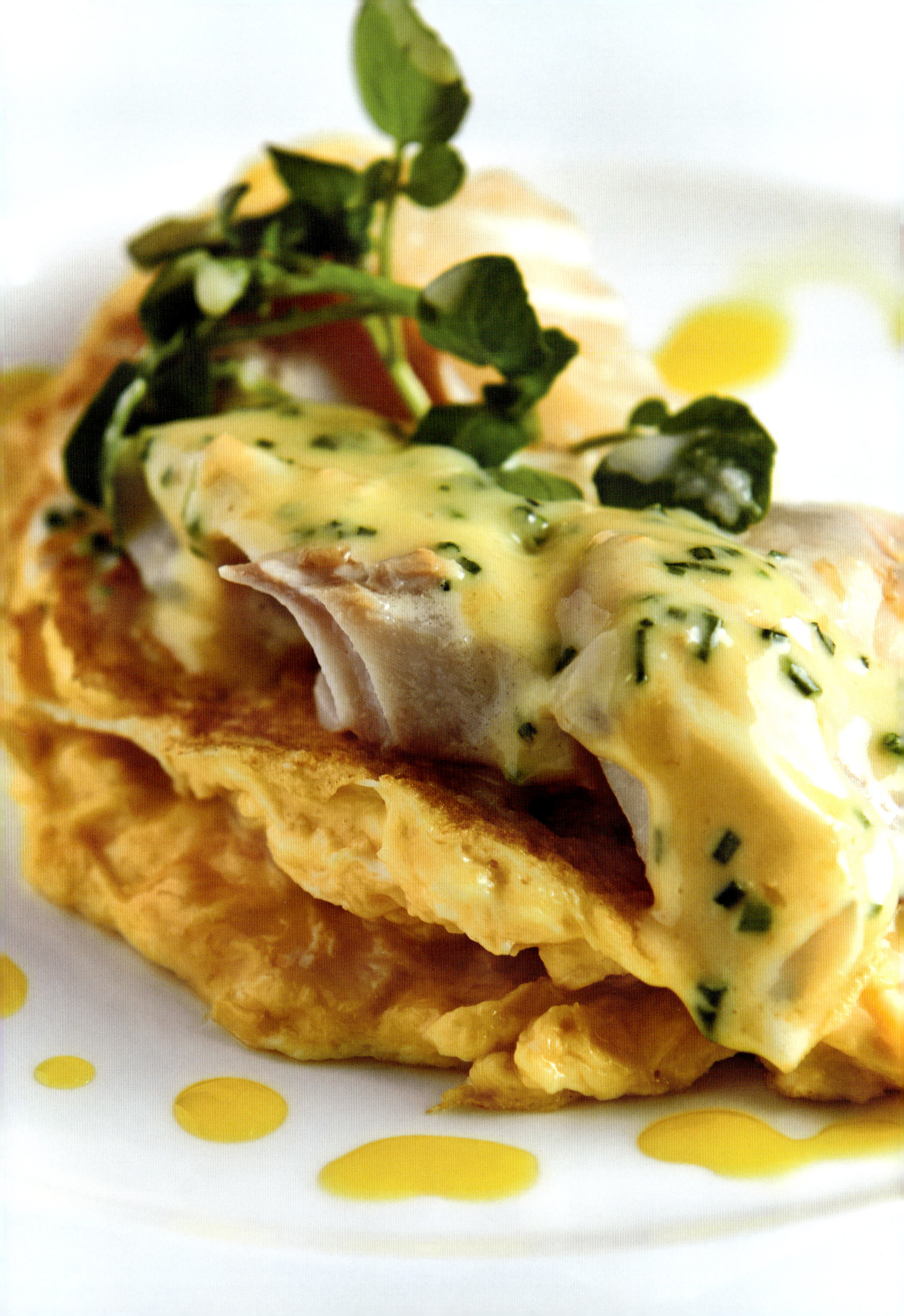

Pan-Fried Sea Bass with Beurre Noisette

INGREDIENTS:
Serves 4

4 x sea bass fillets, de-boned and skin on
60g plain flour seasoned with salt and pepper
20ml rapeseed oil
75g unsalted butter
20g curly parsley, finely chopped
juice of 1 lemon

METHOD:

Coat both sides of the sea bass fillets in the seasoned flour.

Heat the rapeseed oil in a pan and place the fillets in the pan, skin side down. Cook for 2 minutes then turn them over.

Add the butter, curly parsley and then the lemon juice. Cook until the butter foams and takes on a nut-brown colour.

Remove from the pan and serve with a drizzle of the butter.

This is great served with steamed brocolli and new potatoes.

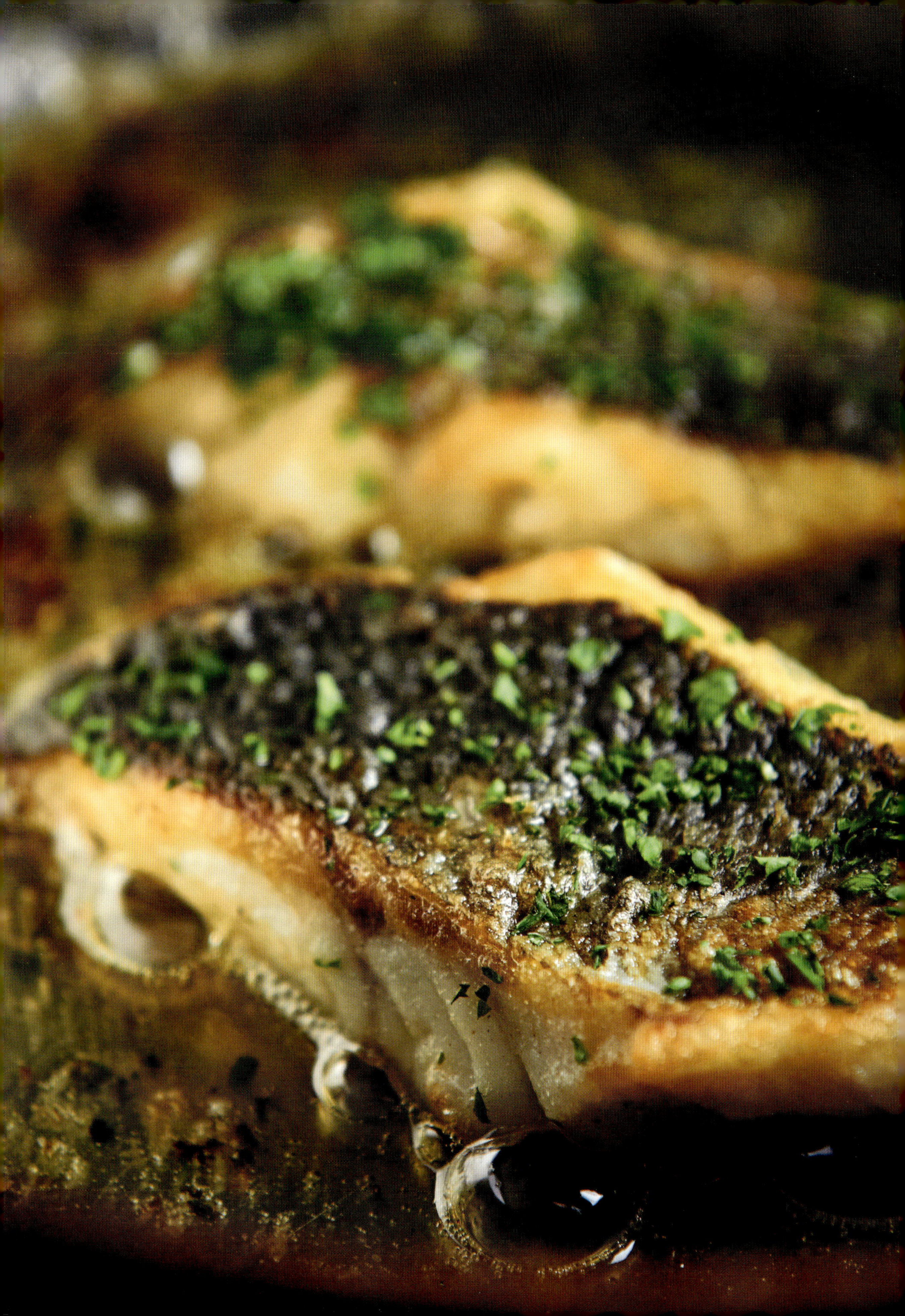

Poached Fillet of Plaice Véronique

INGREDIENTS:
Serves 4

4 fresh plaice fillets, skinned and boned
150ml dry white wine
4 small shallots, finely chopped
24 seedless green grapes
3 parsley stalks
1 bay leaf
1 slice of lemon
20g butter
40g plain flour
200ml fish stock, see page 220
150ml double cream
pinch of salt and ground black pepper
small bunch of curly parsley,
    finely chopped

METHOD:

Roll the plaice fillets into barrels, skin side in, and secure with cocktail sticks.

In a shallow sauté pan, add the wine, shallots, grapes, parsley stalks, bay leaf and lemon and place on the heat. Just before the liquid simmers, add the rolled plaice fillets and cover with a lid. Bring to the simmering point, turn the heat off and leave to one side with the lid on.

Place the butter in a separate pan and heat. When it has melted stir in the flour to make a paste. Add the fish stock, stirring or whisking continuously to avoid any lumps forming, and a ladle of the cooking liquid from the plaice along with the double cream. Reduce the sauce by half and season with the salt and pepper.

Remove the plaice and grapes from the pan and put on your plates. Serve with the sauce and chopped parsley.

This dish is great with seasonal vegetables and potatoes.

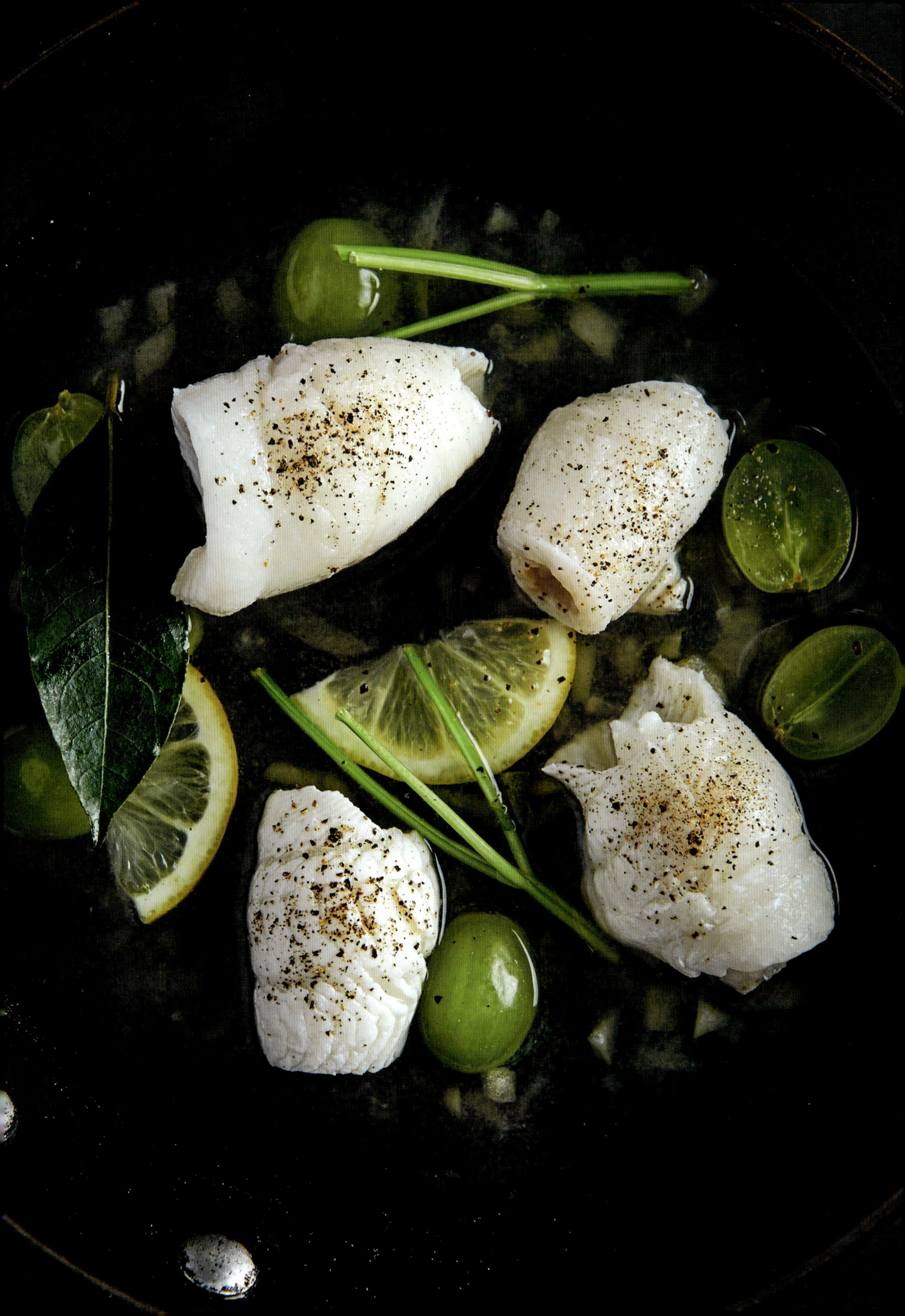

Poached Fillet of Salmon with Mushroom Reduction Sauce

INGREDIENTS:
Serves 4

200ml dry white wine
2 bay leaves
small bunch of parsley stalks
1 slice of lemon
1 stick of celery, sliced or diced
2 shallots, peeled, halved and diced
4 x 250g salmon fillets, skinned and boned
pinch of salt
pinch of white pepper
200ml fish stock, see page 220
16 button mushrooms
200ml double cream
40g unsalted butter, cubed
80g samphire, steamed and buttered

METHOD:

Place the white wine, bay leaves, parsley stalks, lemon, celery and shallots in a pan and warm gently. When the cooking liquid is warm (not simmering), add the salmon portions, skin side down, and season with salt and pepper.

Place a lid on the pan and continue cooking until it begins to simmer. At the point of simmering, turn the heat off and leave the pan to one side with the lid still on.

Place another pan on the heat and add the fish stock, button mushrooms and double cream. Carefully take a ladle of the cooking liquid from the salmon pan and add this to the mushroom sauce. Continue cooking until the liquid has reduced by two-thirds. Gradually add the unsalted butter, one cube at a time, until the sauce has taken on a glossy, thickened, rich appearance.

Remove the salmon portions from the cooking liquid, place on a bed of steamed and buttered samphire and serve with a drizzle of the mushroom reduction sauce.

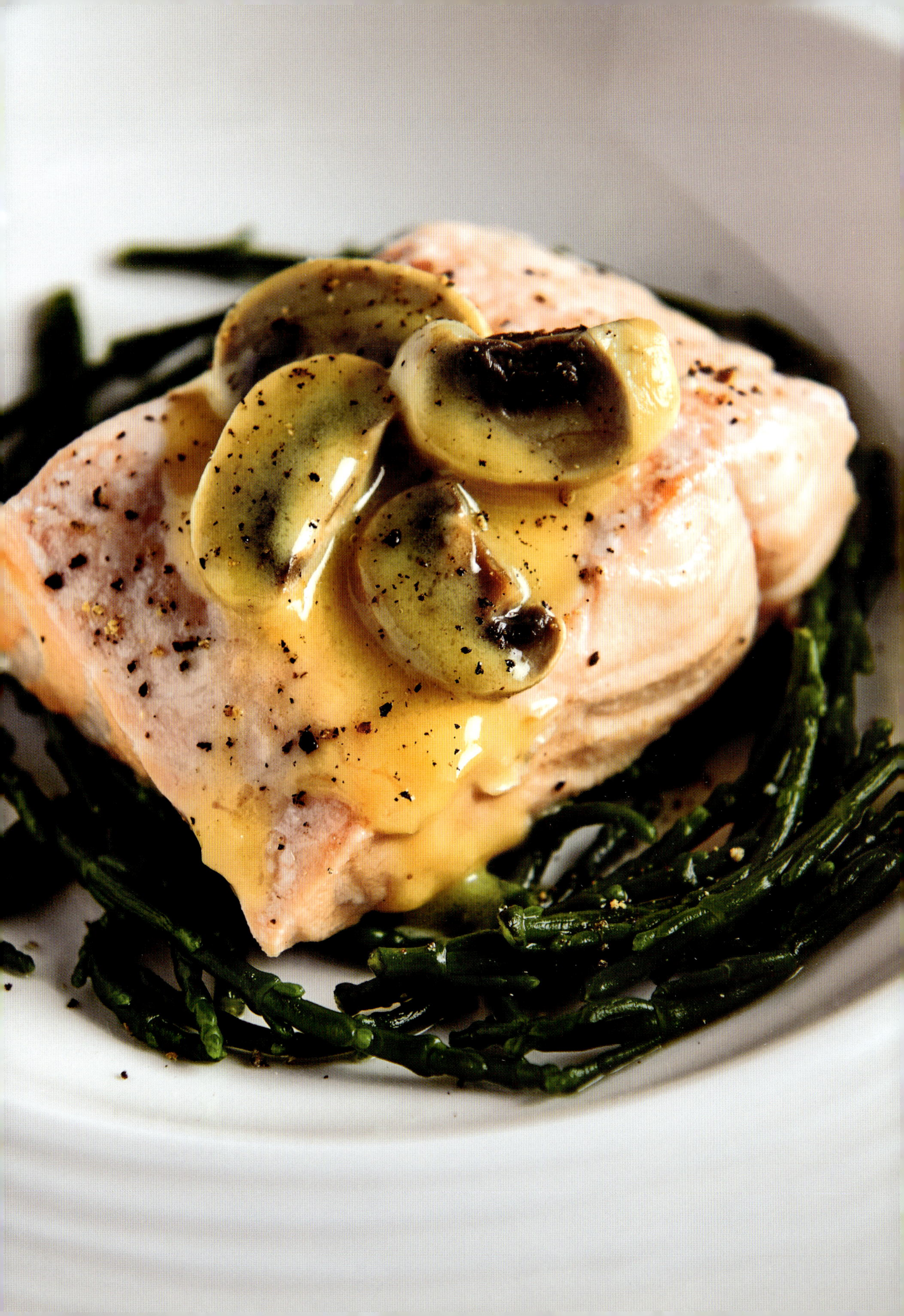

Smoked Mackerel Fishcakes

INGREDIENTS:
Serves 4

300g potatoes, peeled, boiled
   and mashed
30g hot horseradish sauce
500g smoked mackerel fillets,
   skinned and diced
1 bunch spring onions, finely chopped
20g fresh tarragon, chopped
pinch of salt and ground black pepper
60g plain flour, seasoned with salt
   and ground black pepper
2 whole free range eggs, beaten
200g fresh wholemeal breadcrumbs
300ml sunflower oil, for shallow frying
1 lemon
1 small bunch of fresh parsley, chopped

METHOD:

In a large mixing bowl combine the potatoes, horseradish sauce, diced mackerel, spring onions, tarragon and seasoning.

Divide and shape the mixture into 8 fishcakes.

Coat the fishcakes in flour, then egg, then breadcrumbs and reshape if necessary.

Shallow fry the fishcakes in the sunflower oil for just a minute on each side. Transfer to a baking tray and bake in the oven at 180°C for approximately 12 minutes.

Serve with freshly sliced lemon and chopped parsley.

This book is dedicated to my parents who, over the years, have been there to help, guide and advise me with the utmost of unconditional love and affection. To my children for their help and support. To those who've unknowingly helped me through my journey of life's trials and tribulations of which there have been many! To my good friend Jean-Christophe who has been so supportive and kind, and finally to Lisa, my wife, who saw the potential in me not only as a husband, soulmate and best friend, but also as someone with the drive and passion to succeed.

Lisa, this book is a culmination of both our visions, commitment, hard work, early starts and the latest of nights. You've had to listen to me ramble on about my ideas for years, this book being the latest! It's not just another cookery book Lisa: it's everything that we stand for and our recipe for success.

Special thanks to Tim Green, whose photography has brought every recipe in this book to life through his unique way of capturing the true essence of the dishes and ingredients that I've produced and used. From specialist location shoots to hot and steamy kitchens, Tim's dedication to his work and his unquestionable expertise can be clearly seen throughout this book through his ability to create the most stunning imagery.

Thanks also to Anthony Hodgson at Face Publications, whose ability to bring this book to life through his vision and understanding of the complexities that were faced when my initial thoughts were discussed, is truly inspirational.

The design and delivery has been managed seamlessly and certainly shows in the end results that you are now holding. No corners have been cut, no stones left unturned in the quest to use the highest standard of materials.

And finally, thanks to Dan Wright for all his help prepping ingredients for the photography, and to Nick Green at Villeroy & Boch who kindly supplied all of the crockery for the photography.

NB.
CREDITS

HOW TO COOK

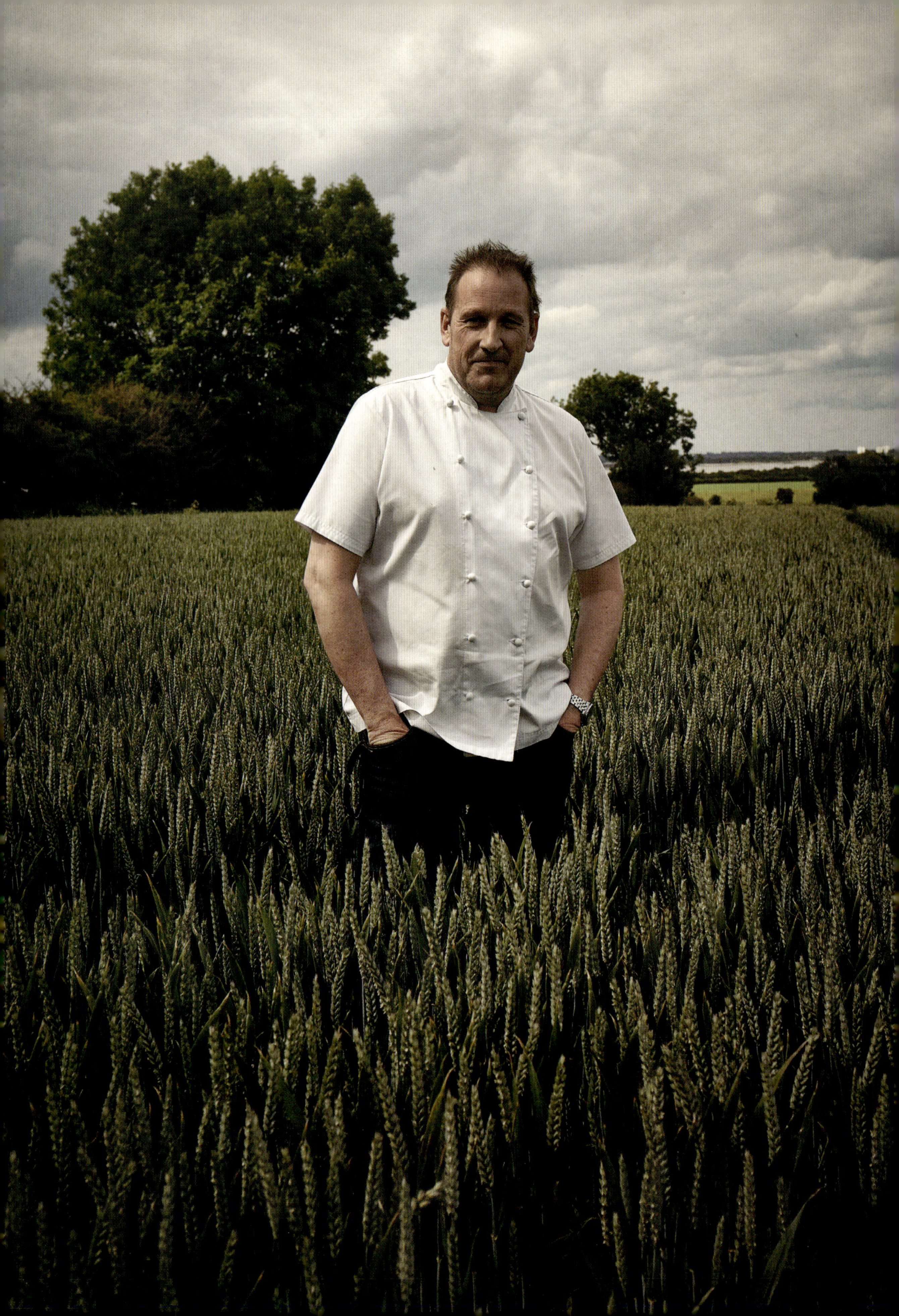

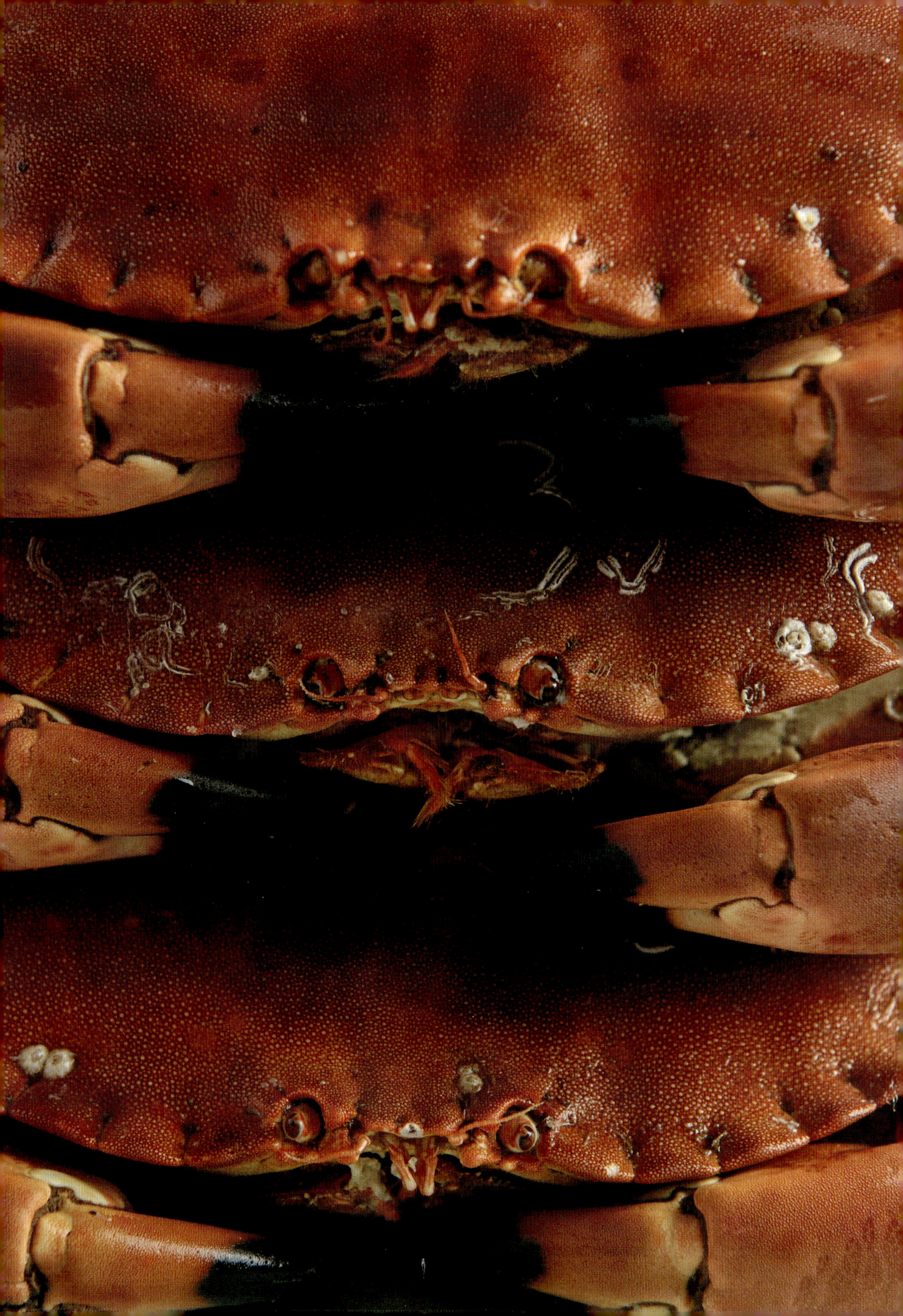

Bridlington Bay Dressed Brown Crab

INGREDIENTS:
Serves 4

4 medium-sized crabs
1 lemon, zest and juice
pinch of salt
pinch of ground black pepper
2 sun-ripened vine tomatoes, chopped
3 hard-boiled eggs, shelled, separated into whites and yolks, and sieved
20g finely chopped curly parsley
brown bread and butter
1 lemon

METHOD:

Remove the claws and legs from the main bodies of the crabs and set to one side.

Carefully but forcefully separate the shell from the main body of the crab. Discard the main body and the small legs that were previously removed.

Remove all the dead men's fingers (these are small pointed grey fin-like inedible parts). Using a spoon, scoop out the brown meat from the shell into a dish. Mix this together with lemon zest and juice, salt, pepper and chopped tomatoes.

Scrub and clean the empty shells before replacing the crab meat.

Using a crab claw cracker or heavy implement, carefully but forcefully crack the claws to remove the meat. In a bowl, flake the meat and season with salt and pepper.

Using the white crab meat, dress the crab down the centre of the shell. Using the sieved egg white, egg yolk and chopped parsley, alternate rows of ingredients each side of the white crab meat.

Serve with a hearty serving of brown bread and butter and a slice of lemon.

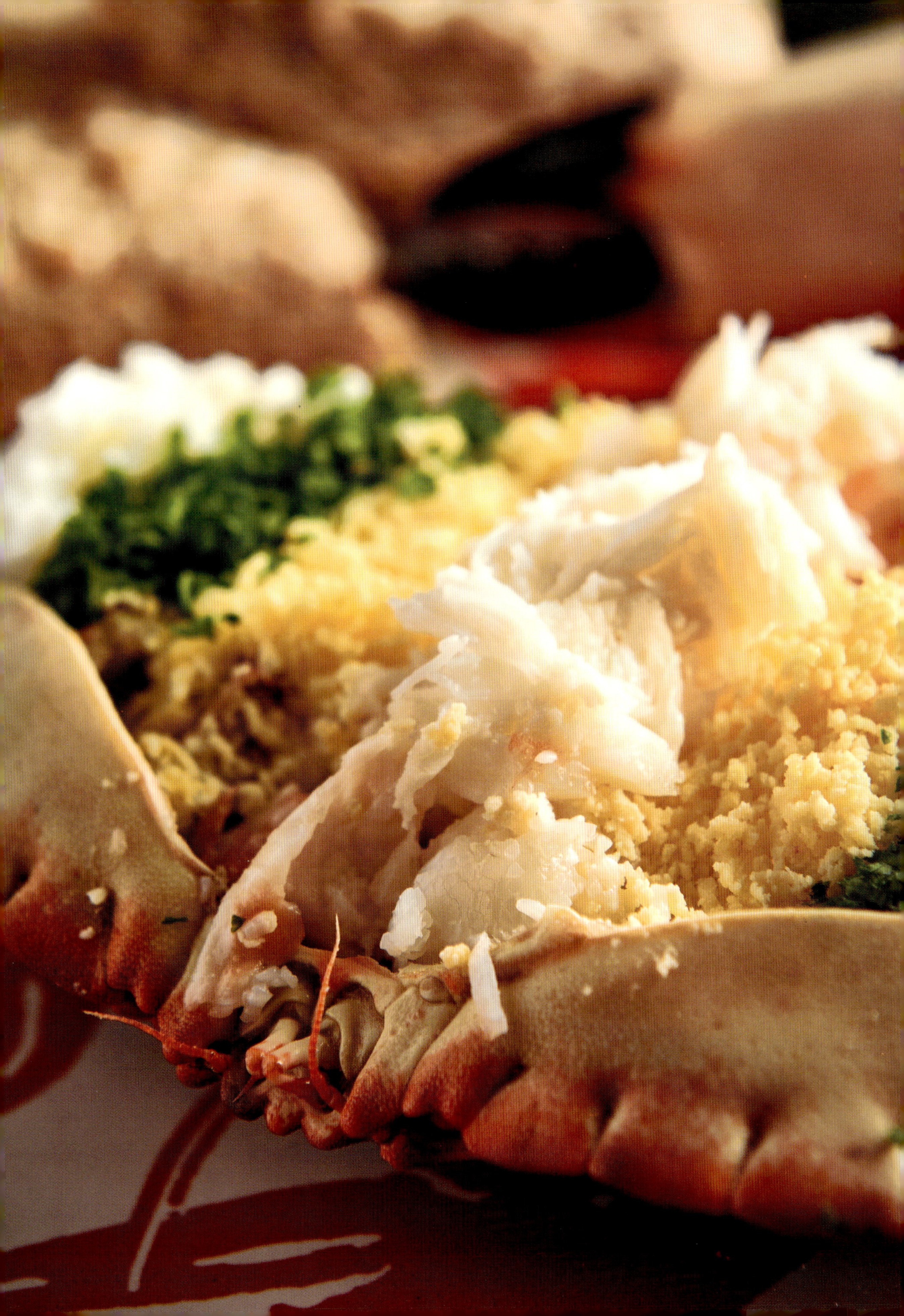

Hot Lobster Salad

INGREDIENTS:
Serves 4

4 small cooked lobsters
1 whole garlic bulb, roasted
20ml olive oil
50g samphire, blanched
12 baby leeks, blanched
12 asparagus tips, blanched
12 baby carrots, peeled and cooked
100g freshly shelled broad beans, blanched
pinch of salt

For the chilli dressing
30ml rapeseed oil
1 small red chilli, deseeded, finely diced
20ml white wine vinegar

METHOD:

Remove the meat from the lobster claws and tails, wash under running water and keep chilled.

Cut the top off the whole roasted garlic bulb and squeeze the purée into a large dish. Add the olive oil, samphire, leeks, asparagus, carrots and beans.

Toss gently and spoon a portion onto each of your serving plates.

To make the dressing, place all the ingredients in a small food processor and blend. Pass through a sieve to remove any debris.

Arrange the cooked lobster on top of the salad and sprinkle with salt. Finish with a drizzle of chilli dressing and rapeseed oil

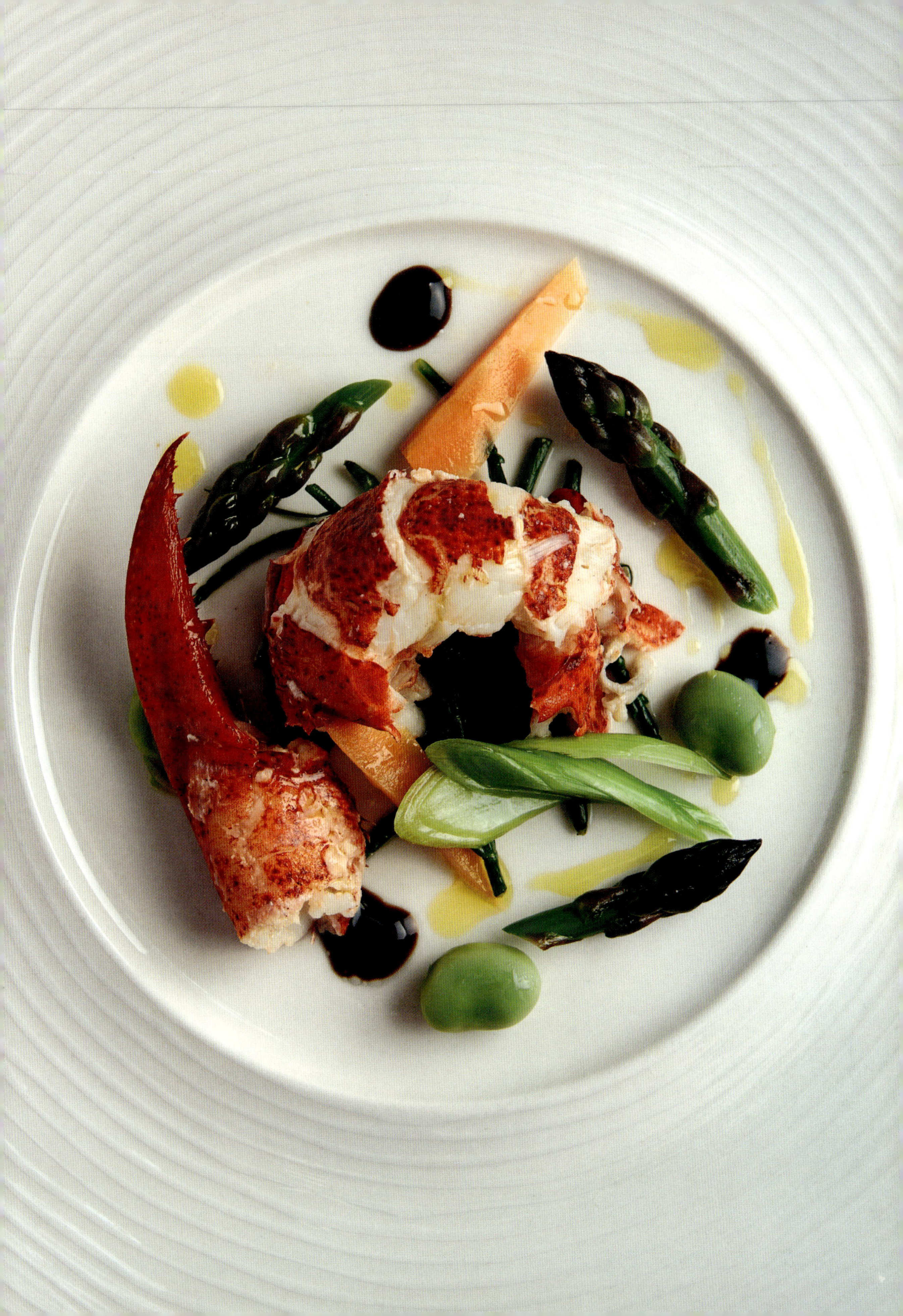

Lobster Thermidor

INGREDIENTS:
Serves 4

2 medium cooked lobsters
30g butter
6 shallots, finely chopped
60ml white wine
60ml double cream
20g English mustard
1 lemon, juice only
pinch of salt and ground black pepper
325ml fish stock, see page 220
40g parmesan, grated
20g fresh sprigs of dill

METHOD:

Cut the cooked lobsters in half lengthways. Remove the legs, the tail meat, and the contents of the body (this needs discarding). Wash the shells and the meat in cold water, then return the meat to the tail section of the shells.

Carefully, with a lobster claw cracker or a heavy implement, crack the remaining claws and remove the meat. Wash the meat under cold water and place it in the lobster's main shell.

Keep your prepared lobsters in the fridge until ready to use.

Place the butter into a sauté pan with the shallots and fry. Add the white wine, double cream, English mustard, lemon juice, salt, ground black pepper and fish stock, and reduce by two-thirds. Remove the sauce from the heat and spoon over each of the lobster halves, saving some to serve on the plate. Sprinkle with parmesan and place under a hot grill for 4-6 minutes.

Serve with fresh sprigs of dill and remaining sauce.

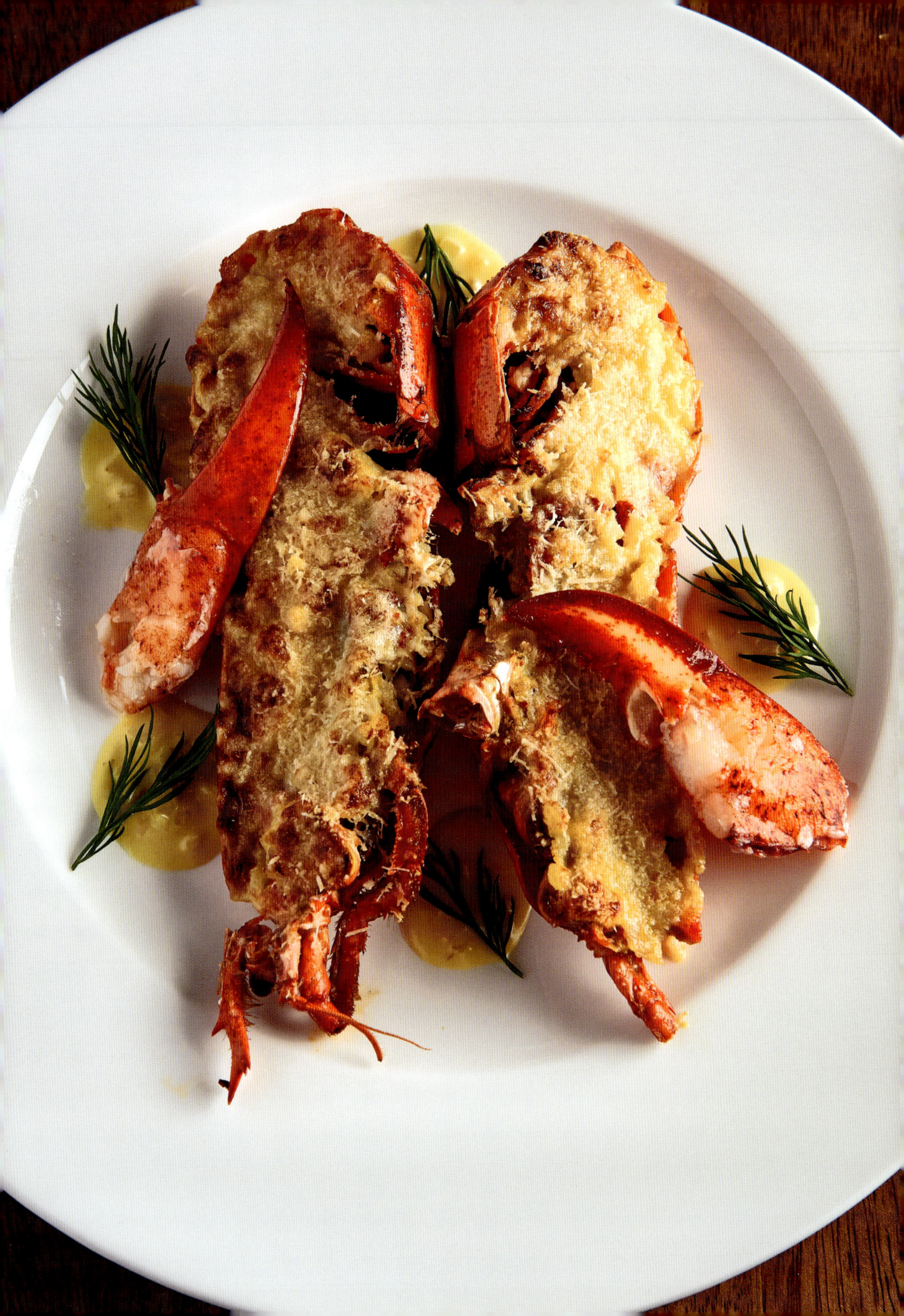

Seared Scallops with Asparagus Spears and Saffron Sauce

INGREDIENTS:
Serves 4

100ml dry white wine
100ml fish stock, see page 220
100ml double cream
pinch of saffron
40g unsalted butter
salt and ground black pepper
10ml rapeseed oil
12 large scallops, cleaned and prepared
12 asparagus spears, trimmed and prepared

METHOD:

Place the white wine, fish stock and double cream into a thick-bottomed pan and bring to the boil.

When the sauce is boiling, add a pinch of saffron and reduce the sauce by two-thirds. Gradually add the butter to the sauce in small cubes, stirring continuously. This will create a glossy sauce that coats the back of a spoon. Season with salt and pepper and keep the sauce warm until the scallops are cooked.

Add the rapeseed oil to a shallow sauté pan and heat. Add the scallops and cook for approximately 2 minutes on each side, or until the scallops take on a seared golden brown appearance. Remove the scallops from the pan and replace with the asparagus spears; cook for 2 minutes, or until tender.

Place the scallops and asparagus together on a plate and serve with the saffron sauce.

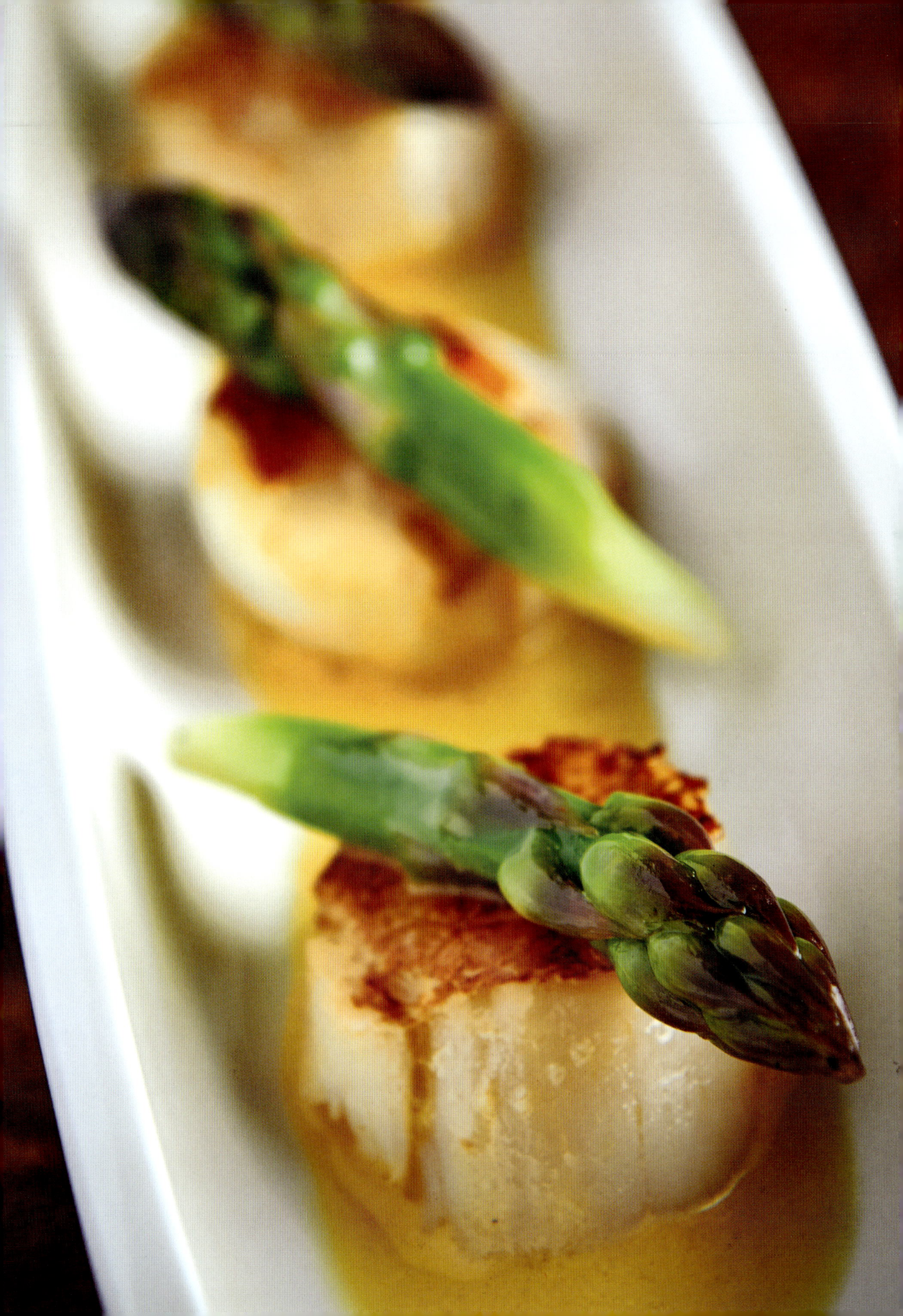

WE WERE CARRYING THE DEER WITH STICKS AND SHACKLES LIKE CAVEMEN - ALWAYS ONES FOR THE GREAT OUTDOORS AND WITH MORE THAN A HINT OF MISCHIEF, MY BROTHER PAUL AND I USED TO GO SHOOTING IN THE WOODLANDS AND FIELDS BEHIND THE HOUSE WHERE WE LIVED AS KIDS.

Meat

BEEF STROGANOFF.62
BRAISED LAMB SHANKS IN RED WINE.64
BRAISED STEAK IN BEER.66
PORK AND LEEK SAUSAGES.68
SLOW-ROASTED BELLY PORK WITH SAGE, ONION AND APPLE TART.70
SLOW-ROASTED LEG OF LAMB.72

Poultry

CHICKEN CHASSEUR.74
WHOLE ROAST CHICKEN.76

Game

POT ROAST PHEASANT WITH BEETROOT AND CORN FRITTERS.78
VENISON STEAK WITH STILTON AND PEAS.80

On this occasion we had decided to go to a woodland that was to us, aged 15 and 17, classed as high risk. If we slipped up we could be seen from the farmer's house just a couple of hundred metres away and we knew from previous experience he was a farmer not to be crossed – and neither were his fields for that matter, especially when armed with an air rifle!

Safely into the woodland after following a textbook procedure discussed and planned earlier, we could breathe in the thick undergrowth of thistles, nettles, thorny bushes and trees.

Our mission: to find a duck pond that we suspected of being there. We could see ducks and geese landing in the woodland from our house about a mile away. We were correct; the pond was there – but no ducks or geese today. Not even a wood pigeon: they were all feeding on the farmer's crops of peas and corn.

Our route out was much less risky as we had the cover of the woodland near the farmer's house. As we approached the edge of the woodland we came across a young fallow deer that had fallen trying to jump the barbed wire fence. It had died earlier that morning, and was still warm. It was like finding a pot of gold at the end of a rainbow for two budding young chefs.

We managed to find some bailer twine and some good strong branches and strapped the front and back legs to the branch, then carried it across the fields. We were carrying the deer with sticks and shackles like cavemen.

On our return home we donned our chefs' jackets, and with chopping boards, knives and a bottle of beer each we butchered the beast as best we could.

NB.
MEAT, POULTRY & GAME

CHAPTER 3

Beef Stroganoff

INGREDIENTS:
Serves 4

50g butter
1 onion, finely diced
600g beef fillet, cut into strips
100ml brandy
15g French mustard
pinch of paprika
100g button mushrooms, sliced
200ml double cream
100ml beef stock, see page 216
1 small bunch of curly parsley,
    finely chopped
salt and ground black pepper

METHOD:

In a pan, heat 25g of butter and fry the onion. Add the beef and fry for 1 minute until browned, then add the brandy and ignite with a naked flame to burn off the alcohol.

Add the mustard, paprika, mushrooms, double cream and beef stock. Reduce the sauce by half and add half the parsley and the remaining butter, swirling gently. Season to taste and serve with rice and the remaining chopped parsley.

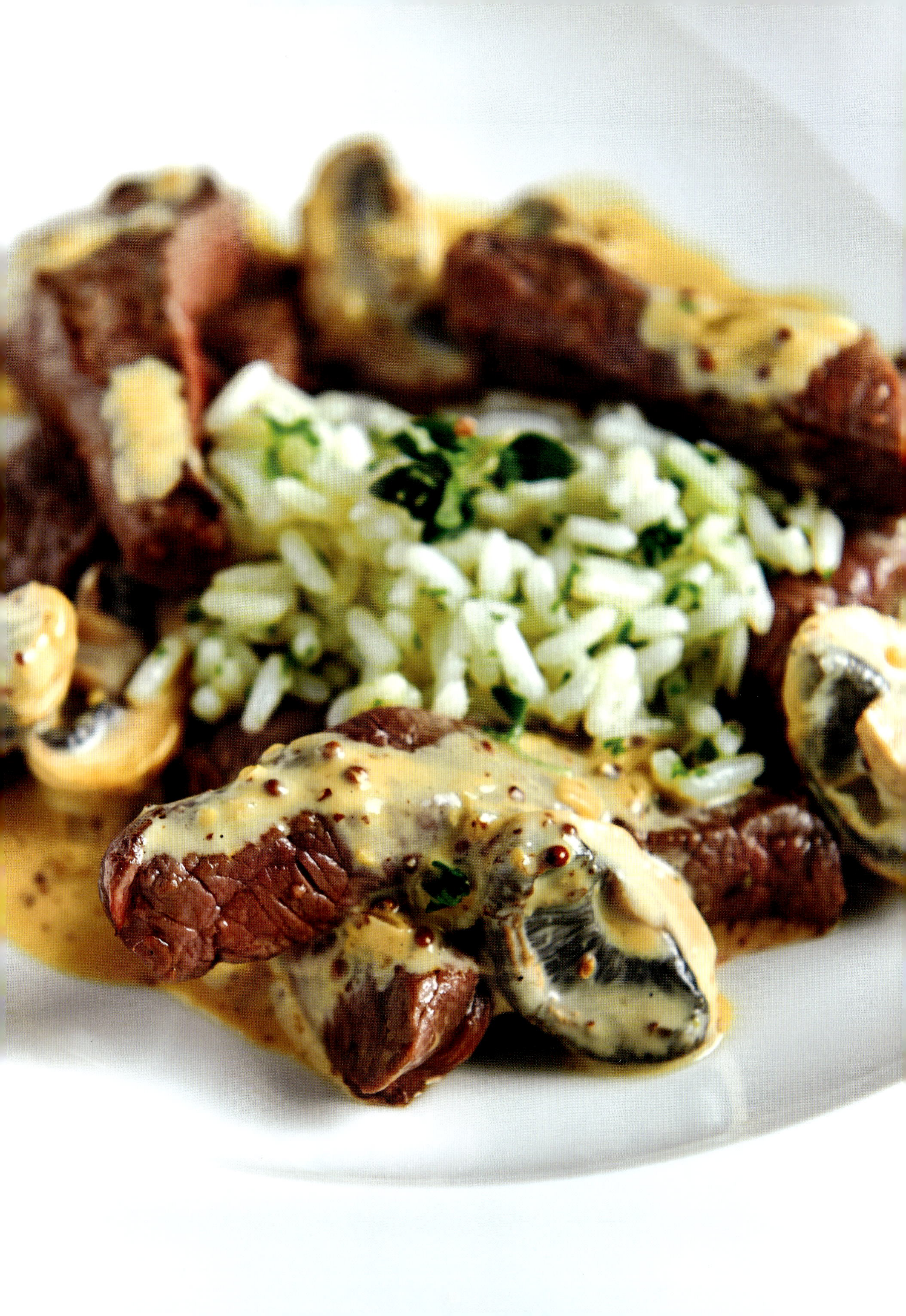

Braised Lamb Shanks in Red Wine

INGREDIENTS:
Serves 4

20ml rapeseed oil
4 medium-sized lamb shanks
16 shallots, peeled, trimmed and whole
16 washed and trimmed Chantenay carrots
2 sticks of celery, washed and quartered
1 fresh sprig of rosemary
4 fresh bay leaves
100g plain flour
60g tomato purée
250ml good red wine
1 litre of chicken stock, see page 218
salt and ground black pepper

METHOD:

Heat the rapeseed oil in your largest thick-bottomed pan. Add the lamb shanks and brown all sides.

Add the shallots, carrots, celery, rosemary, bay leaves and sweat the ingredients with the lid on for 5 minutes on a medium heat. Remove the lid, sprinkle the flour over and stir to coat all the ingredients.

Add the tomato purée, red wine and chicken stock (depending on the size of the lamb shanks you may need to top up with water to cover the ingredients).

Bring the pan to the boil and simmer for 3 hours either on the hob or in the oven at 180°C. Once cooked, remove the lamb shanks from the liquid and keep warm.

Return the cooking liquid to the heat reduce to the point that it coats the back of a spoon. Check the sauce for seasoning. Serve the lamb shanks with the sauce.

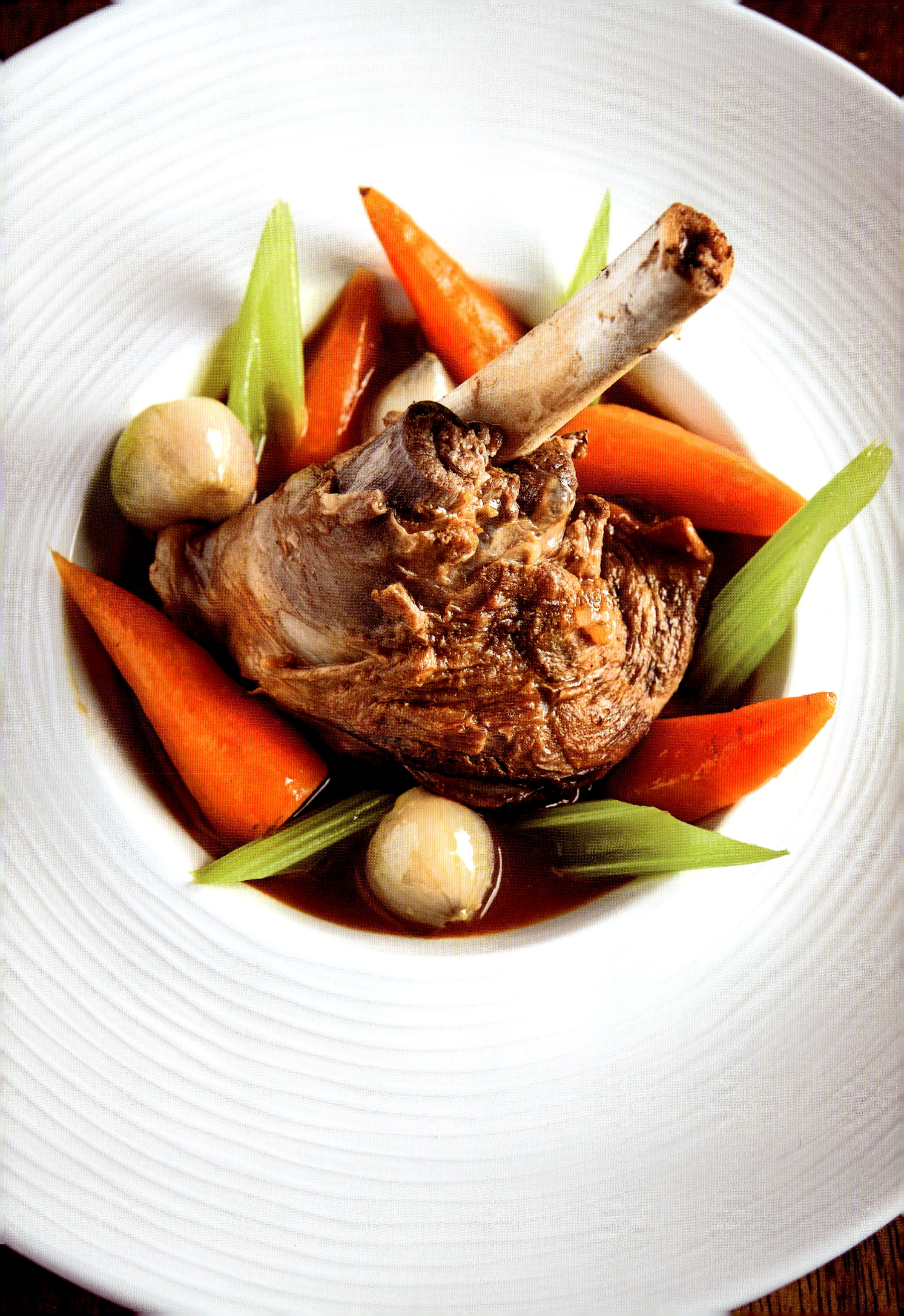

Braised Steak in Beer

INGREDIENTS:
Serves 4

50g rapeseed oil
800g braising steak in 4 thick slices
1 Spanish onion, peeled and sliced
40g plain flour
60g tomato purée
20g English mustard powder
10ml Worcestershire sauce
250ml good dark ale
salt and ground black pepper
4 sprigs of watercress

METHOD:

In a large thick-bottomed pan heat the rapeseed oil and fry the steaks until browned on both sides. Add the onions and fry for a further 2 minutes.

Sprinkle the steaks with plain flour and tomato purée and stir to coat the ingredients. Add the English mustard, Worcestershire sauce and dark ale and top up with water if necessary. Cover the pan with a lid, bring to the boil and simmer for 2 hours.

Remove the lid and the steaks and reduce the sauce to the required consistency by boiling to the point it coats the back of a spoon.

Season the sauce to taste and serve with the braised steaks along with a sprig of watercress.

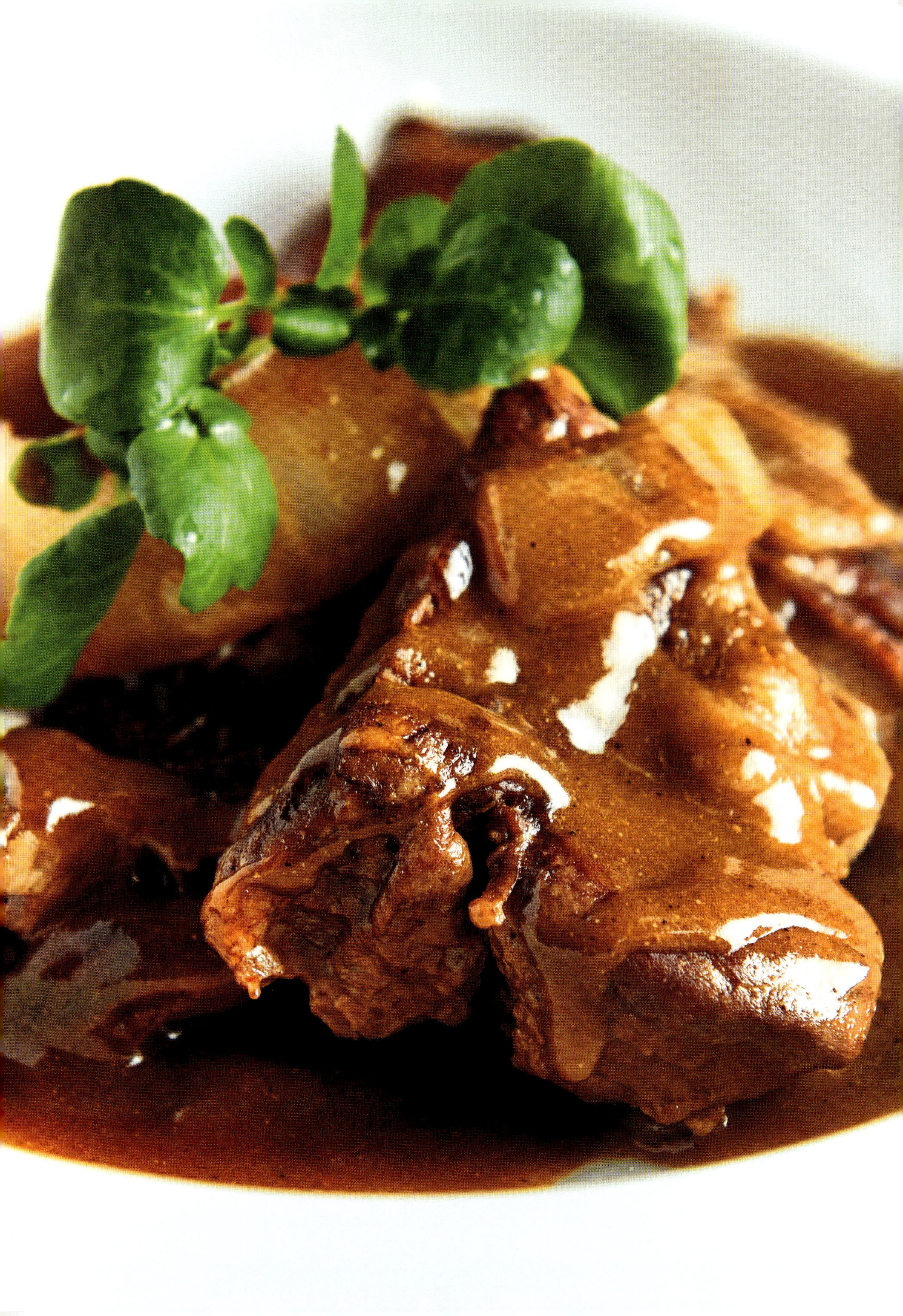

Pork and Leek Sausages

INGREDIENTS:
Serves 4

300g belly pork
300g shoulder pork
1 large leek, washed and finely diced
1 small sprig of thyme, leaves only
pinch of salt and ground black pepper
30g wholegrain mustard
1 small bunch curly parsley,
    finely chopped
50g rolled oats
1 free range egg white
4 small sprigs of thyme

For the sauce
2 small Spanish onions, peeled,
    sliced and fried until golden
300ml Española sauce, see page 238

METHOD:

Finely dice the pork by hand or with a food processor. Add the leek, thyme, salt, pepper, mustard, parsley and oats to the mixture and mix well.

Add the egg white to bind the ingredients together.

Divide the recipe into 4 equal portions and shape each to form a sausage.

Either pan fry or oven bake at 180°C for 10 minutes or until juices run clear.

To make the sauce, combine the onions with the Española sauce and re-heat. Serve with the cooked sausages and a fresh sprig of thyme.

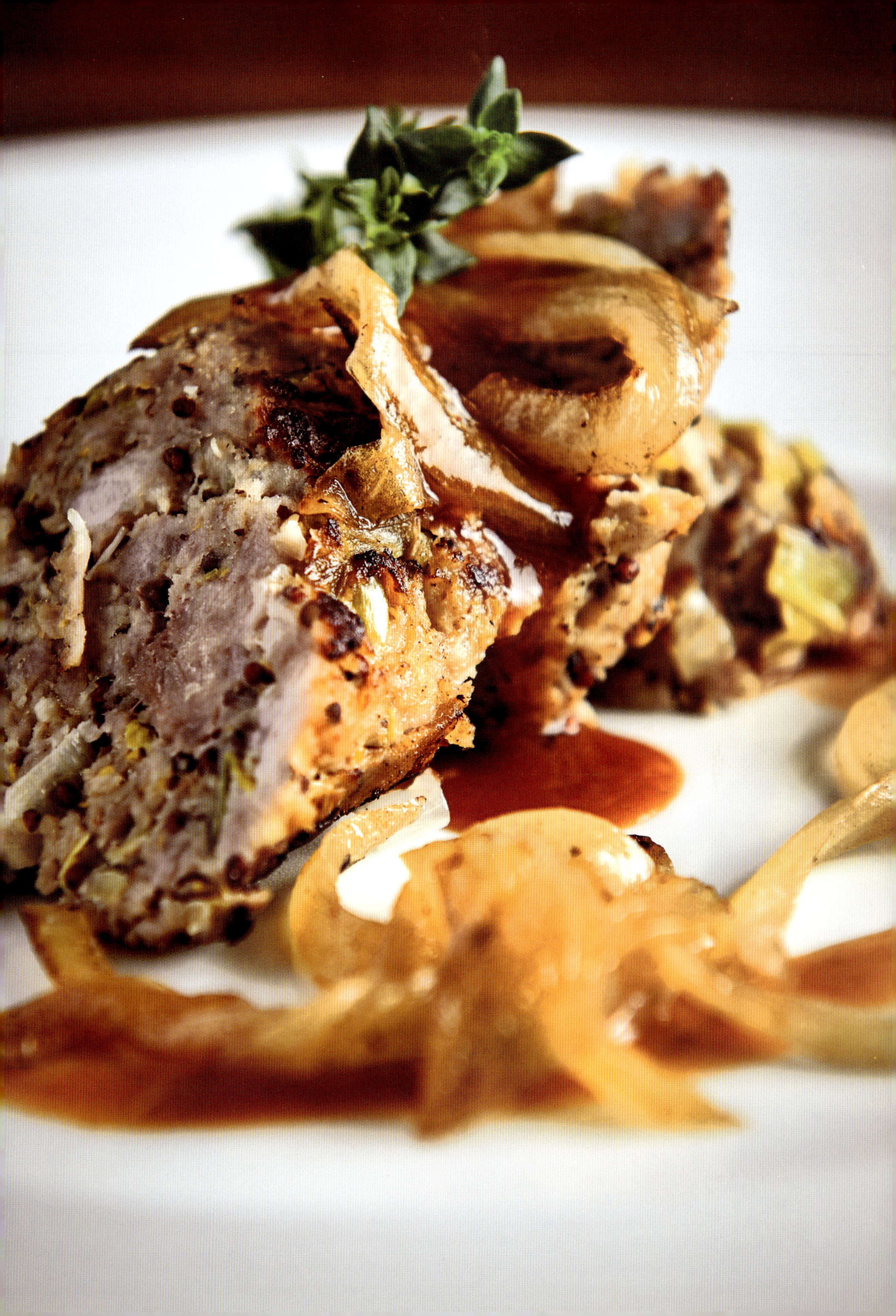

Slow-Roasted Belly Pork with Sage, Onion and Apple Tart

INGREDIENTS:
Serves 4

1 parsnip, peeled and chopped into large dice
1 carrot, peeled and chopped into large dice
1 leek, halved, washed and chopped into large dice
1 celery stick, washed and diced
600g scored belly pork
20ml rapeseed oil
20g salt
200g shortcrust pastry, see page 228
1 large onion, peeled, chopped into large dice and cooked
1 large Bramley apple, peeled, diced and cooked
1 small bunch fresh sage
50g salted butter, melted

METHOD:

Place all the vegetables in a roasting tray and sit the belly pork on top. Brush the pork with the rapeseed oil. Sprinkle the salt on the rind.

Cook at 180°C for 30 minutes, then reduce the temperature to 160°C for an hour-and-a-half.

When the pork is cooked, remove from the oven and rest for 15 minutes before serving.

To make the sage, onion and apple tarts, line 4 small tart tins with shortcrust pastry. Fill each tart with the diced onion, Bramley apple and chopped sage and drizzle with melted butter. Bake the tarts in the oven at 180°C until the pastry is golden.

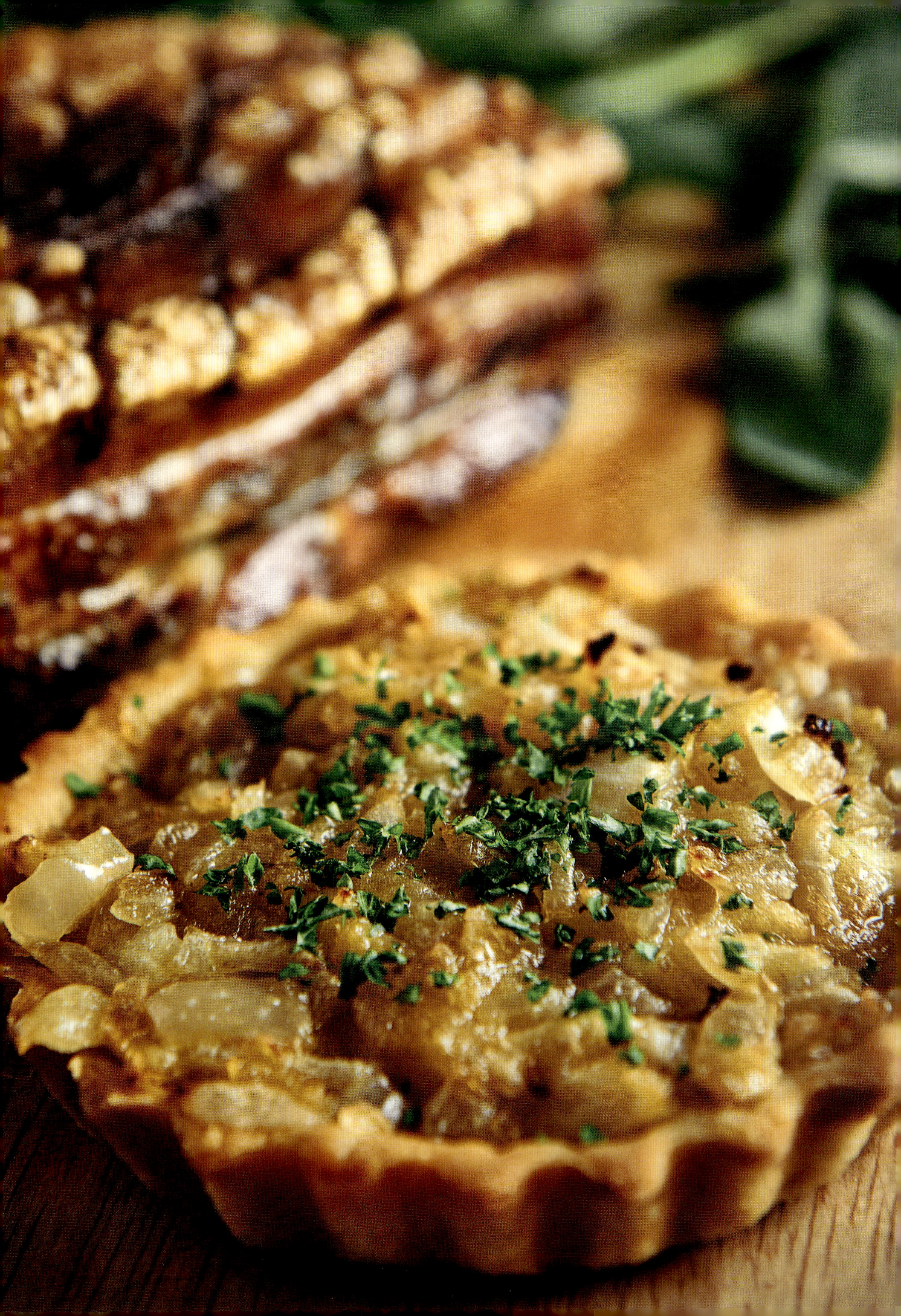

Slow-Roasted Leg of Lamb

INGREDIENTS:
Serves 4

2 sticks of celery, halved
2 carrots, halved
2 Spanish onions, peeled and quartered
1.5kg leg of lamb, on the bone
1 sprig of rosemary
4 bay leaves
1 sprig of thyme
20ml rapeseed oil
pinch of salt and black pepper
100ml port

METHOD:

In a roasting tin, make a bed of vegetables using the celery, carrots and onions.

To prepare the leg of lamb for roasting, with a sharp knife remove approximately 1 inch of flesh from the top of the bone and scrape clean. Cover the scraped bone with foil. Make several short incisions in the lamb and pack with rosemary, bay leaves and thyme. Place the lamb on top of the bed of vegetables.

Brush the leg of lamb with the rapeseed oil and season with salt and pepper. Pour the port into the tray and cover the whole tray with foil. Roast in the oven at 160°C for 3 hours 40 minutes. After 3 hours remove the foil to allow the meat to brown, basting occasionally.

When the lamb is cooked, rest for 15 minutes before serving with the vegetables.

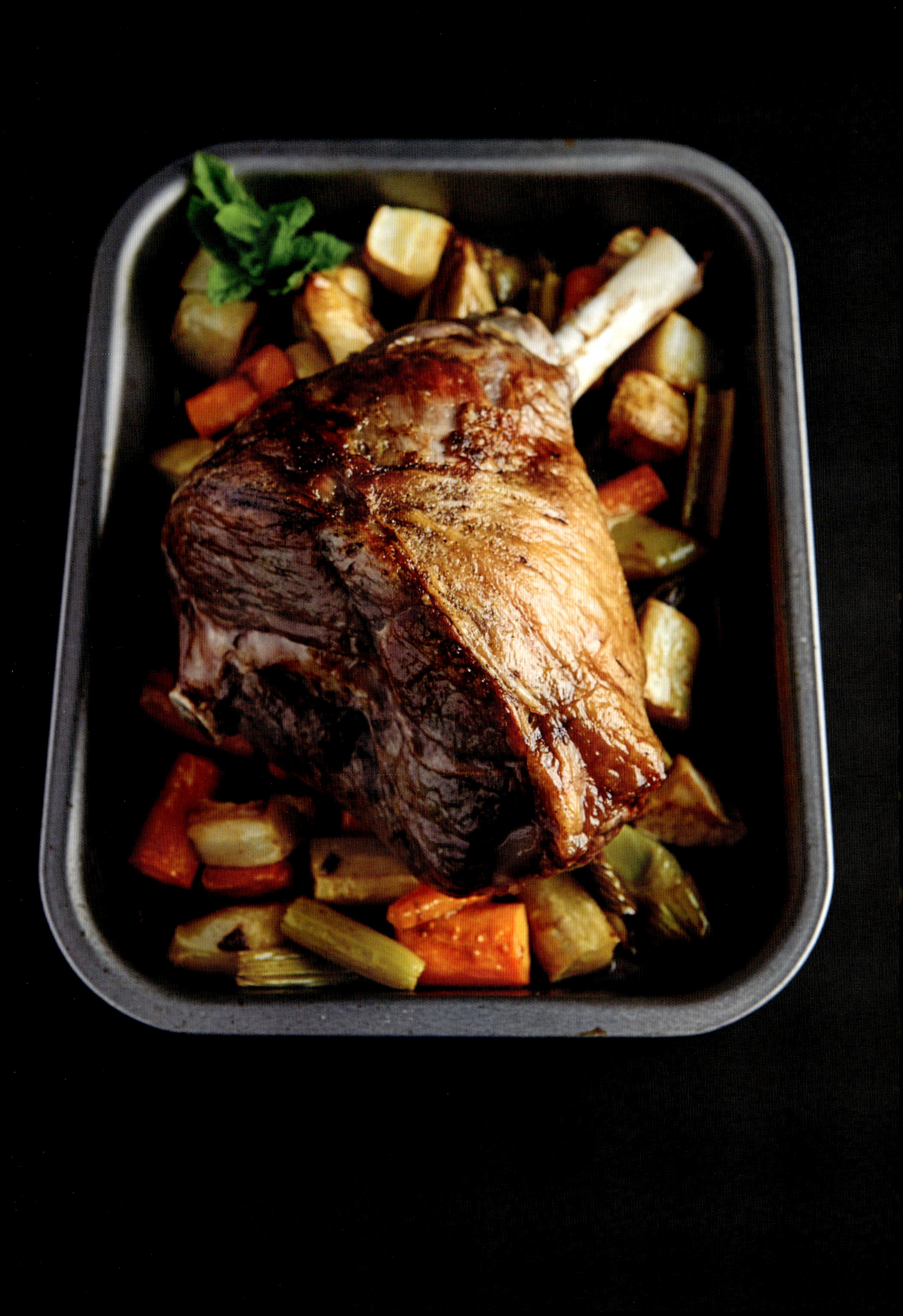

Chicken Chasseur

INGREDIENTS:
Serves 4

20ml rapeseed oil
1 whole chicken, cut into 8 portions
16 small shallots, peeled, trimmed and whole
100g button mushrooms
60g plain flour
200ml dry white wine
300ml chicken stock, see page 218
4 tomatoes, blanched, skinned, seeded and chopped
50g tomato purée
1 small bunch of tarragon, chopped
salt and ground black pepper
100g streaky bacon, sliced into lardons and fried

METHOD:

Place the rapeseed oil in the pan and on a medium heat fry the chicken portions, starting with the thighs and the drumsticks, and adding the breast portions last. Turn the chicken portions to seal and create a golden, crisp colour.

Add the shallots and button mushrooms and cook for 5 minutes on a medium heat.

Sprinkle the plain flour over the chicken and vegetables to coat. Add the wine and chicken stock followed by the tomatoes and tomato purée.

Add some of the chopped tarragon and place a lid on the pan. Cook for 30 minutes on a low heat.

Remove the lid and increase the heat to medium. Reduce the sauce to a consistency that coats the back of a spoon. Season with salt and pepper and serve with the lardons and the remaining tarragon.

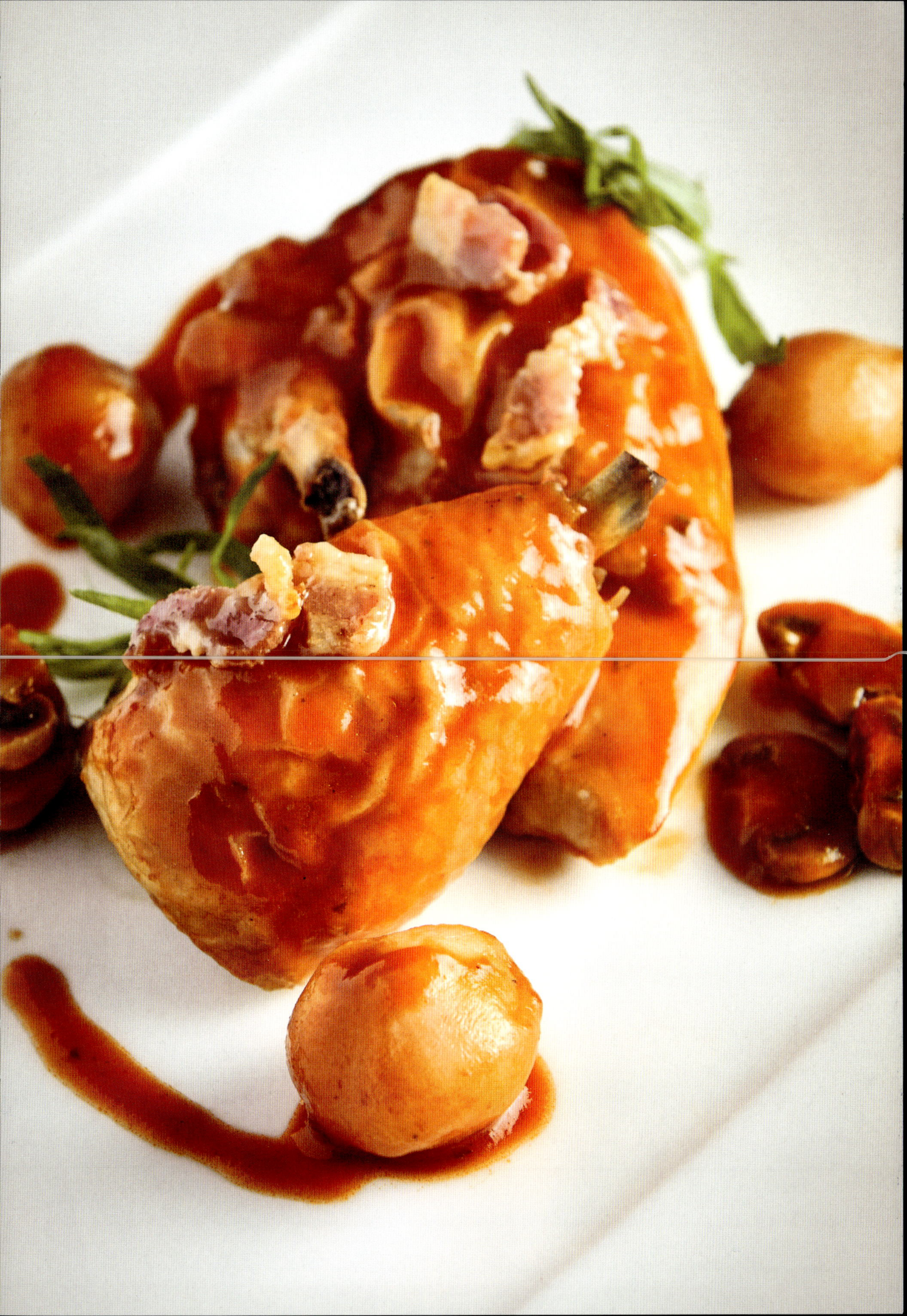

Whole Roast Chicken

INGREDIENTS:

Serves 4

2 leeks, washed, trimmed and quartered
2 medium carrots, peeled, trimmed and quartered
1 whole chicken, around 1.5kg
2 small bunches of thyme
20ml rapeseed oil
salt and ground black pepper
200ml dry white wine
1 small bunch of parsley

METHOD:

Take a large roasting tray and make a bed of vegetables with the leek and carrots.

Place the whole chicken on the bed of vegetables. Add 1 bunch of thyme to the open cavity of the chicken. Brush the skin of the chicken with rapeseed oil followed by a sprinkling of salt and pepper.

Pour the white wine into the roasting tray and sprinkle the remaining thyme and parsley onto the vegetables. Cover the whole tray with foil and roast in the oven at 200°C for the first 20 minutes. Then reduce the temperature to 180°C and remove the foil for the remaining 1 hour or until the juices run clear.

Allow to rest for 10 minutes before serving.

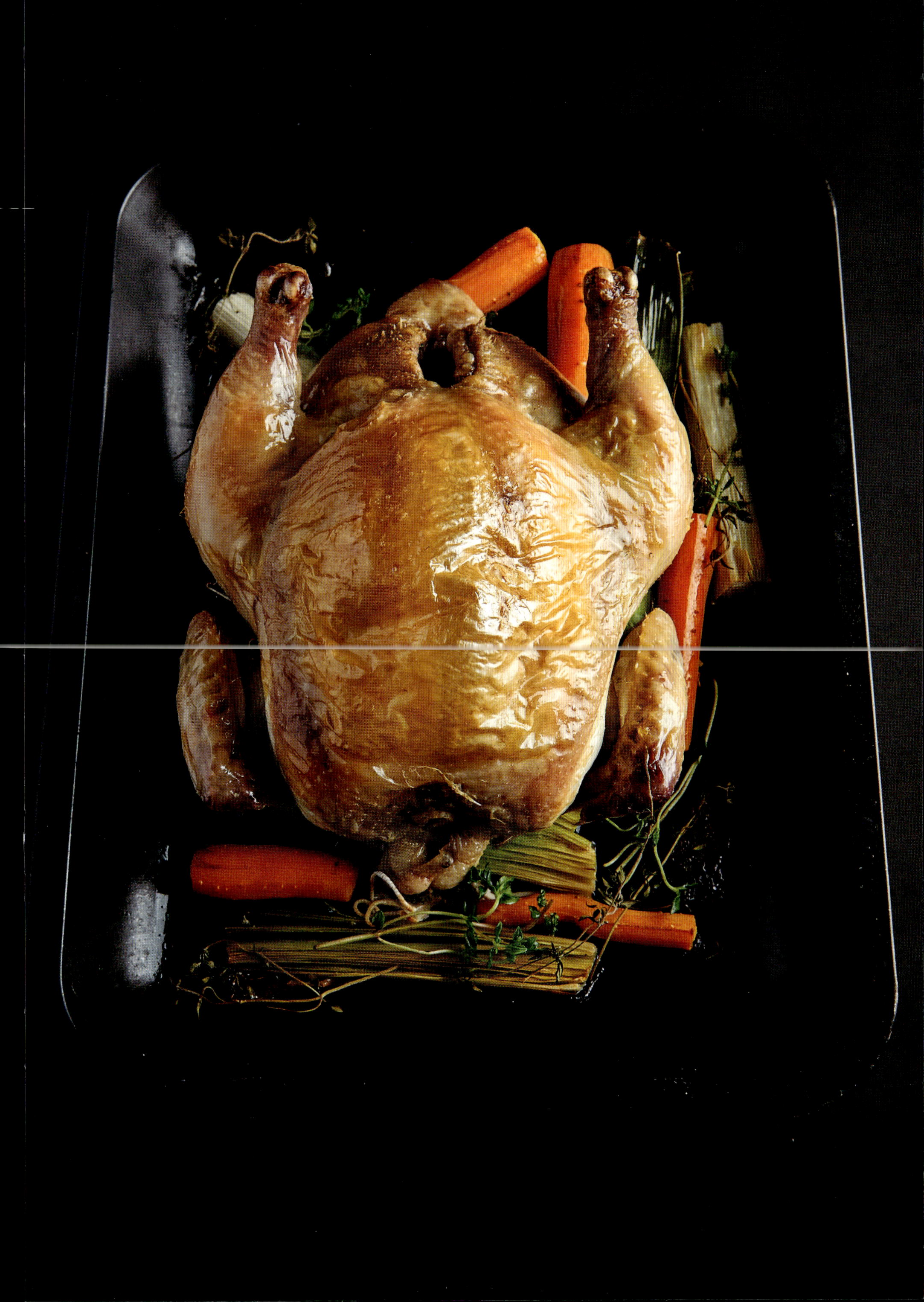

Pot Roast Pheasant with Beetroot and Corn Fritters

INGREDIENTS:
Serves 4

50g salted butter
2 whole pheasants, quartered
16 small shallots peeled, trimmed and whole
4 whole raw beetroot, peeled and quartered
200ml port
300ml chicken stock, see page 218
50g tomato purée
salt and ground black pepper
50g streaky bacon, cut into lardons and fried
4 small sprigs of sage

For the corn fritters
100g sweetcorn
50g plain flour
1 free range egg white
1 small bunch of curly parsley
pinch of salt and ground black pepper
30ml rapeseed oil

METHOD:

Melt the butter on a medium heat in a sauté pan and cook the pheasant portions until browned. Transfer them to an earthenware pot.

Sprinkle the shallots and beetroot over the pheasant portions followed by the port, chicken stock and tomato purée. With the lid on, roast in the oven at 170°C for 2 hours.

To make the corn fritters, while the pheasant is roasting, in a separate bowl combine the sweetcorn, plain flour, egg, parsley, salt and pepper until it reaches a loose batter consistency and refrigerate until needed.

After 2 hours, remove the pheasant from the pot and place the cooking liquid in a thick-bottomed saucepan on a medium heat. Reduce the consistency until it coats the back of a spoon. Season with salt and pepper.

Place the rapeseed oil in a frying pan on a medium heat and carefully, one at a time, place a dessert spoonful of the corn batter into the pan and cook on both sides until golden brown. Repeat the process until you have the required number of fritters.

Serve the pot roast pheasant with the cooking sauce, beetroot and corn fritters, lardons of bacon and a small sprig of fresh sage.

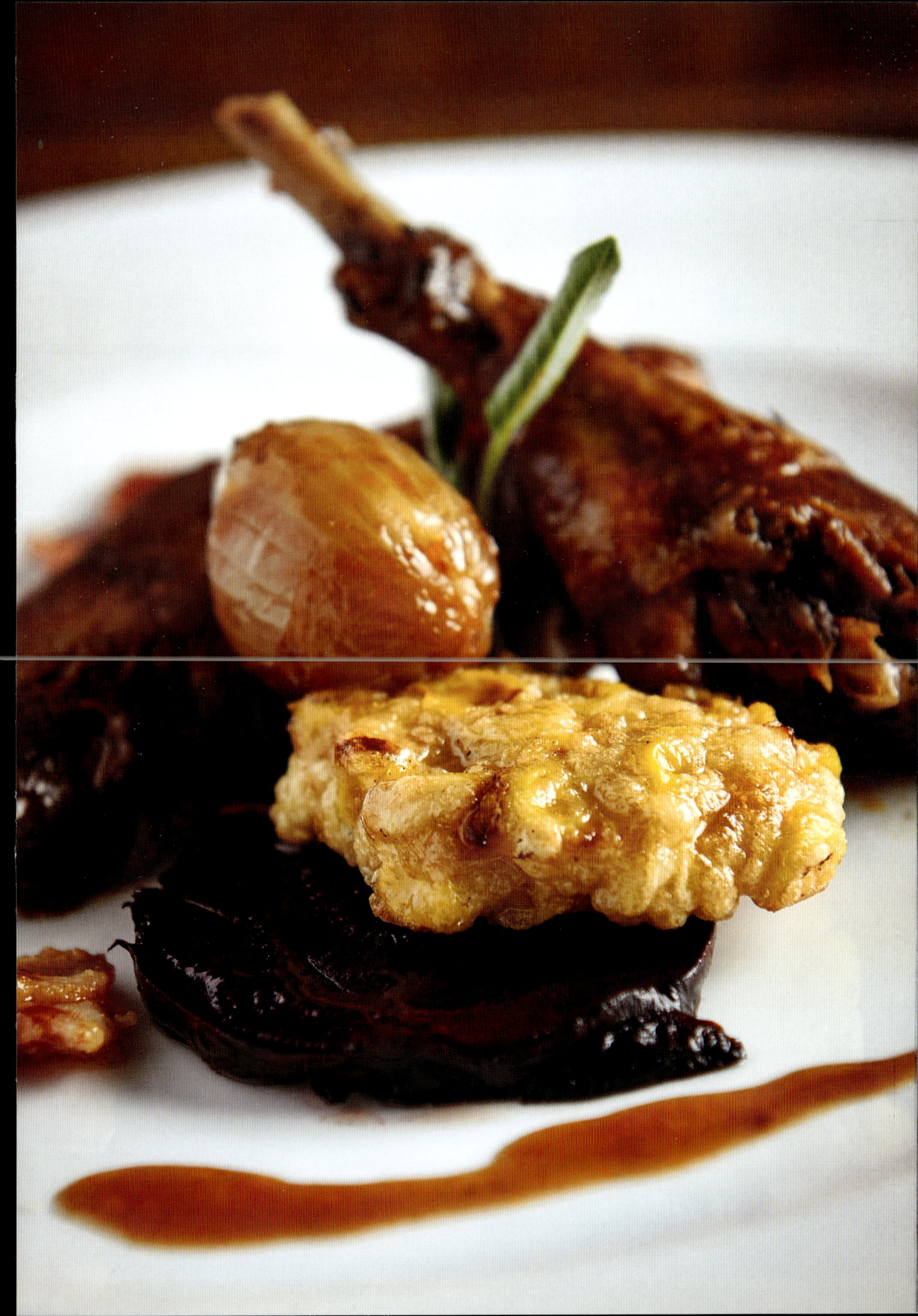

Venison Steak with Stilton and Peas

INGREDIENTS:
Serves 4

20ml rapeseed oil
4 wild venison haunch steaks
salt and ground black pepper
6 juniper berries, crushed
2g fennel seeds, crushed
4g harissa paste
20ml red wine vinegar
200ml beef stock, see page 216
50g unsalted butter
100g Stilton cheese, crumbled
200g peas, cooked

METHOD:

Place the rapeseed oil in a thick-bottomed sauté pan on a medium heat. Season the venison steaks and pan fry them to your liking.

While the steaks are frying, in a separate pan add the juniper berries, fennel seeds and harissa paste and heat for 1 minute on a high heat then add the red wine vinegar and beef stock and reduce the heat by half.

Reduce the sauce to the point at which it coats the back of a spoon, adding small chunks of the butter to create a glossy finish.

Sprinkle the Stilton cheese over your cooked steaks and place under the grill for 1-2 minutes or until melted.

Serve the steaks with the reduction sauce and freshly cooked peas.

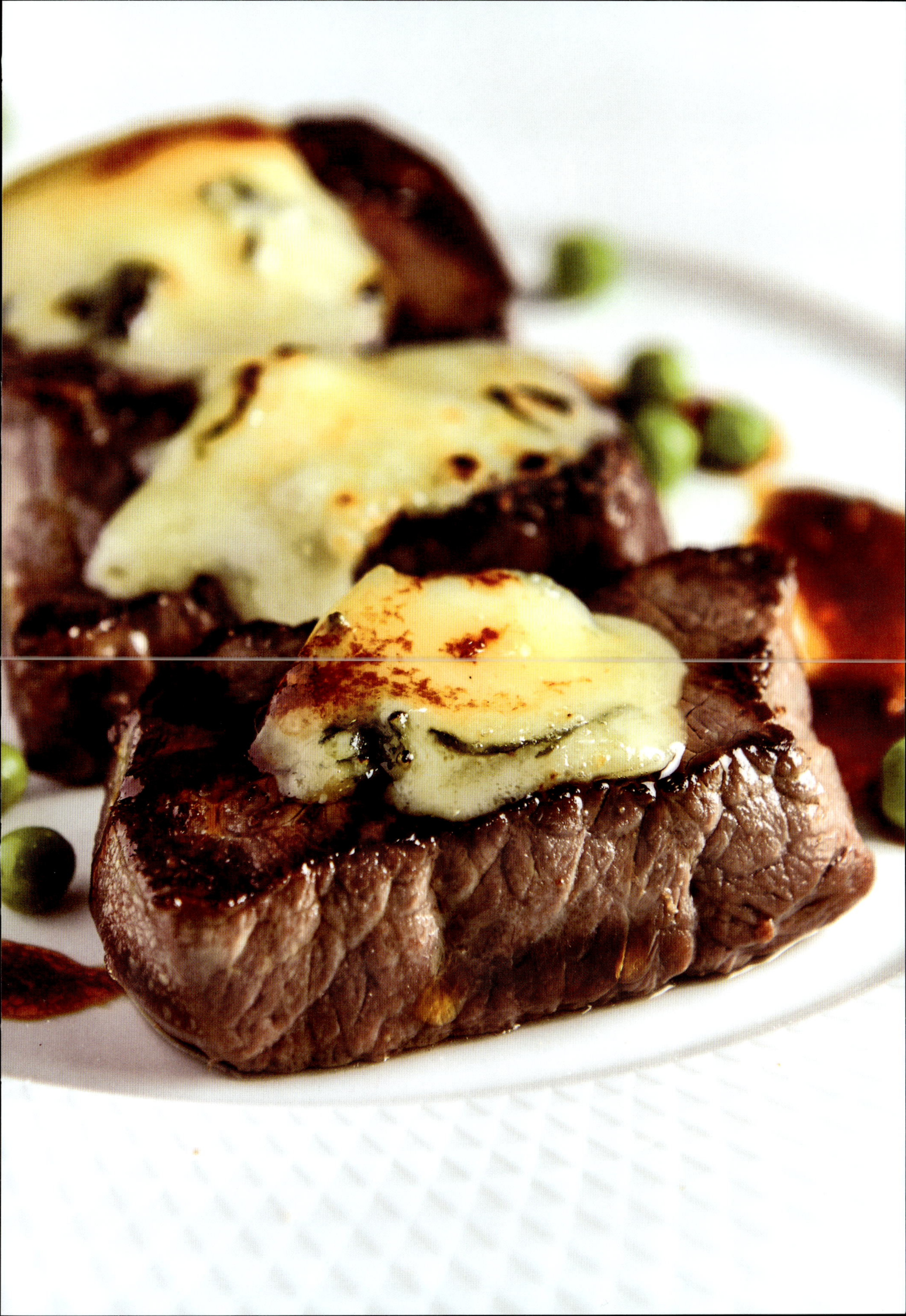

IT'S NOT EVERYDAY THAT YOU GET TO COOK FOR ROYALTY! I ONCE WON A CONTRACT TO SUPPLY THE CATERING FOR A ROYAL VISIT TO A COMPANY THAT HAD WON THE QUEEN'S AWARD FOR EXPORT FOR THE SECOND TIME. I HAD TO PRODUCE SAVOURY CANAPÉS AND AFTERNOON TEA FOR 80 GUESTS INCLUDING THE PRINCESS ROYAL.

Savoury Puddings

STEAK AND KIDNEY PUDDING.84
YORKSHIRE PUDDING.86

Pies

CHICKEN AND LEEK PIE.88
PORK PIE.90

Casseroles

BEEF BOURGUIGNON.92
LAMB HOTPOT.94

The food had to be prepared in an office kitchen that was more used to the sound of the kettle boiling and the microwave dinging for a pot noodle. With the bare minimum of staff and a lot of stress, we pulled it off and produced the goods. There was, though, a moment where the word 'awkward' springs to mind.

The event was taking place in the head office boardroom. The food was displayed and enjoyed by all. Following service, HRH the Princess Royal was taken on a tour of the sales office where she was to meet some of the key members of the company. The Lord Lieutenant accompanied her.

As the caterer, we had work to do and continued as normal; however a waitress and I somehow managed to become trapped between some office tables, a filing cabinet and the line-up of meet-and-greet dignitaries.

Talk about being in a tight spot: we were about one minute away from being introduced to the Princess. Luckily, just in the nick of time the official in charge of the line-up spotted the situation. They all discreetly shuffled a couple of spaces to the left and the waitress and I made a swift but co-ordinated escape!

Later, one of the royal protection squad came to see me. I thought I was in big trouble but no, far from it. As the Princess had not managed to eat anything during her visit, could I assemble an afternoon tea on a tray for her to have during her flight to her next engagement?

Naturally I obliged and off she flew. I wonder if my tray and linen napkin are in her kitchen cupboard now? At least they've gone to a good home and I've got the story to tell.

NB.
SAVOURY PUDDINGS, PIES & CASSEROLES

CHAPTER 4

Steak and Kidney Pudding

INGREDIENTS:
Serves 4

20ml rapeseed oil
500g braising steak, cut into 3cm cubes
200g beef kidneys, cut into 3cm cubes
1 onion, diced
4 celery stalks, diced
1 sprig fresh thyme
4 fresh bay leaves
40g plain flour
10ml Worcestershire sauce
200ml dark ale
200ml beef stock, see page 216
300g suet pastry, see page 230

METHOD:

Place the rapeseed oil into a large thick-bottomed saucepan and onto a medium heat. Add the diced steak and kidney, and cook until browned all over.

Add the onion, celery, thyme, bay leaves and plain flour and stir to coat all the ingredients evenly in the pan. Finally, add the Worcestershire sauce, dark ale and beef stock and bring to the boil. Simmer for 2 hours.

Allow the steak and kidney filling to cool completely before use.

On a floured surface, roll out 200g of the suet pastry to a 1cm thickness and line a 1/1.5 litre pudding basin. Fill the pudding with the steak and kidney mixture.

Roll the remaining pastry to the same thickness to make the lid. Brush the rim of the pudding with water and seal with the lid. Trim the excess pastry from around the edge.

Cover the whole pudding and dish with cling film and foil and steam for 2 hours. Alternatively, to bake your pudding, place in a hot oven at 170°C covered with foil for 90 minutes.

Serve with a hearty portion of seasonal vegetables and potatoes.

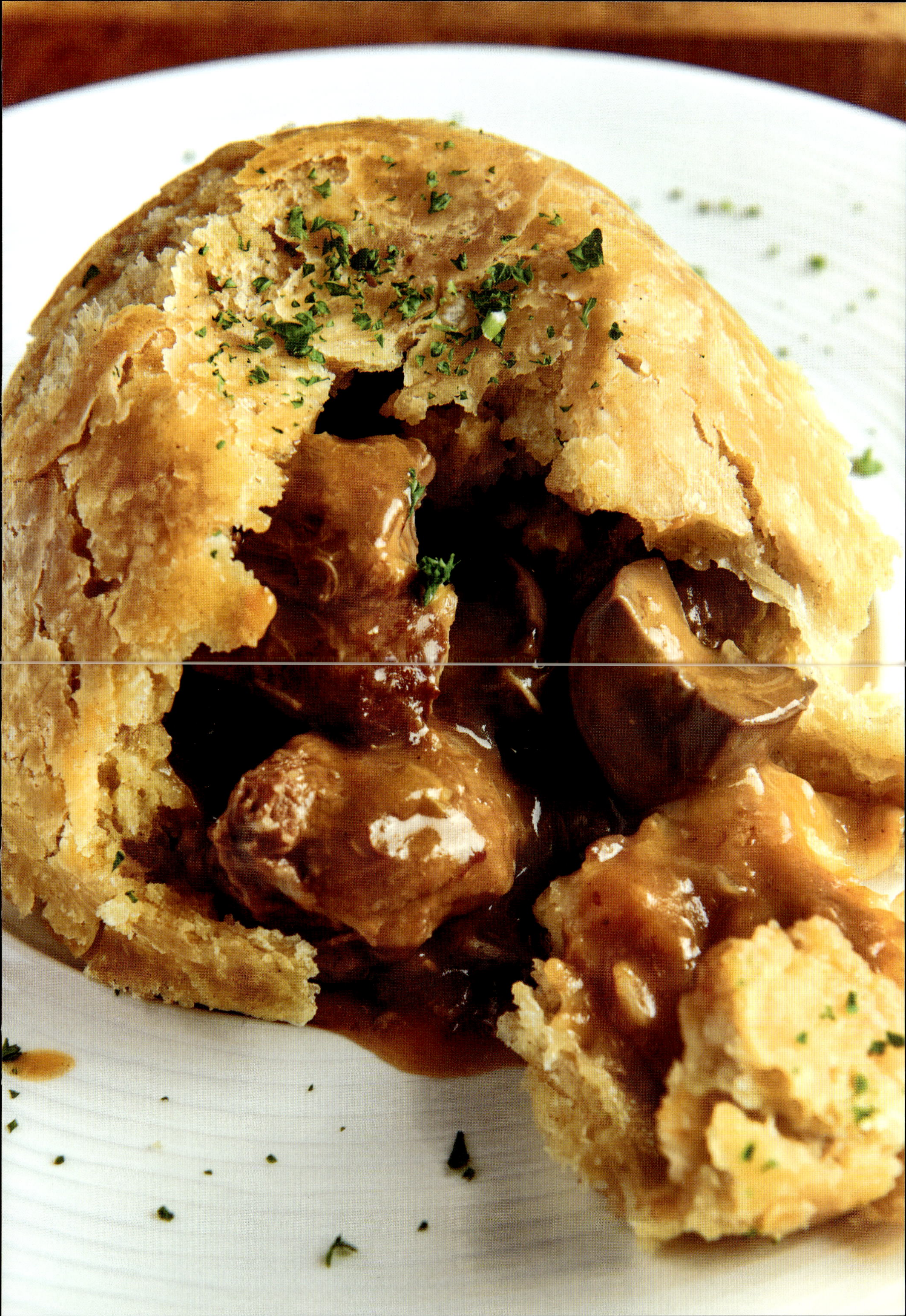

Yorkshire Pudding

INGREDIENTS:

Makes 4 large or 8 small Yorkshire puddings

3 large free range eggs
pinch of salt
150ml whole milk
100g plain flour
40g beef dripping or lard

METHOD:

Crack the eggs into a bowl, add the salt and whisk for 1 minute.

Add the milk and flour and whisk vigorously.

After whisking for 2 minutes, strain the batter through a sieve into a measuring jug and rest for 10 minutes.

While the batter is resting, divide the beef dripping or lard into your chosen number of Yorkshire pudding tins and place in the oven at 200°C for 5 minutes.

Give the batter a final whisk and pour into the hot Yorkshire pudding tins swiftly so as not to lose too much heat from the tins, and return to the oven.

When the puddings have risen sufficiently, reduce the temperature of the oven to 180°C until they are golden brown all over.

Remove from the oven and serve immediately.

This is the perfect accompaniment to a roast rib of beef or simply on their own with onion sauce.

To make an onion sauce, combine 2 small Spanish onions, peeled, sliced and fried until golden, with 300ml Española sauce, see page 238, and re-heat.

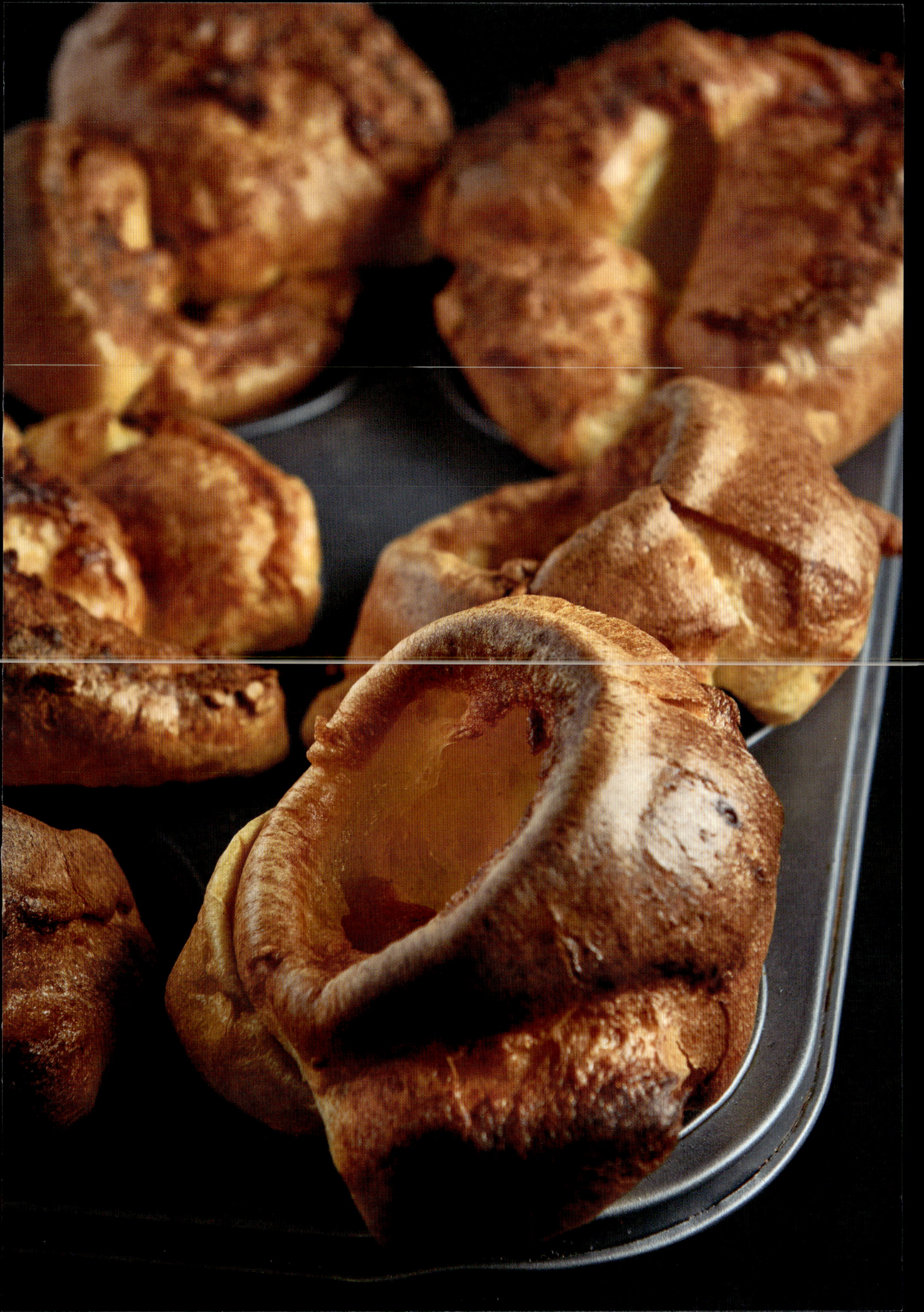

Chicken and Leek Pie

INGREDIENTS:
Serves 4

55g butter
1 onion, peeled and diced
1 leek, washed, sliced and diced
1 small bunch of fresh curly parsley, chopped
40g plain flour
400ml chicken stock, see page 218
150ml whipping cream
1 roasted chicken, meat stripped from the carcass and skin removed
salt and ground black pepper
600g shortcrust pastry, see page 228
1 free range egg, beaten for eggwash

METHOD:

Place the butter in a large thick-bottomed pan and heat. Add the onion, leek and parsley and cook for 5 minutes on a medium to low heat until the ingredients have softened without browning.

Add the plain flour to coat all the ingredients followed by the chicken stock and cream while stirring the sauce continuously to thicken. When the sauce is thickened, remove from the heat and place in a clean bowl.

Cool completely. Stir in the prepared chicken, season with salt and pepper and leave to one side.

Using 350g of the pastry, roll out on a floured surface to 7mm thickness and line a large buttered pie dish. Place the filling into the dish and egg wash the rim of the pastry.

Using the remaining 250g of the pastry, roll out the pie lid to 1cm thickness. Seal, crimp and decorate the pie with the pastry trimmings. Make a vent hole in the centre of the pie lid and egg wash the surface.

Bake in the oven at 180°C for 35-45 minutes until golden brown.

Serve with seasonal vegetables and potatoes.

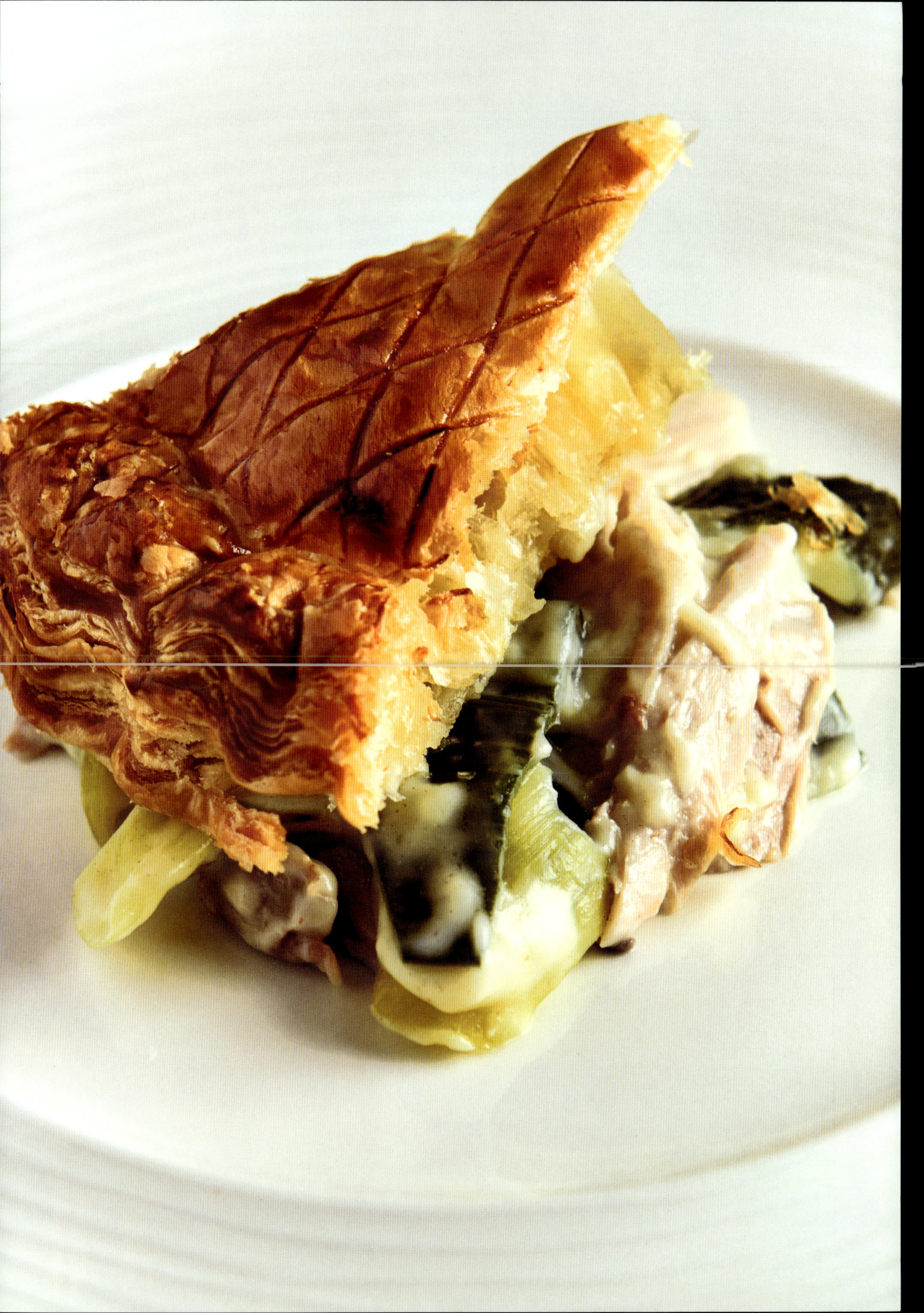

Pork Pie

INGREDIENTS:
Makes 4 small or 1 large pork pie

800g hot water pastry, see page 224
150g belly pork, diced
450g pork shoulder, diced
1 small sprig of fresh chopped fresh sage
1/4 teaspoon ground mace
pinch of salt and ground black pepper

To glaze your pies
2 free range egg yolks
1g salt

METHOD:

To make 4 small pork pies, weigh out 150g of pastry for the base and 50g for the lid.

On a floured surface, using 150g of pastry, make a pie case by hand, moulding to approximately 3-5mm thickness.

Using a rolling pin, roll out the lids for your pies to the required diameter and the same thickness as the base.

For the filling, combine and mix well the belly pork, pork shoulder, sage, mace, salt and pepper in a bowl. Divide the filling into 4 portions and place in the centre of each pie.

Egg wash the rims, place the lids on, seal and trim any excess pastry. Use this to decorate your pies as you wish, then egg wash the top and sides. Make a vent hole in the centre of the lids using a plain piping bag nozzle or similar.

For 4 small pies, place on a non-stick baking tray and bake in the oven at 170°C until golden brown all over. Cool before serving.

To bake one large pie, egg wash the lid and wrap a double layer band of tin foil tied with string around the circumference. Place on a non-stick baking tray and bake at 170°C for 40 minutes. Remove the foil, egg wash the sides, and continue baking until the whole pie is golden brown.

Cool before serving with your favourite pickles, chutney and salad.

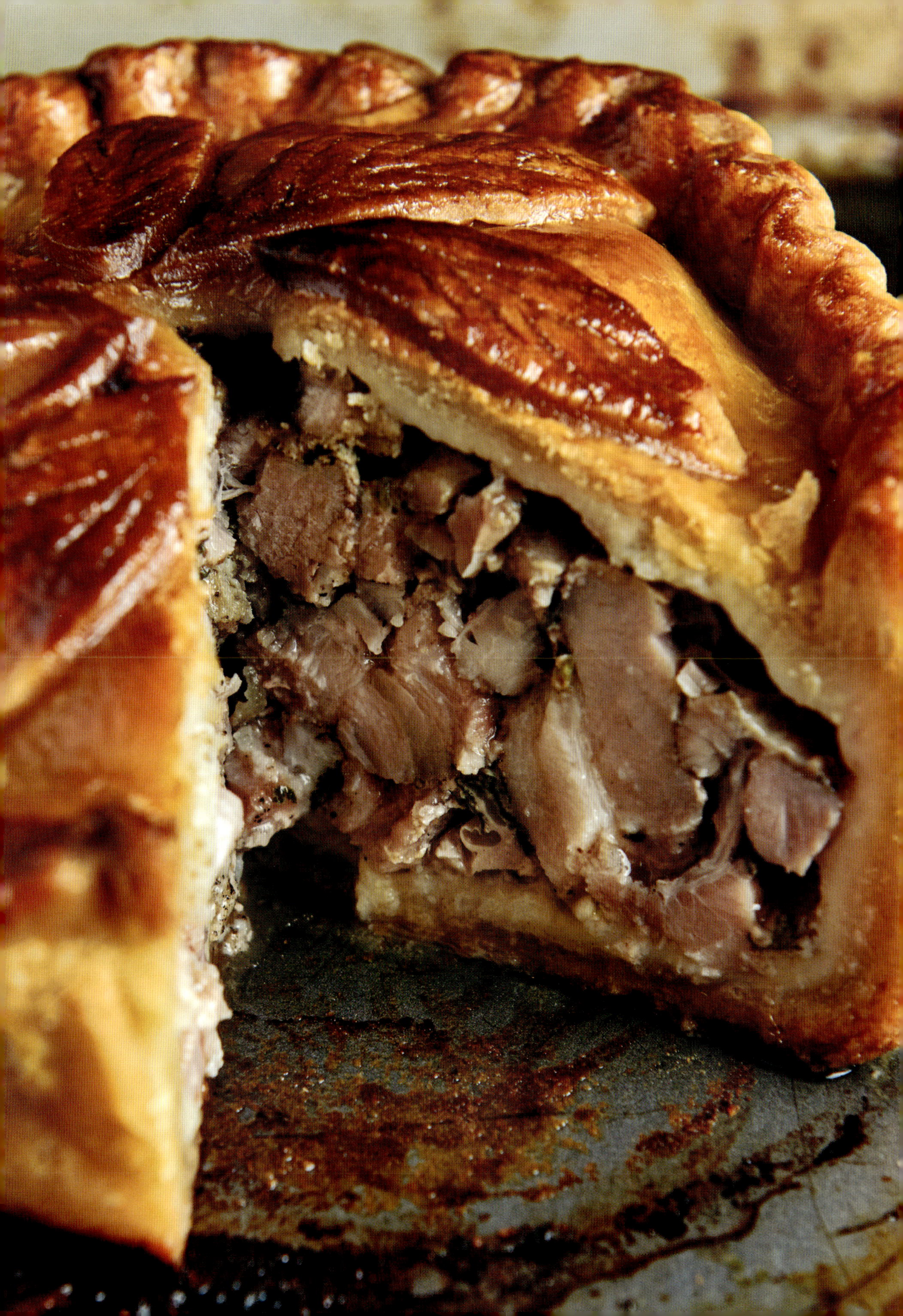

Beef Bourguignon

INGREDIENTS:
Serves 4

20ml rapeseed oil
750g stewing steak, 3cm diced
16 baby shallots, peeled, trimmed and whole
16 baby carrots, washed, peeled and trimmed
16 button mushrooms
1 clove garlic, crushed
1 sprig of fresh thyme
40g tomato purée
40g plain flour
200ml good red wine
400ml beef stock, see page 216
2 bay leaves
salt and ground black pepper
150g smoked bacon, cut into lardons and fried

METHOD:

Place the rapeseed oil in a large thick-bottomed sauté pan on a medium heat.

Fry the stewing steak until browned on all sides.

Add the shallots, carrots and mushrooms and cook for a further 5 minutes on a medium to low heat.

Add the garlic, thyme, tomato purée and plain flour. Stir to coat all the ingredients. Add the red wine, beef stock and bay leaves. Bring to the boil and simmer for 90 minutes until the beef is tender and the sauce has thickened.

Season with salt and pepper and serve with the lardons of bacon.

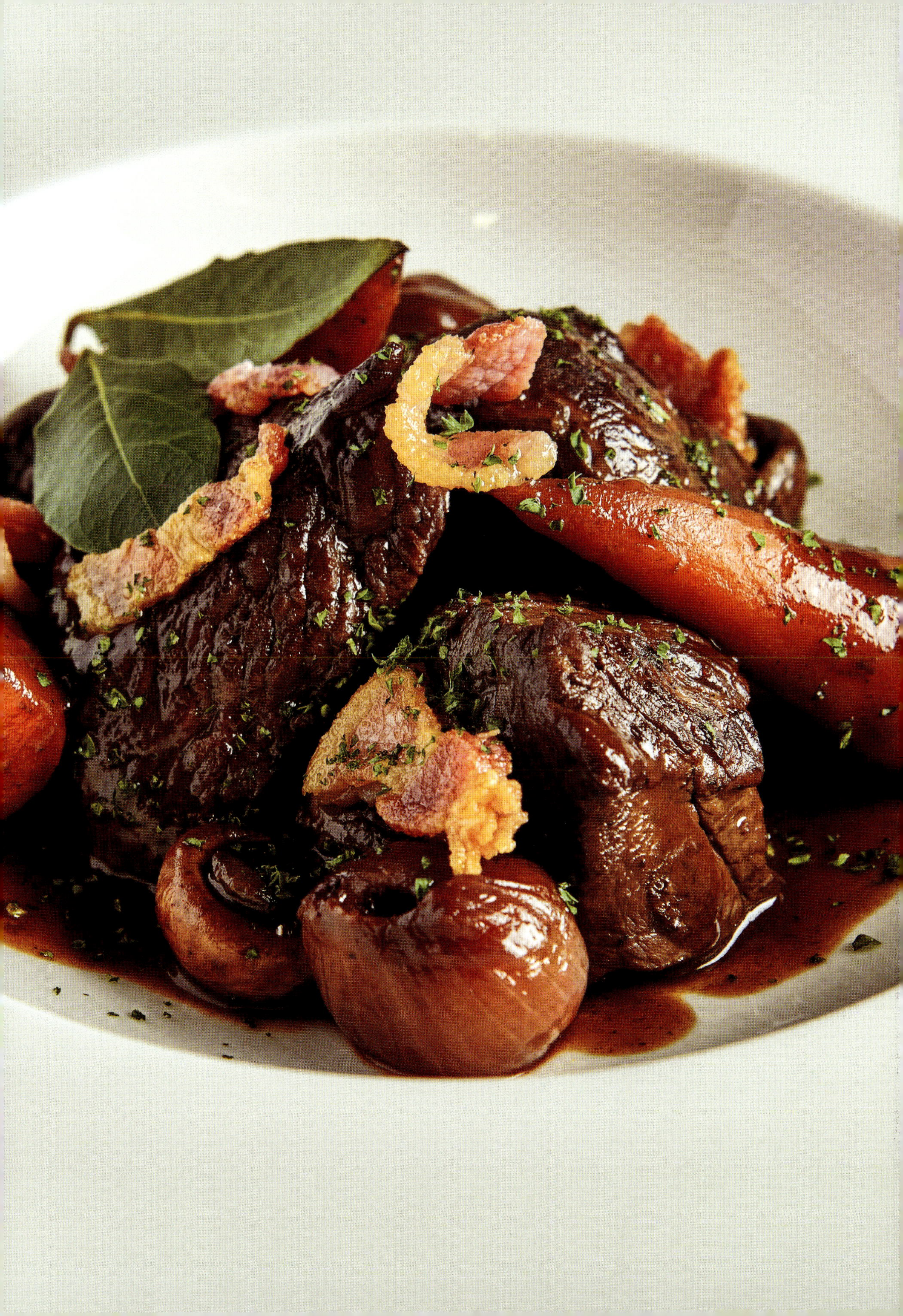

Lamb Hotpot

INGREDIENTS:
Serves 4

2 carrots, washed, peeled, trimmed and diced
2 onions, thinly sliced
1 sprig of thyme, leaves picked
2 bay leaves
50g pearl barley
2 small bunches of curly parsley, finely chopped
8 lamb cutlets or 300g diced lamb or mutton shoulder
salt and ground black pepper
3 Maris Piper potatoes, washed, peeled and thinly sliced
500ml chicken stock, see page 218
30g butter, melted

METHOD:

Take a large casserole dish and make a mixed layer of half the carrots, onions, thyme, bay leaves, pearl barley, and a third of the parsley. Put a layer of lamb cutlets, diced lamb or mutton on top of this and season with salt and pepper. Top with another layer the same as the first.

Top with the thinly sliced potatoes. Flood the dish with the chicken stock and drizzle with butter. Bake in the oven at 180°C for 2 hours uncovered. Check the casserole occasionally and if necessary, top up with chicken stock.

After baking, sprinkle with the remaining parsley and serve.

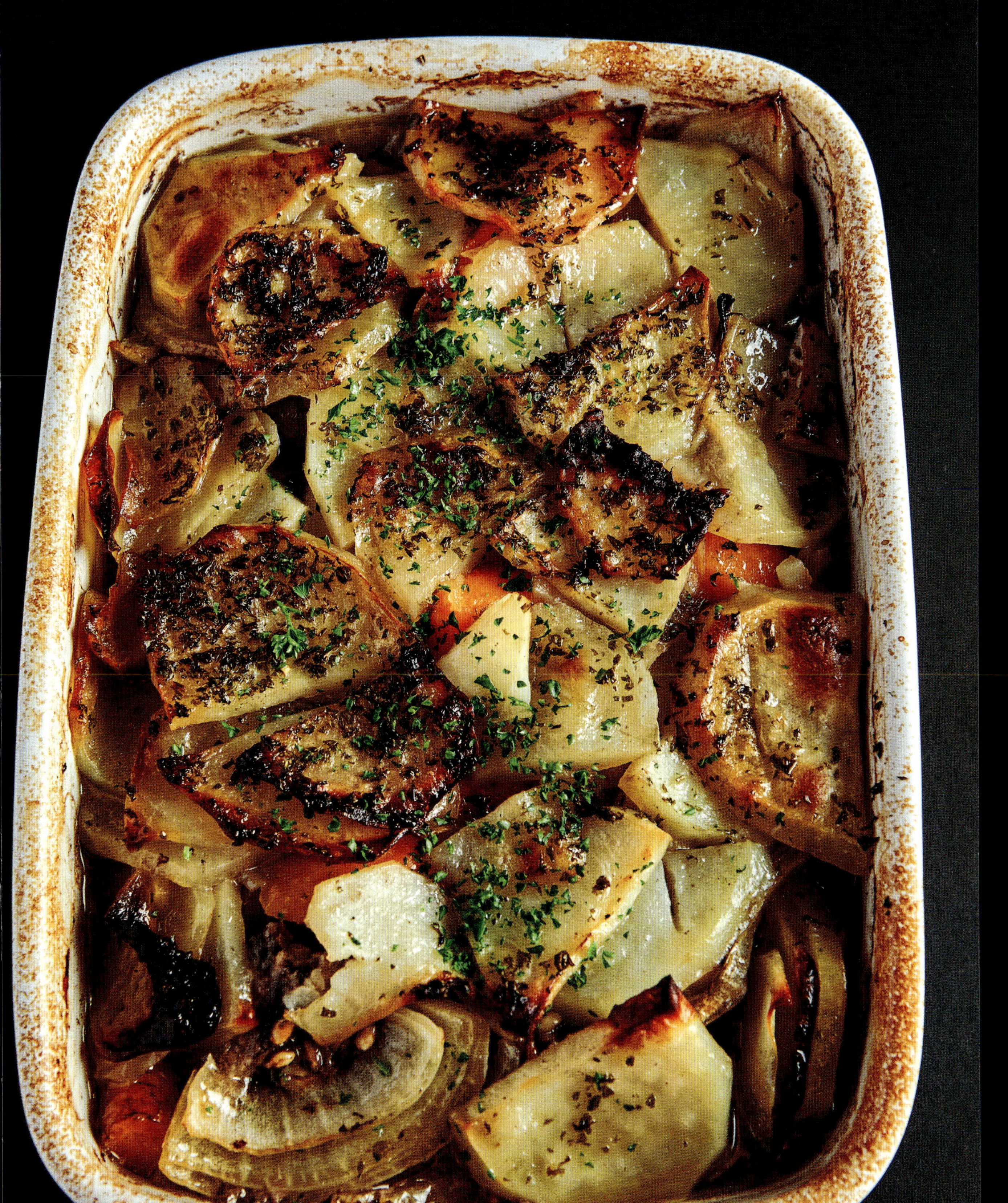

WHEN IT COMES TO DINNER PARTIES THAT I DO IN PEOPLE'S HOMES, EVERYONE LOVES SOMETHING A LITTLE SPICY. I NEVER DO AN EXTRA PORTION; IT KEEPS ME ON MY TOES!

Nicely Spicy

EGG FRIED RICE.98
JALFREZI CHICKEN.100
NAAN BREAD.102
STIR FRIED GINGER BEEF.104
SWEET AND SOUR PORK.106

It's just too safe and complacency can set in; then we're into the realms of compromised quality. If you've got spares you're more likely to overcook the first one as it's not at the front of your mind because you know you have a plan B. The way I operate carries risk, but it works for me and has never failed me yet.

It's all about discipline and trusting yourself to deliver the goods to the highest standard that you can. An artist commissioned to paint a portrait wouldn't have two easels and canvases, would they? So why should I have an extra portion of chicken?

NB.
NICELY SPICY

CHAPTER 5

Egg Fried Rice

INGREDIENTS:
Serves 4

50ml sesame oil
2 large free range eggs, beaten
100g fresh peas, blanched
1 red pepper, deseeded and diced
1 bunch spring onions, trimmed and sliced on the diagonal, 5cm long
1 garlic clove, crushed
3g Chinese five spice powder
300g long grain rice, cooked
salt and ground black pepper
fresh chives, chopped

METHOD:

In a wok, heat the sesame oil.

Pour the eggs into the hot oil, and using a fork or a spatula, mix and stir over a high heat continuously to keep the egg separated and frying.

When the egg starts to turn to a fried and golden appearance, season with salt and pepper and add the peas, pepper, spring onions, garlic, Chinese five spice and rice.

Continue stirring and cooking over a medium heat until the rice is hot and ready to serve.

Finish the dish with fresh chopped chives.

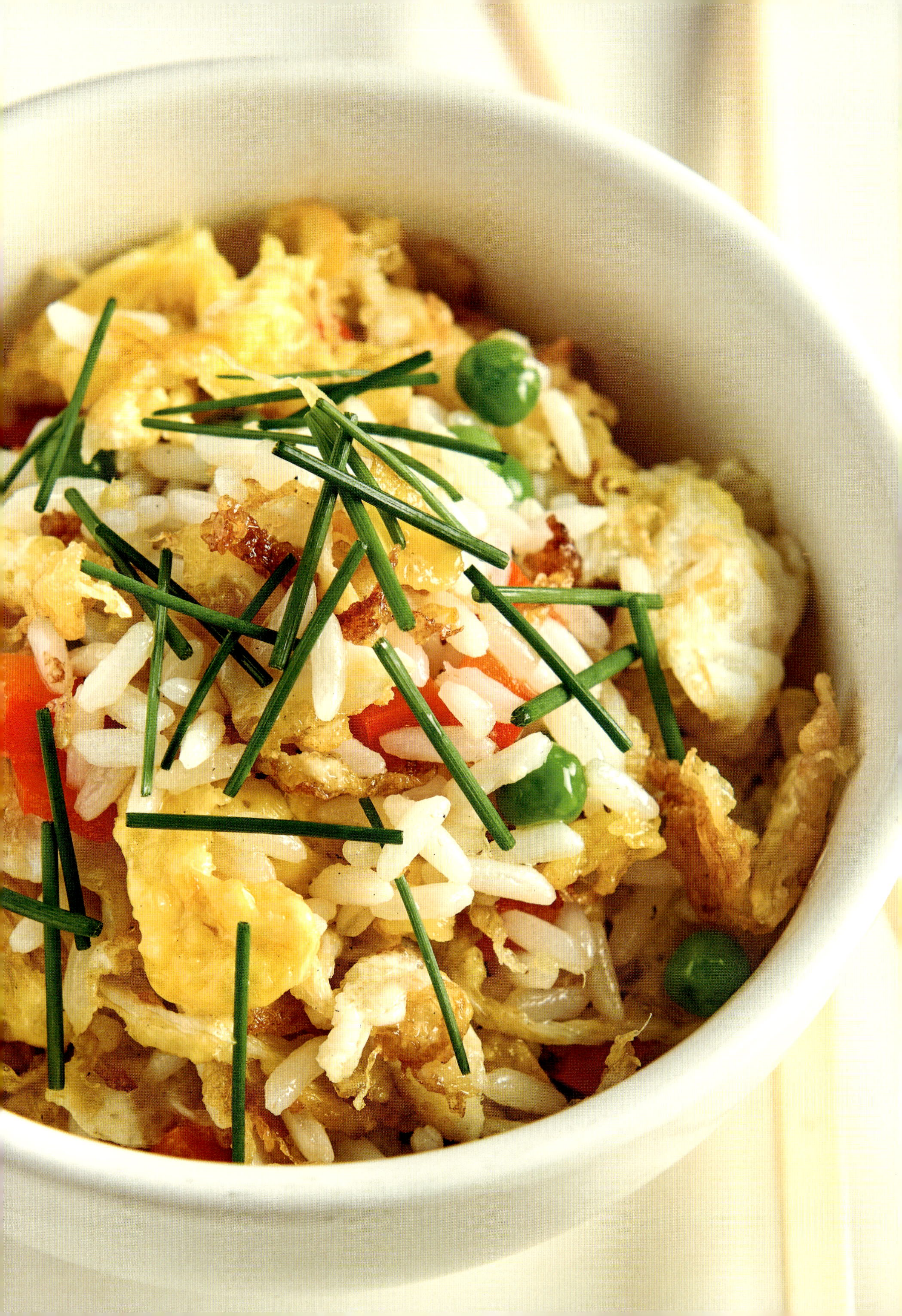

Jalfrezi Chicken

INGREDIENTS:
Serves 4

4 skinless chicken breasts and 4 thigh portions, on the bone
50g ground turmeric
5g harissa paste
20g ground cumin
20g grated fresh ginger root
20g garam masala
30g ground coriander
4 cloves of garlic, crushed
10ml vegetable oil
2 onions, peeled and quartered and separated
2 red peppers, sliced and cut into large chunks
30g plain flour
20g tomato purée
12 tomatoes, blanched, skinned, deseeded and chopped
1 litre chicken stock, see page 218
salt and ground black pepper
1 bunch fresh coriander

METHOD:

Place the chicken portions, turmeric, harissa paste, cumin, ginger, garam masala, ground coriander and garlic in a large bowl. Rub the spices into the chicken and allow to marinate for 2 hours in the fridge.

Put the vegetable oil in a thick-bottomed saucepan and on a medium heat. Cook the chicken and spices for 5-6 minutes, or until sealed. Add the onions and peppers and continue cooking for a further 3 minutes on a low to medium heat. Add the plain flour and tomato purée to coat all the ingredients, followed by the chopped tomatoes and chicken stock, and season to taste.

Bring the jalfrezi to the boil and allow to simmer for 75 minutes, stirring occasionally, topping up with chicken stock if necessary.

Once cooked, transfer to a serving dish and finish with fresh chopped coriander.

Serve with naan bread, see page 102.

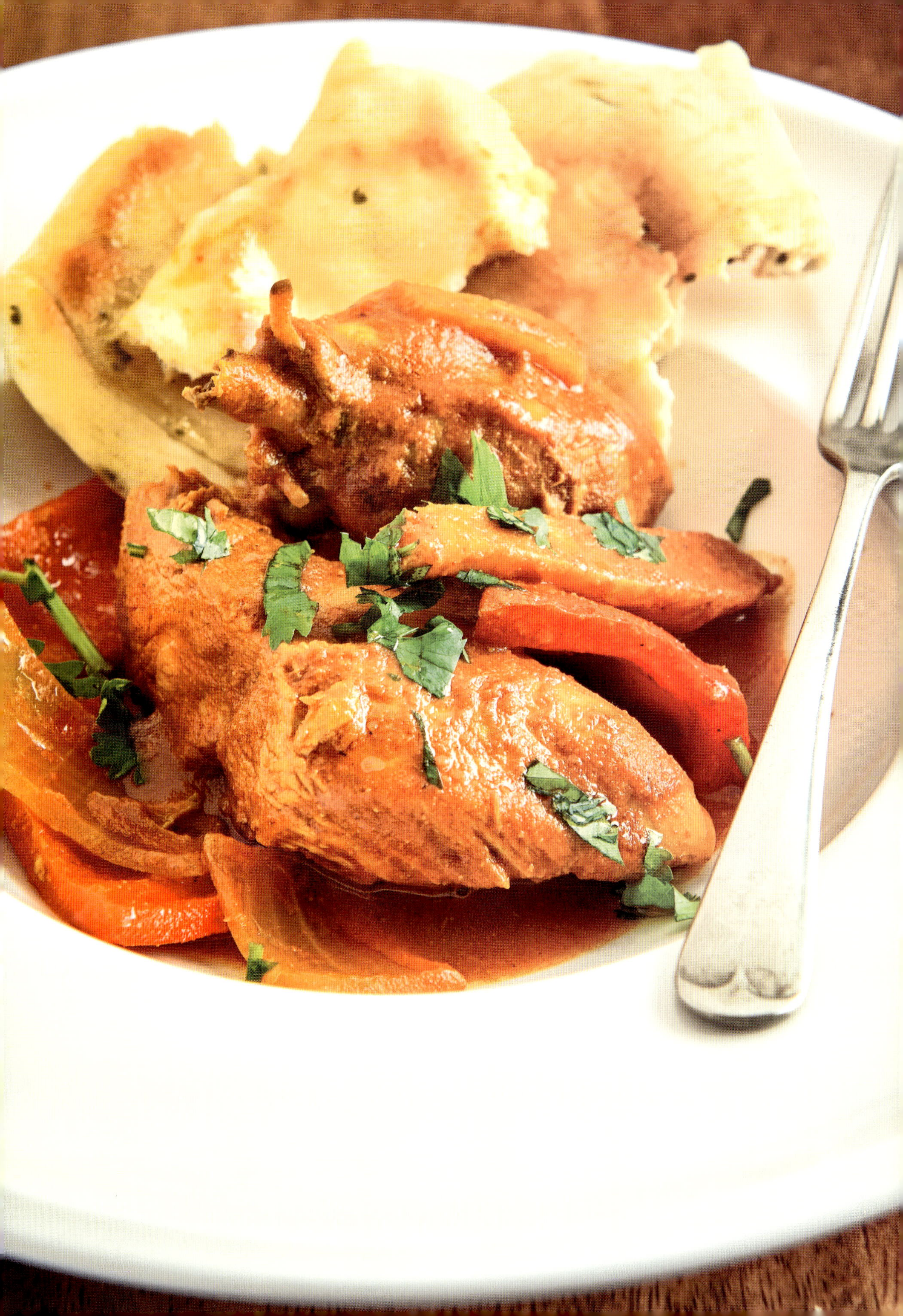

Naan Bread

INGREDIENTS:
Serves 4

400g strong white bread flour
pinch of salt
1 small bunch fresh coriander, chopped
7g fresh or dried yeast
150ml whole milk
50ml natural yoghurt
100ml ghee, melted

METHOD:

Sieve the flour into a large bowl and add the salt and chopped coriander.

In a separate dish, add the yeast, milk and natural yogurt, and stir until dissolved.

Make a well in the centre of the flour and pour in two-thirds of the yeast liquid. Using a small butter knife, bind the ingredients together to form a soft dough, using the remaining yeast liquid if required.

When a soft dough is formed, knead for 3 minutes and allow to rest until doubled in size.

Pre-heat the oven to 190°C. Divide the dough into 8 portions and roll with a rolling pin to the shape of a naan bread (pear-shaped), approximately 7.5mm thick. Place onto an oiled baking tray, allow to rest for 5 minutes then bake until slightly risen and golden. Once cooked, brush with melted ghee and serve.

Serve with jalfrezi chicken, see page 100.

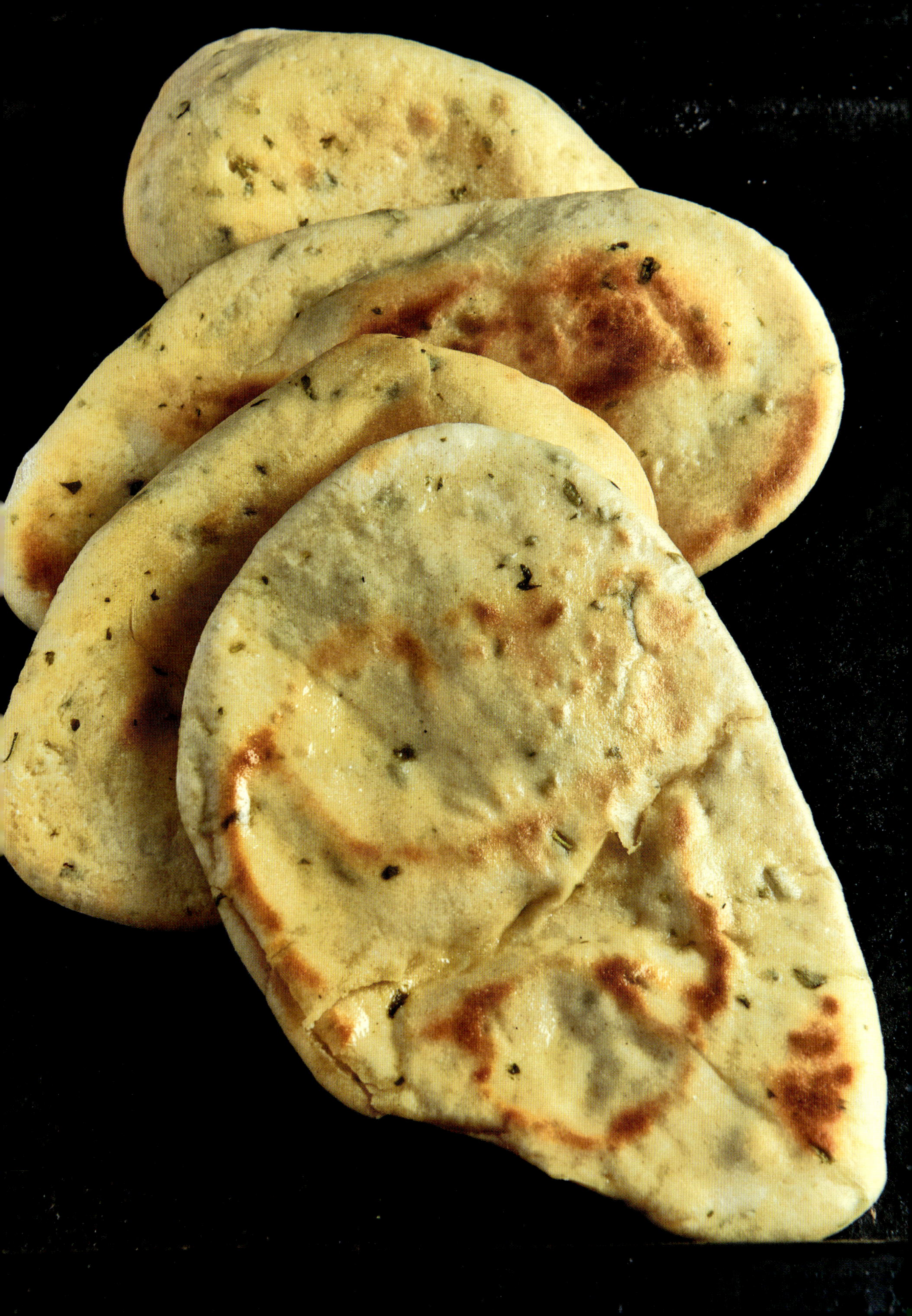

Stir Fried Ginger Beef

INGREDIENTS:
Serves 4

500g beef fillet, trimmed and cut into thin strips (approx. 5cm x 2cm)
3g Chinese five spice powder
1 large red chilli, deseeded and cut into strips
1 garlic clove, crushed
40g fresh ginger root, grated
juice of 1 lime
20ml soy sauce
10ml fish sauce
20ml sesame oil
1 stick lemongrass, trimmed and sliced
100g sugar snap peas, cut into thin strips
8 baby sweetcorns, sliced
6 spring onions, trimmed and sliced on the diagonal, 5cm long
30g cashew nuts, roasted
100g fresh rice noodles, cooked
1 small bunch of fresh coriander, chopped
1 lime

METHOD:

Place the beef fillet, Chinese five spice, red chillies, garlic, ginger, lime juice, soy sauce and fish sauce in a bowl. Marinate for 1 hour in the fridge.

Drain the beef, keeping the marinade for later.

Take a large thick-bottomed sauté pan and add the sesame oil. On a high heat, fry the beef with the lemongrass, sugar snap peas, baby sweetcorn, spring onions and cashew nuts for one minute.

Add the marinade juices and the noodles and cook for a further minute.

Transfer to a serving dish and sprinkle with fresh coriander.

Serve with fresh wedges of lime.

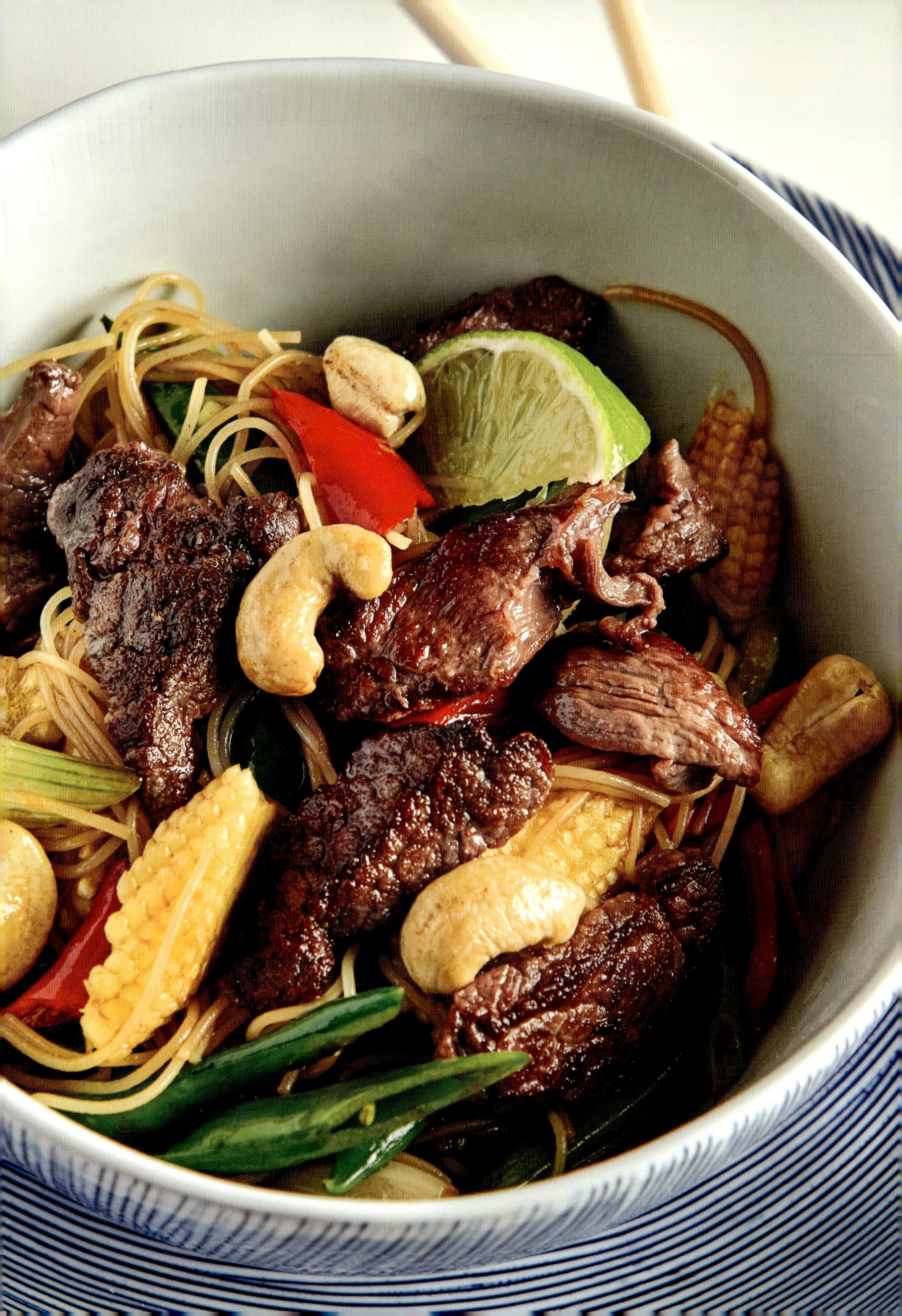

Sweet and Sour Pork

INGREDIENTS:
Serves 4

450g pork fillet, trimmed and cut into 5cm x 1cm strips
20g plain flour
sunflower oil for deep frying

For the batter
40g plain flour, sifted
30ml rice wine
1 medium free range egg, lightly beaten
200ml cold water
pinch of salt

For the sauce:
1tsp sesame oil
1 red pepper, quartered and deseeded
1 bunch spring onions, trimmed and sliced on the diagonal, 5cm long
100g bamboo shoots
50g water chestnuts, sliced
1/4 fresh pineapple, trimmed and cut into chunks
1 star anise
1 cinnamon stick
20g grated fresh ginger root
3g harissa paste (optional)
100ml plum sauce
100ml oyster sauce
10ml soy sauce
50ml rice wine vinegar
10ml Worcestershire sauce

METHOD:

Roll the pork fillet strips in the plain flour and set to one side.

For the batter, beat all the ingredients together to a smooth batter, and strain through a sieve into a bowl.

For the sauce, place a small saucepan onto the heat with the teaspoon of sesame oil. Add the red pepper, spring onions, bamboo shoots, water chestnuts and pineapple. Cook for 1 minute on a high heat then add the star anise, cinnamon stick, ginger and harissa paste (if using). Cook for a further minute. Add the plum sauce, oyster sauce, soy sauce, rice wine vinegar and Worcestershire sauce, bring to the boil and remove from the heat.

Heat the sunflower oil to 180°C. Dip the pork strips in the batter, allow the excess batter to drain off, then gently place into the oil to cook. The strips should take no longer than 3 minutes to cook. During this time, reheat the sauce if necessary. Drain the pork on kitchen paper and serve together with the sauce.

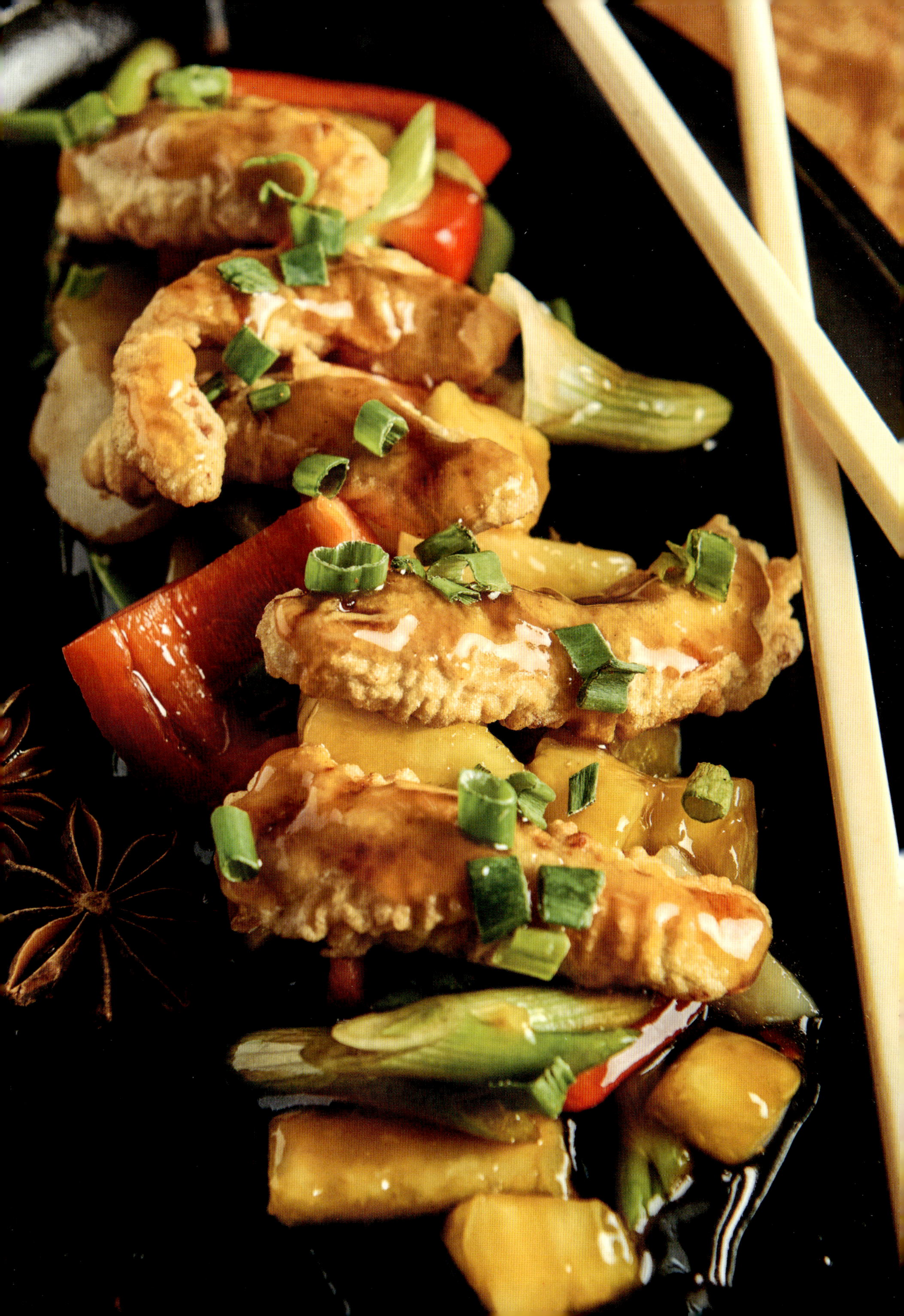

WE ALL TAKE ITALIAN, CHINESE, THAI AND TURKISH RESTAURANTS AND SO ON FOR GRANTED NOWADAYS; THEY ARE SO READILY AVAILABLE TO US EVERYWHERE WE GO. EVERY TOWN AND CITY SEEMS TO HAVE SUCH A WIDE SELECTION OF EUROPEAN AND INTERNATIONAL CUISINES BUT I REMEMBER WHEN IT WAS EXCITING TO HEAR OF AN ITALIAN RESTAURANT POPPING UP IN YOUR LOCAL TOWN OR CITY.

Pizza

PIZZA DOUGH.110
MOZZARELLA, PARMA HAM AND OLIVE PIZZA.112

Pasta

PASTA DOUGH.114
SALMON RAVIOLI WITH TOMATO AND DILL DRESSING.116
SMOKED HAM AND MUSHROOM TAGLIATELLE.118

My first experience of an Italian restaurant and pizza was when as a family we were dining out at new Italian restaurant just outside Hull back in the mid 1970s. The name of the restaurant escapes me now; but the memory of the mozzarella will stay with me forever.

The drama of seeing an Italian chef spinning your pizza base 17 feet high in the air at 1,600 revolutions a minute suggested eating it would be a real experience.

The freshly-baked pizza base with its rich tomato paste, parma ham and mushrooms was so tasty; and the mozzarella and oregano were completely new to me. It was a delicious flavour combination.

The problem was that the chef was so generous with this new and exciting ingredient, mozzarella, it was impossible to swallow and almost choked me. When it comes to mozzarella, less is more!

NB.
PIZZA
& PASTA

CHAPTER 6

Pizza Dough

INGREDIENTS:
Makes 4 x 24cm pizza bases

225g Italian 00 flour
pinch of salt
pinch of caster sugar
7g yeast
150ml water
25ml whole milk
15ml olive oil

METHOD:

Sieve the flour into a large bowl and add the salt and sugar.

In a separate bowl, dissolve the yeast in the water, milk and olive oil. Make a well in the centre of the flour and add two-thirds of the yeast liquid. Using a small butter knife, stir the ingredients to make a dough consistency, adding additional yeast mixture if required.

Remove the dough onto a floured surface and knead until it takes on a smooth, soft texture. Allow to rest for half an hour or doubled in size before use.

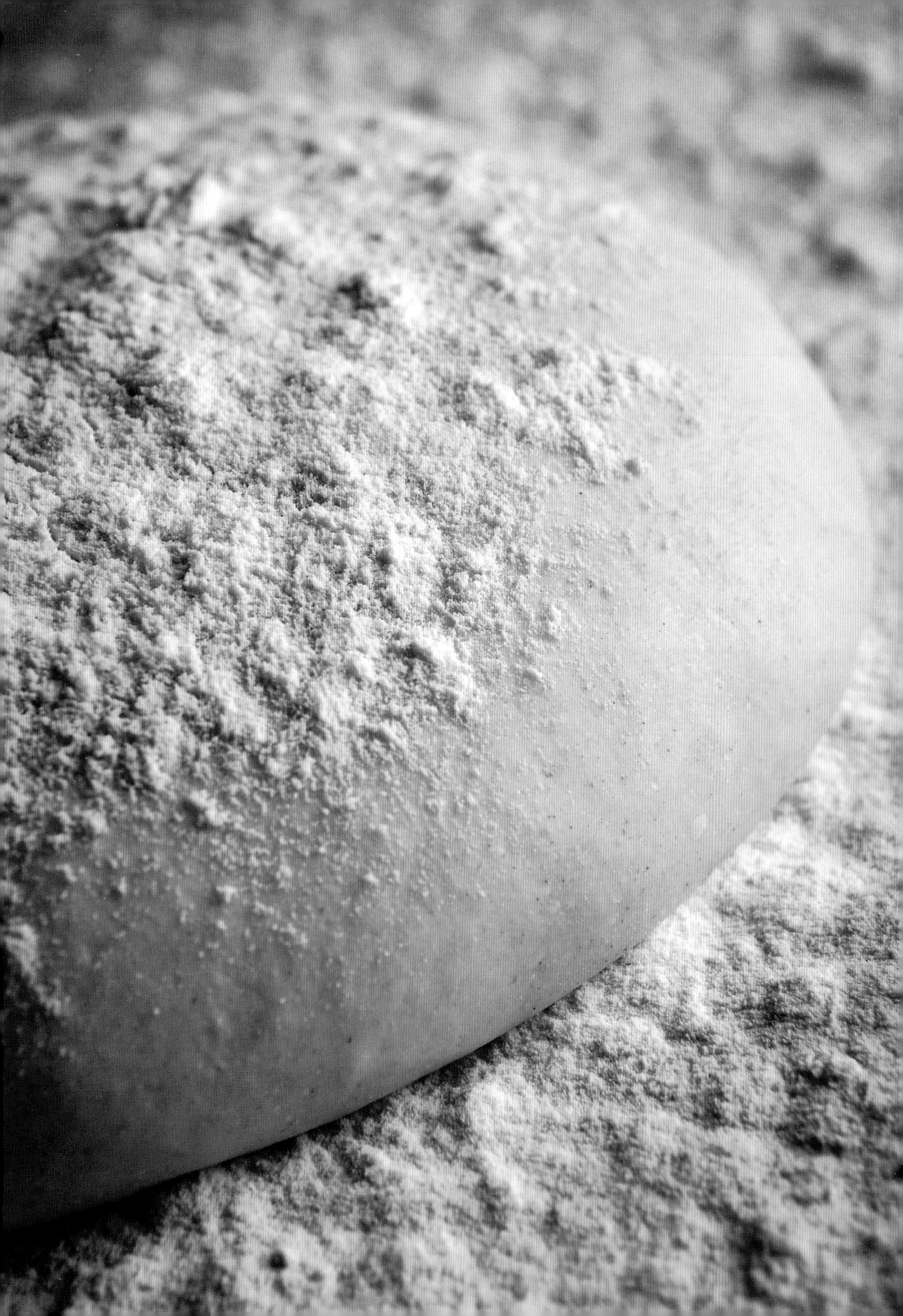

Mozzarella, Parma Ham and Olive Pizza

INGREDIENTS:
Makes 4 x 24cm pizzas

400g pizza dough, see page 110
80g tomato purée
1 small bunch of fresh or dried oregano
2 garlic cloves, crushed
4 large vine-ripened tomatoes, thinly sliced
300g Parma ham
150g black olives, pitted
200g mozzarella, sliced or torn
100g parmesan shavings
20ml olive oil
1 bunch of fresh basil

METHOD:

Pre-heat oven to 200°C.

Divide the pizza dough into 4 x 100g and roll into 24cm bases.

Spread the tomato purée onto the pizza bases leaving a 2cm plain crust around the edge. Sprinkle with oregano and crushed garlic cloves.

Divide the tomatoes between the pizza bases followed by the Parma ham, black olives, mozzarella and parmesan shavings.

Bake in the oven for 8-10 minutes. Once cooked, drizzle with olive oil and decorate with fresh picked basil leaves.

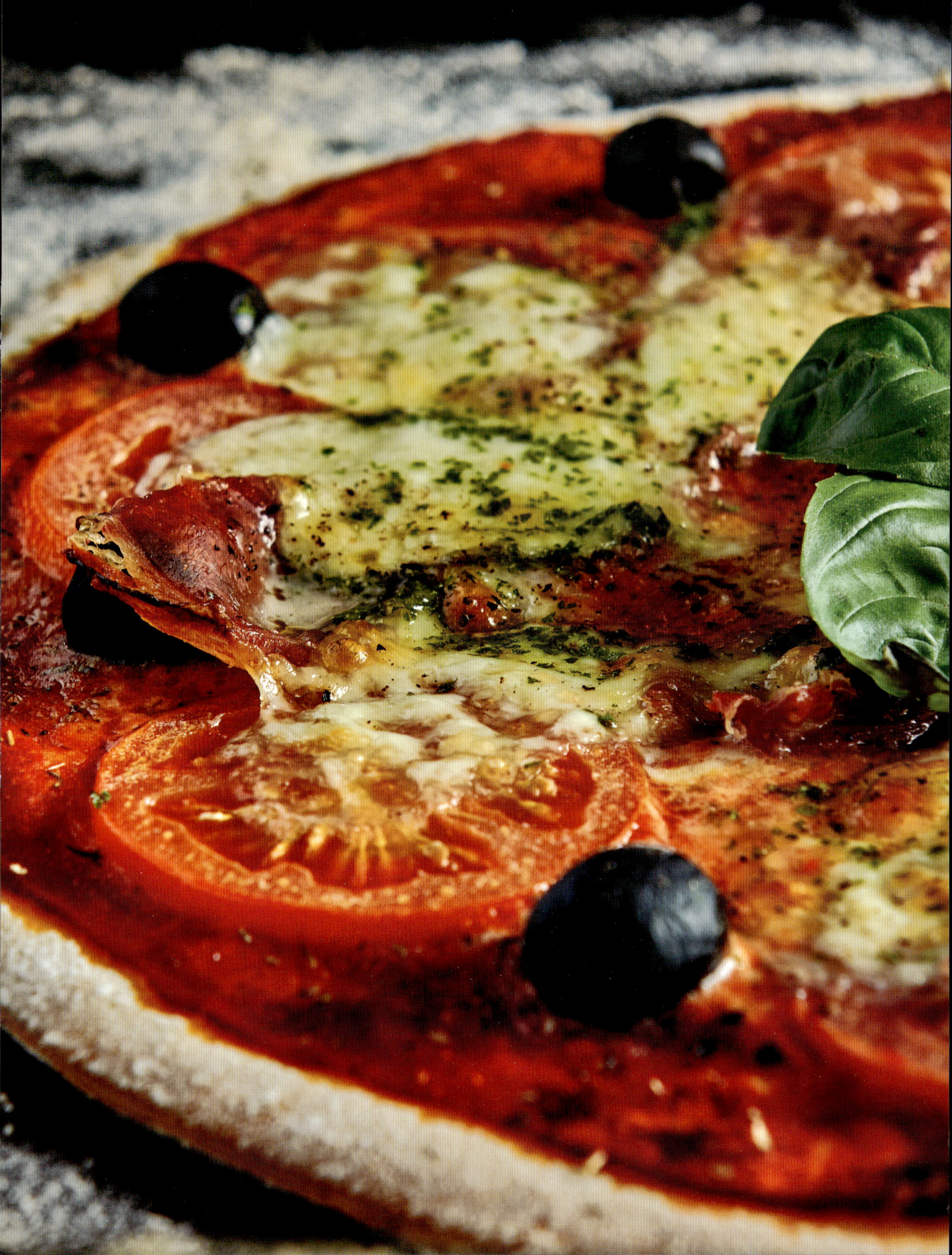

Pasta Dough

INGREDIENTS:

Makes 200g pasta dough

200g fine ground semolina or 00 grade flour
2 large free range eggs

METHOD:

Place the semolina or flour into a large bowl. Make a well in the centre and add the eggs.

Using a small butter knife, mix the ingredients together until a dough is formed. Knead the dough on an unfloured surface for 5 minutes.

Wrap the dough in cling film, rest for a minimum of 30 minutes before use.

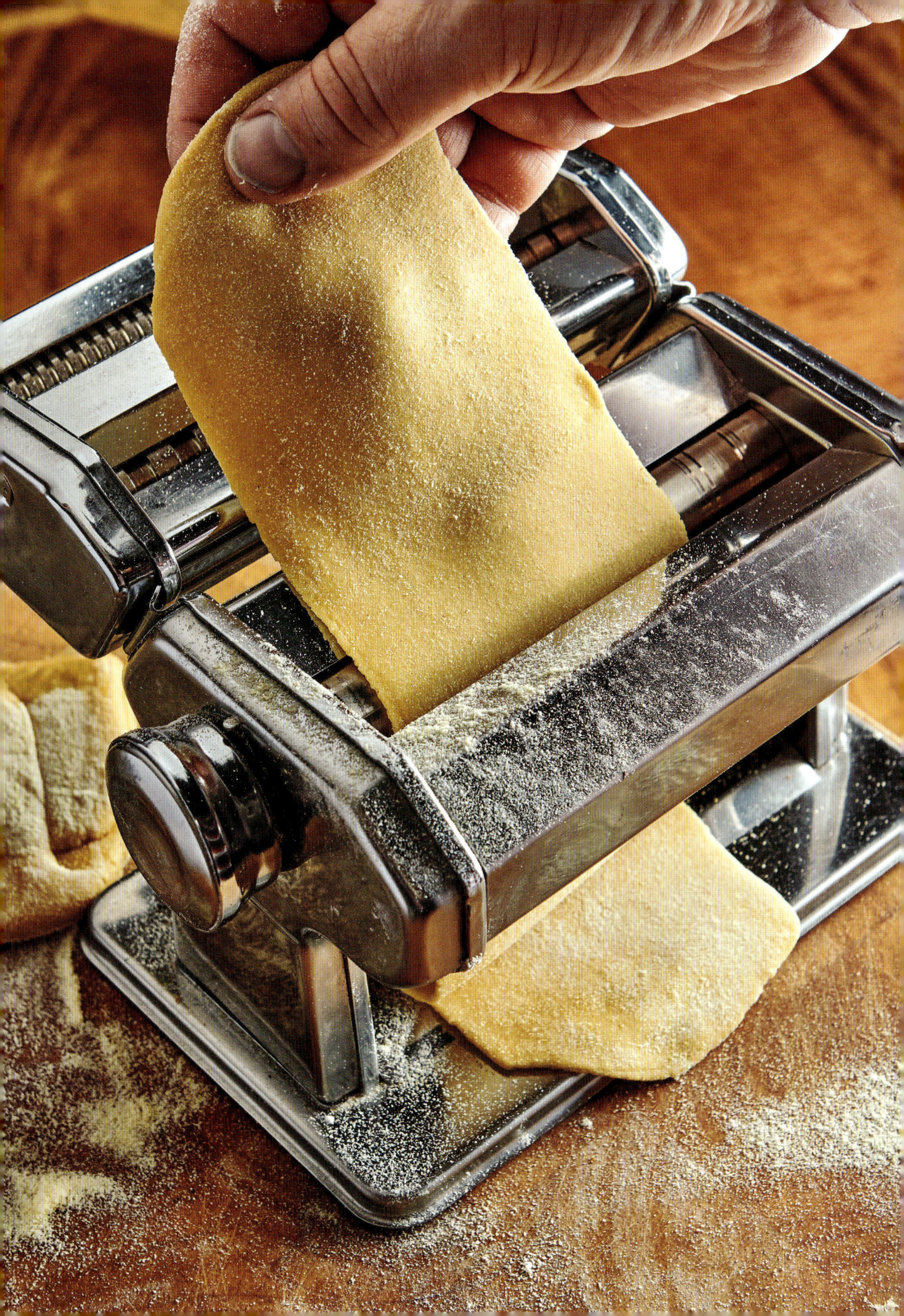

Salmon Ravioli with Tomato and Dill Dressing

INGREDIENTS:

Serves 4

200g pasta dough, see page 114
1 egg, beaten for egg wash
400g salmon fillets, skinned and cut into 20g portions
pinch of salt and ground black pepper
zest of 1 lemon

For the dressing

120g sun-dried tomatoes, sliced into strips
30ml of oil from a jar of sun-dried tomatoes
1 garlic clove, crushed
pinch of nutmeg
1 small bunch of fresh dill

METHOD:

Divide the pasta dough into 4 x 50g portions.

Using a pasta machine, pass each piece of pasta dough through the machine, rolling from the thickest setting to the thinnest to achieve the lasagne sheets.

To make the dressing, mix all the ingredients together and chill in the fridge.

Egg wash half of each sheet. Place the salmon portions on the egg-washed sheets at 4cm intervals. Season with salt, pepper and lemon zest. Carefully fold the remaining part of the pasta sheet over the salmon and gently press and seal around the portions. Using a fluted pastry cutter of a suitable size, cut out each ravioli from the pasta sheet and cook in a pan of salted water for 2-3 minutes and drain.

Serve the ravioli with a good serving of the dressing.

This is perfect with tomato and parmesan ciabatta, see page 150.

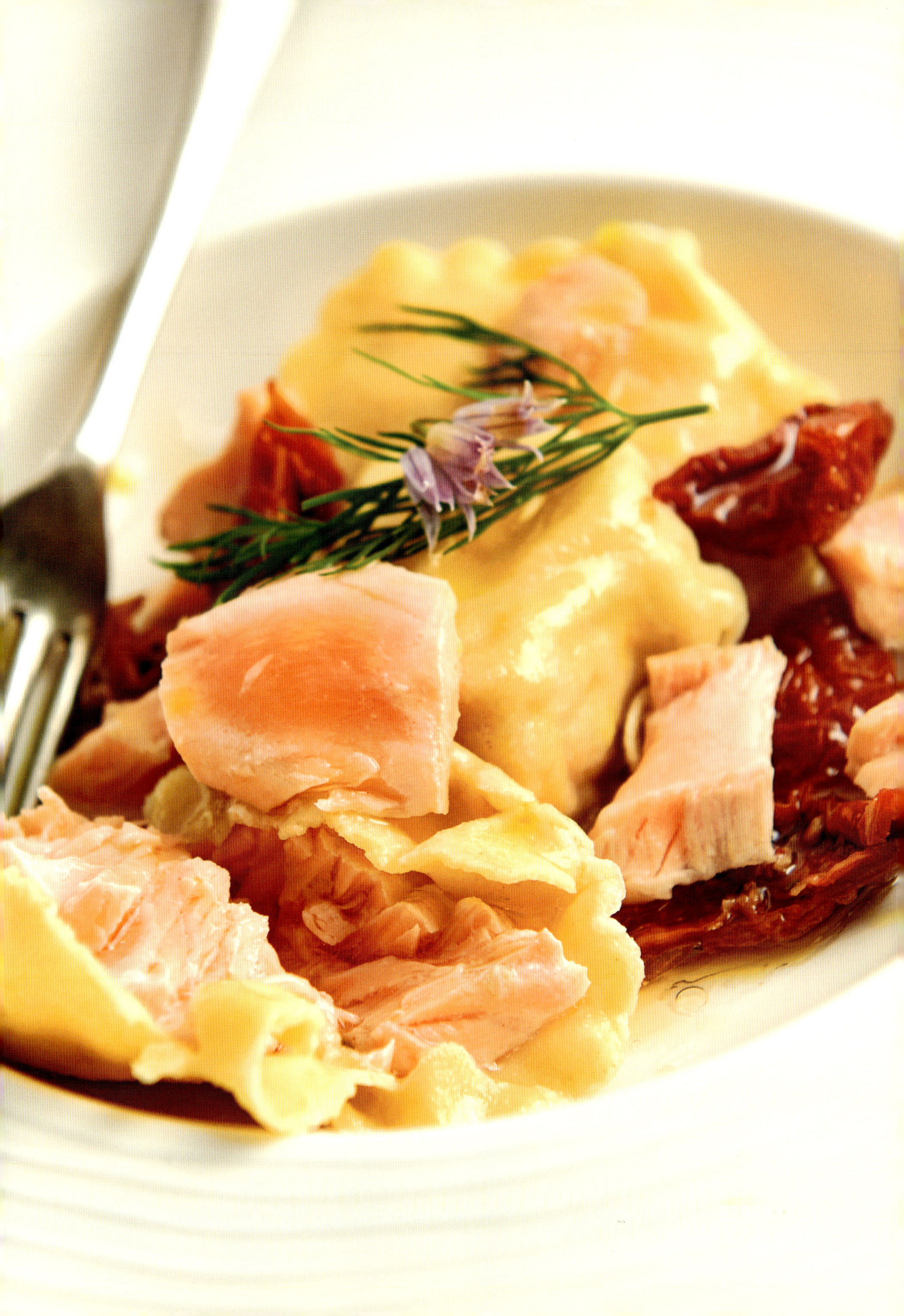

Smoked Ham and Mushroom Tagliatelle

INGREDIENTS:
Serves 4

200g pasta dough, see page 114

salt and ground black pepper
20ml olive oil
200g button mushrooms, sliced
200g thick-cut smoked ham, sliced
100ml dry white wine
100g mascarpone cheese
20g salted butter
20g wild mushrooms
50g fresh parmesan, shaved
1 small bunch of fresh basil

METHOD:

Divide the pasta dough into 4 x 50g portions.

Using a pasta machine, pass each piece of pasta dough through the machine, rolling several times from the thickest setting to the thinnest to achieve lasagne sheets. Then pass it through a tagliatelle attachment or cut into long strips by hand, approximately 5mm wide. Set to one side.

Half fill a large saucepan with water and a pinch of salt. Place onto the heat and bring to the boil.

In a separate sauté pan, add the olive oil and place on a medium heat. Gently fry the button mushrooms for 2 minutes then add the smoked ham and white wine. Reduce the wine by half then add the mascarpone cheese. Season with salt and pepper.

Place the tagliatelle into the boiling salted water and cook for 2 minutes. Strain and toss with the butter. Add the wild mushrooms to the sauce and bring together with the tagliatelle.

Serve with shaved parmesan and fresh basil leaves.

This is perfect with tomato and parmesan ciabatta, see page 150.

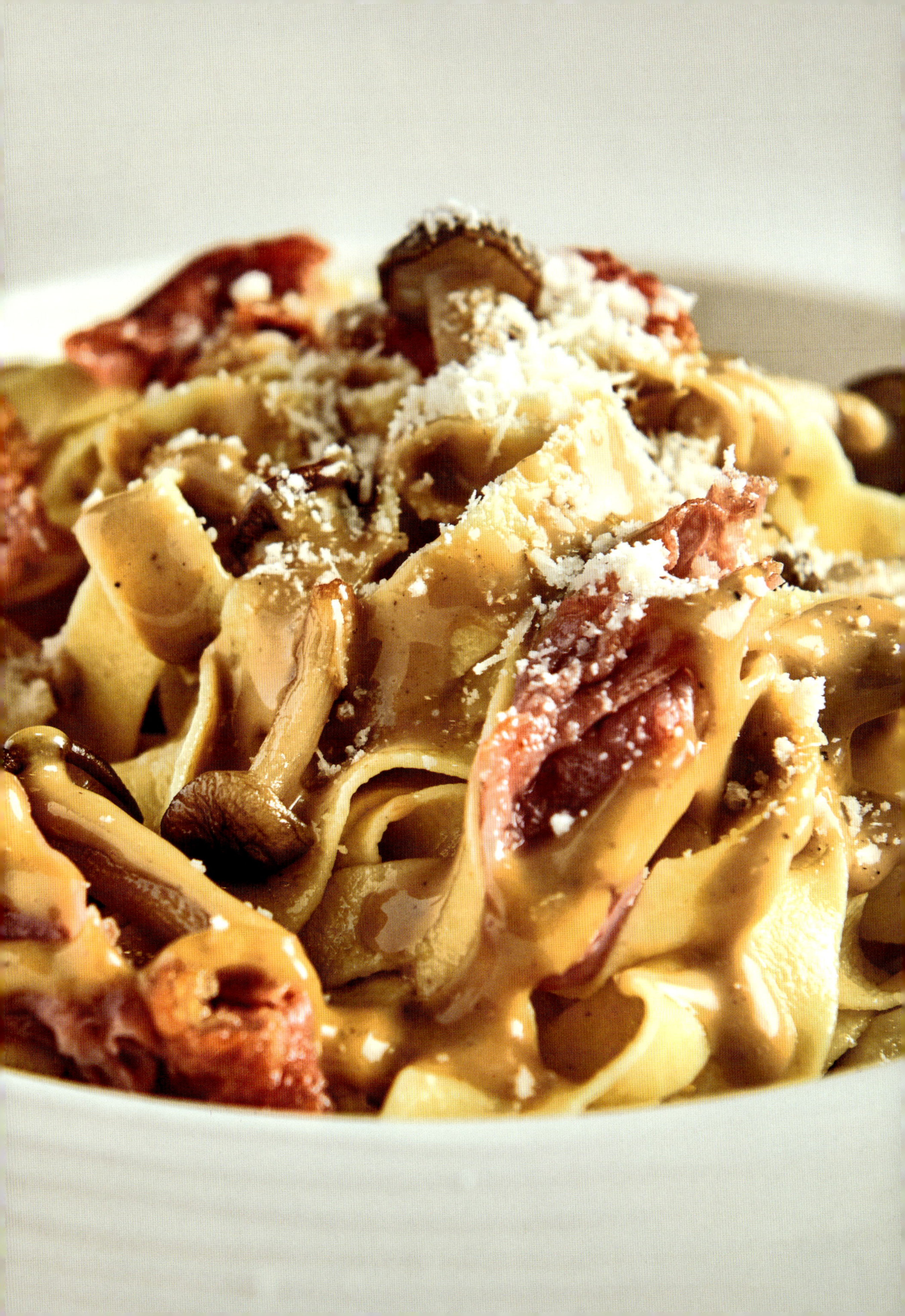

IN THE LATE EIGHTIES I HAD THE FABULOUS OPPORTUNITY TO SPEND A MONTH AT THE HIGHLY ACCLAIMED FRENCH PATISSERIE SCHOOL LENÔTRE. IT WAS, AND STILL IS, JUST ON THE OUTSKIRTS OF PARIS. THE BUSINESS STARTED AS A SMALL BAKERY RUN AND OWNED BY GASTON LENÔTRE AND HAS SINCE DEVELOPED INTO ONE OF FRANCE'S FINEST COOKERY SCHOOLS.

Just Desserts

BREAD AND BUTTER PUDDING.122
CHOCOLATE FONDANT PUDDING.124
CRÈME CARAMEL WITH CARAMELISED ORANGES.126
PASSION FRUIT SOUFFLÉ.128
STICKY TOFFEE PUDDING WITH SALTED CARAMEL SAUCE.130

It was an amazing experience with much responsibility; I was one of a select few chosen to be upgraded in their patisserie work to then return and help improve the standards of our respective hotels' pastry sections.

I couldn't believe how meticulous our French cookery tutors were with their recipes: they even had a recipe for egg wash, which was unheard of in an English hotel or restaurant kitchen.

Their precision in presentation extended to the choice of crockery for each recipe – presentation was considered in depth. 'Colour is flavour' and 'we eat with our eyes' were phrases drummed in to us and which I still use today.

From ice carvings to blown sugar decorations to restaurant-plated desserts and even as far as a spectacular croquembouche, no stone was left unturned.

I remember sitting in a tiny little traditional French bar with my colleagues on the last day before we came back to England. We were reflecting on our experience while we drank pastis, and lots of it; great if you liked aniseed. I soon learned to like it. If I had a glass of pastis now I'd say 'Santé' to Lenôtre!

NB.
JUST DESSERTS

CHAPTER 7

Bread and Butter Pudding

INGREDIENTS:
Serves 4

80g butter
3 whole free range eggs
225ml whole milk
10g caster sugar
seeds from 1 vanilla pod
8 slices of brioche, see page 148
40g sultanas
ground or grated nutmeg (optional)
40g golden syrup
20g icing sugar

METHOD:

Take a medium-sized earthenware dish or 4 small ramekins and butter the inside using 10g of the butter.

Place the remaining butter in a bowl over a pan of hot water and allow it to melt to liquid.

In a separate bowl add the eggs, milk, sugar and vanilla seeds. Whisk and strain the egg custard mixture through a sieve into a pouring jug and set to one side.

Slice the brioche to the required thickness depending on the dish size and arrange it in the dish or dishes while randomly scattering the sultanas and an occasional drizzle of the melted butter. Continue filling the dish in this manner until it's full to the top.

Flood the dish or dishes with the egg custard to cover and allow them to stand for 10-15 minutes. Finally, grate the nutmeg and drizzle the golden syrup over the top.

Bake the pudding(s) in the oven at 180°C.

When they have a golden brown top and a firm wobble, remove from the oven, dust with icing sugar.

Serve with a scoop of your favourite ice cream.

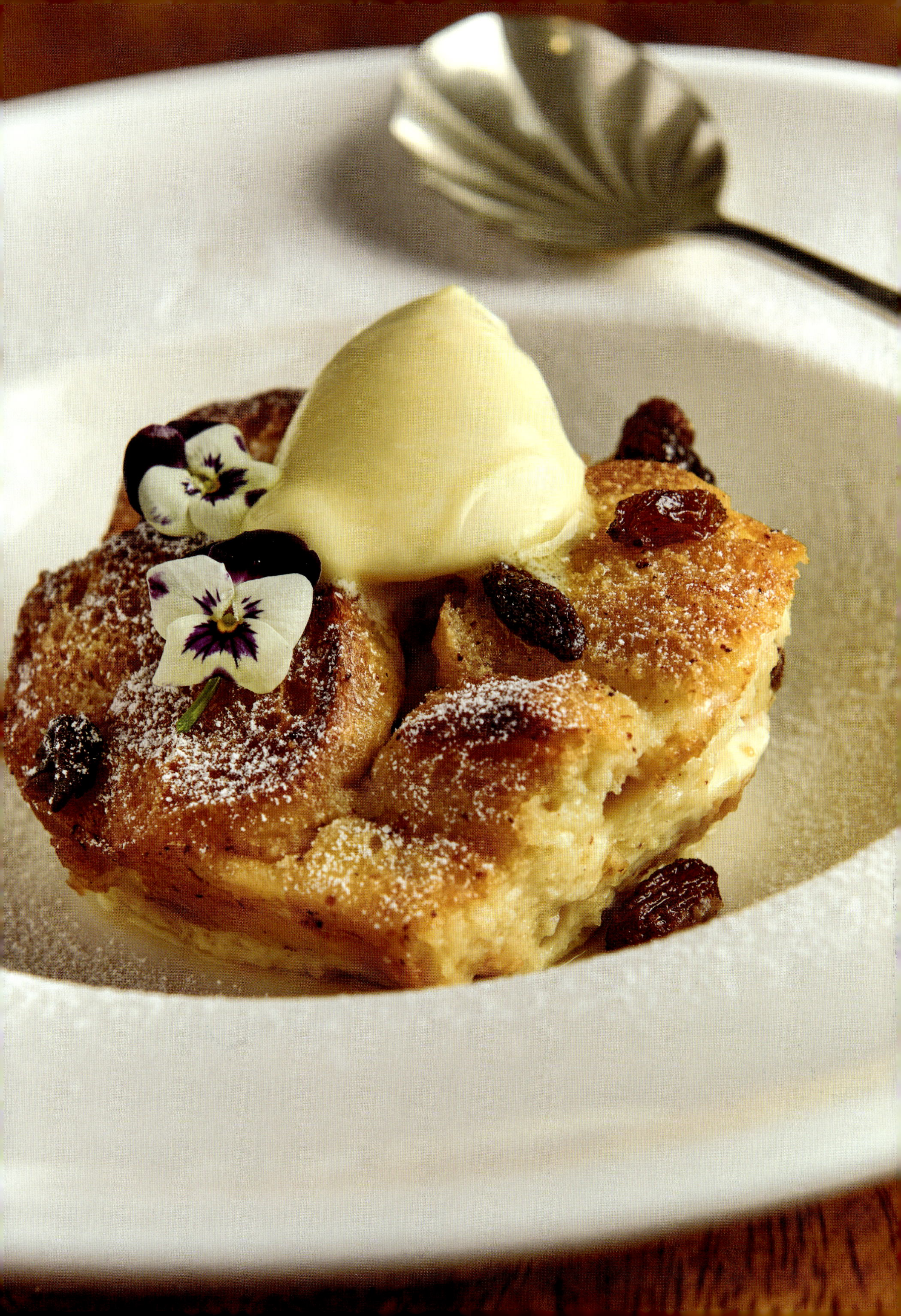

Chocolate Fondant Pudding

INGREDIENTS:
Serves 4

25g butter, softened
35g caster sugar
150g dark chocolate, melted
5g vanilla paste
2 large free range eggs, beaten
40g plain flour
15g icing sugar, for dusting
12 fresh raspberries
4 small sprigs of fresh mint

METHOD:

Butter the insides of 4 ramekins or dariole moulds using 10g of the butter. Coat the butter with 10g of the caster sugar and shake out the excess.

Place the chocolate in a heatproof bowl and heat gently over a pan of hot water until melted.

In a separate bowl cream the remaining butter, sugar and vanilla paste to a light and fluffy consistency. Beat in the eggs one at a time, then add the flour and melted chocolate. Allow the mixture to cool to a dropping consistency and divide between your prepared moulds.

Place them in a roasting tin and add cold water to halfway up the sides of the moulds. Bake in the oven at 180°C for approximately 12 minutes. When cooked, turn them out of the moulds.

Dust the puddings with the icing sugar. Finish with fresh raspberries and a sprig of mint. Alternatively, turn the puddings out of the moulds onto a plate and serve with the raspberries and a quenelle of clotted cream.

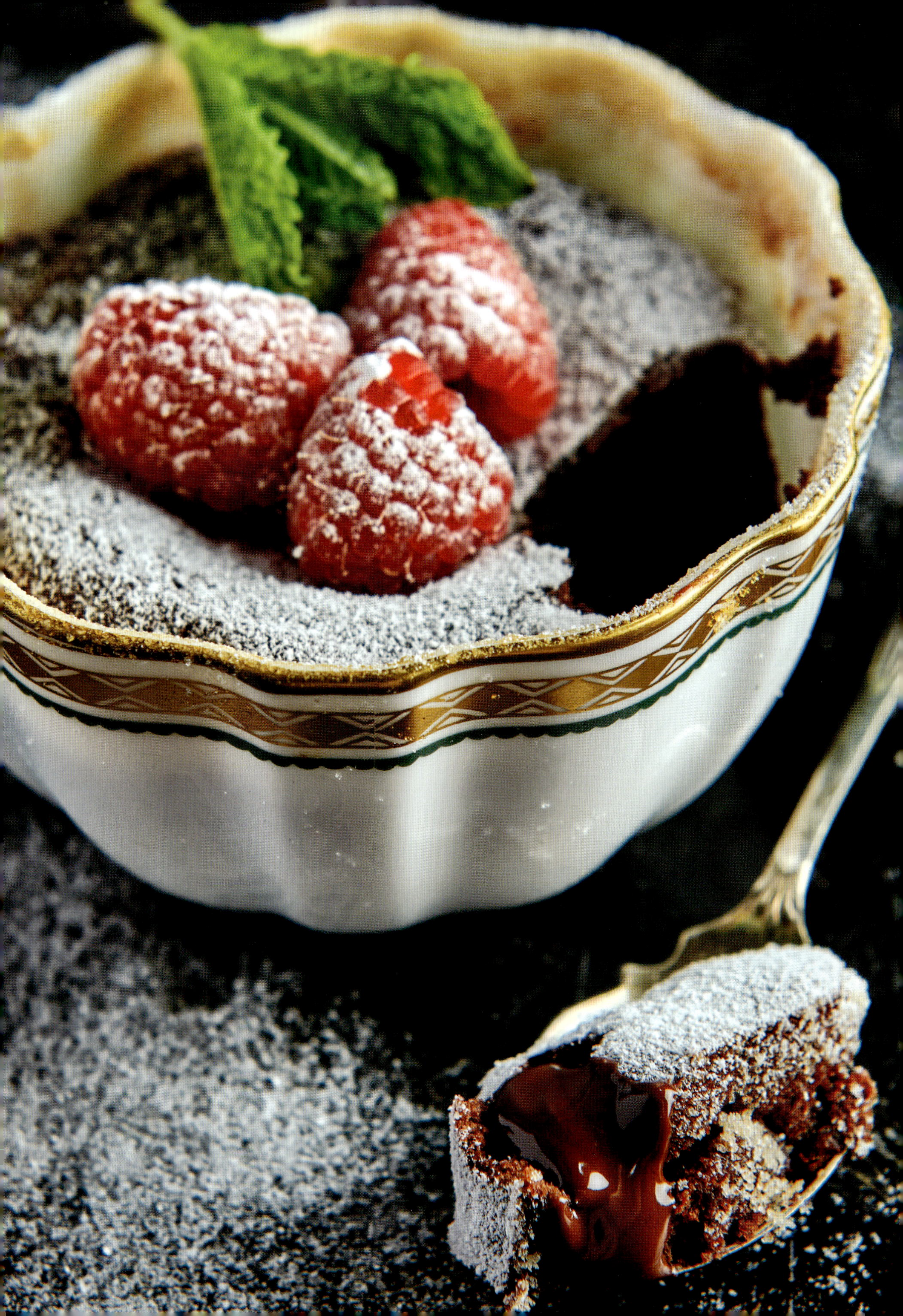

Crème Caramel with Caramelised Oranges

INGREDIENTS:
Serves 4

100g caster sugar
200ml water
4 large free range eggs
30g vanilla sugar
seeds of 1 vanilla pod
450ml whole milk
marigold petals

For the caramelised oranges
50g soft light brown sugar
2 large oranges
100ml brandy

METHOD:

Put the caster sugar and water in a thick-bottomed pan and on a medium heat, gently bring to the boil. Boil until all the water has evaporated and you are left with a caramel-coloured sugar syrup. At this point, plunge the base of the pan into a bowl of cold water to stop the cooking process. Pour the caramel into the base of four dariole moulds and allow to cool.

Place the eggs, vanilla sugar, vanilla seeds and milk in a bowl and whisk together. Strain into a jug and pour the egg mixture into the moulds to the top.

Place them in a roasting tin and add cold water to halfway up the sides of the moulds. Bake in the oven at 170°C for approximately 35 minutes or until the egg custard has set. Cool in the roasting tin with the water. Once cool, remove from the tin and refrigerate for 1 hour prior to serving.

For the caramelised oranges, place the brown sugar into a pan. Peel and slice the oranges then place them on top of the brown sugar. Place the pan on a medium heat. When the sugar has dissolved and caramelised, turn the heat off, pour the brandy over the orange slices and ignite with a naked flame to burn off the alcohol. Allow the oranges to cool in the pan before serving.

Decorate with small marigold petals and serve.

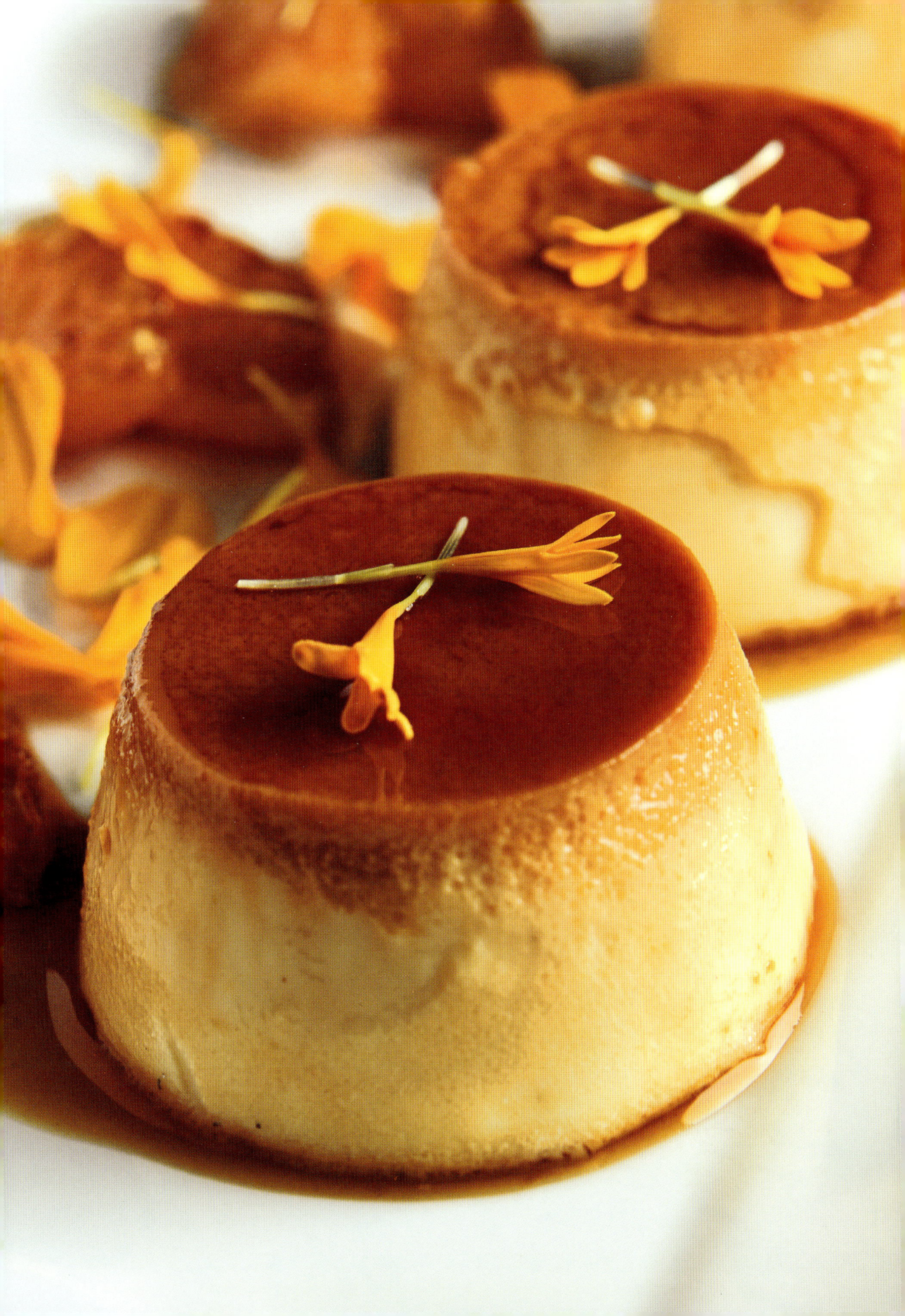

Passion Fruit Soufflé

INGREDIENTS:
Serves 4

120g melted butter, to grease
50g butter
70g caster sugar
4 large free range eggs, separated
40g plain flour
150ml whole milk
6 large passion fruit, scooped and strained, or around 80ml juice
15g icing sugar, to dust

METHOD:

Grease four dariole moulds with butter, and using 20g of the caster sugar coat the butter and shake out the excess.

Place the egg yolks and the rest of the caster sugar into a large bowl. Put the bowl over a pan of hot water and whisk the mixture continuously until light and fluffy and the whisk leaves a trail. Remove the bowl from the pan and leave to one side to cool.

In a separate pan, melt the remaining butter and add the flour, stirring for 1 minute over the heat. Add the milk and stir until a thick white sauce is reached. Stir in the passion fruit juice and pour into a clean bowl.

Whisk the egg whites to a stiff peak. When all the ingredients are cold, combine the egg yolk and sugar sabayon with the passion fruit sauce. Gently fold in the egg whites and divide the mixture between the prepared moulds.

Place the soufflés onto a baking tray and bake at 180°C for approximately 12 minutes or until risen with a golden top. Serve immediately dusted with icing sugar.

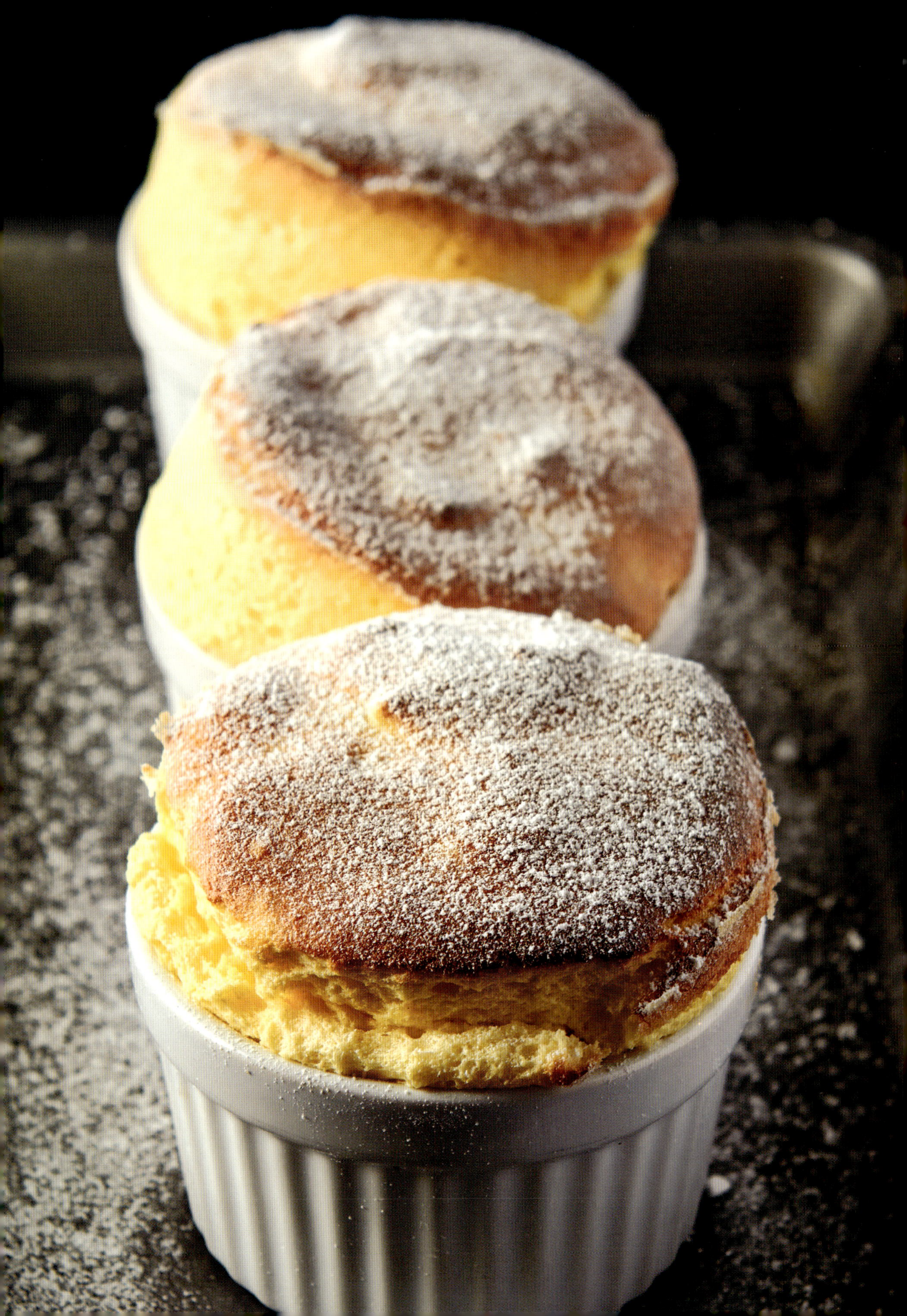

Sticky Toffee Pudding with Salted Caramel Sauce

INGREDIENTS:
Serves 4

80g butter, softened
20g caster sugar
140g soft brown sugar
2 whole free range eggs, beaten
160g self-raising flour
150g dates, de-stoned, roughly chopped and soaked in 150ml hot water with 3g bicarbonate of soda for 2 hours
120g clotted cream

For the salted caramel sauce
125g butter
175g dark soft brown sugar
10g vanilla paste
150ml double cream
1g salt

METHOD:

Butter the insides of 4 large dariole moulds using 10g of the butter. Coat the butter with the caster sugar and shake out the excess.

Place the soft brown sugar and the remaining butter in a bowl and cream together to a light brown, soft and fluffy consistency. Beat in the eggs one at a time, then add the flour. When the soaked dates are completely cold, stir them through the sponge batter. Divide the recipe between the moulds and wrap each one in cling film. Steam for 25 minutes.

For the sauce, place the butter, soft brown sugar and vanilla paste into a thick-bottomed sauté pan and heat until the sugar and butter has dissolved. Add the double cream and salt. Reduce the sauce to the desired consistency and serve with the sticky toffee pudding.

Serve with a quenelle of clotted cream.

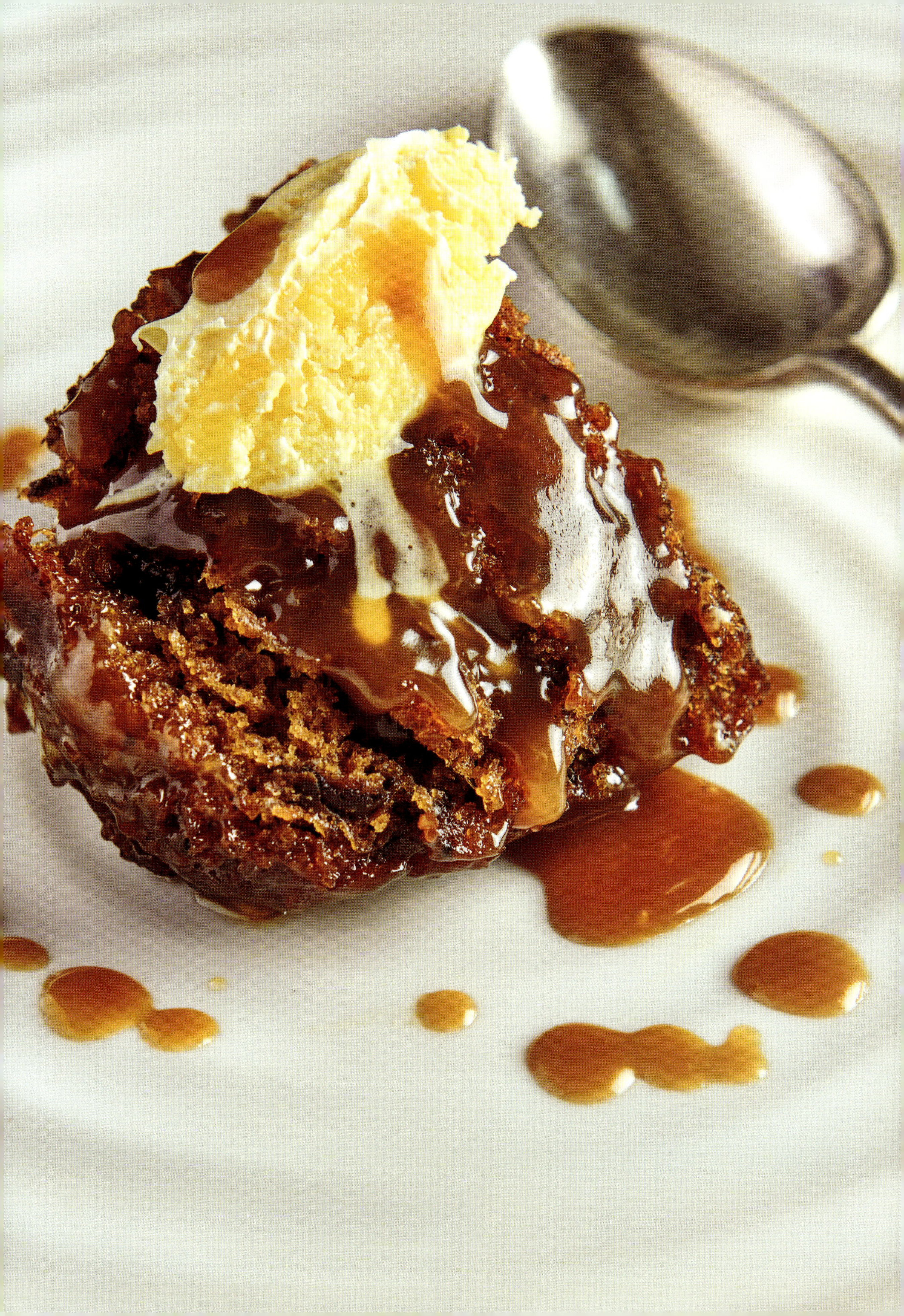

WHEN I WAS A YOUNG CHEF, KEEN TO IMPRESS, I COMPETED IN ONE OF THE UK'S GREATEST CULINARY CHALLENGES, THE SALON CULINAIRE AT HOTELYMPIA IN LONDON, SHOWCASING MY SKILLS IN CHOCOLATE AND SUGARWORK. I HAD THE ENTHUSIASM, AND THE BACKING FROM MY HEAD CHEF TO PRACTISE IN WORK TIME; HE EVEN FUNDED THE INGREDIENTS.

Chocolate

23CT GOLD CHOCOLATE CHAMPAGNE TRUFFLES.134
CHOCOLATE MACAROONS.136
FLORENTINES.138
HAZELNUT PRALINES.140

Sugar Work

CARAMEL CREATIONS.142
RICH BUTTER FUDGE.144

There was only one problem: I needed to find the right crockery for the job. I needed six large plates of a quality and style appropriate to my recipes; but I hadn't the budget to cover what I wanted. However, I did have a credit card!

On my day off I took a shopping trip and found the perfect plates. They were just what I wanted, and in stock. Out came the credit card and the deal was done. Carefully wrapped, they were guarded with my life.

On competition day off I went to London to present my six entries for display and judging. It was a great day and what an experience; but I didn't win any awards. Oh well, it's the taking part that counts.

Off I went to I collect my entries on their plates. I carefully washed the plates without removing the barcode labels on the bottom. I polished and re-wrapped, then took them back to the shop and got my money back: sometimes a chef's got to do what a chef's got to do. Times were hard, but that didn't stop me competing against the rest of them at the Salon Culinaire. I wonder where those plates are now?

NB.
CHOCOLATE & SUGAR WORK

CHAPTER 8

23ct Gold Chocolate Champagne Truffles

INGREDIENTS:
Makes 18 truffles

half a bottle of champagne, or a similar alternative such as Prosecco
10g salted butter
40g dark chocolate
40g milk chocolate
75g clotted cream
3g vanilla paste
23ct edible gold leaves or dust

METHOD:

Pour the champagne into a thick-bottomed pan and boil gently on a medium heat until it has reduced to 5ml. Remove from the pan to a small dish and allow to cool.

In a separate pan, place the butter, all the chocolate, clotted cream and vanilla paste and on a low heat, slowly melt whilst continually stirring. When all the ingredients are bound together, pour in the champagne syrup and stir thoroughly.

Remove the truffle mixture to a clean bowl and cool, stirring occasionally. Once the mixture is firm enough to roll, divide into the required number of truffles, roll into small balls and refrigerate for 15 minutes.

Before serving, brush each truffle with edible gold leaves or dust.

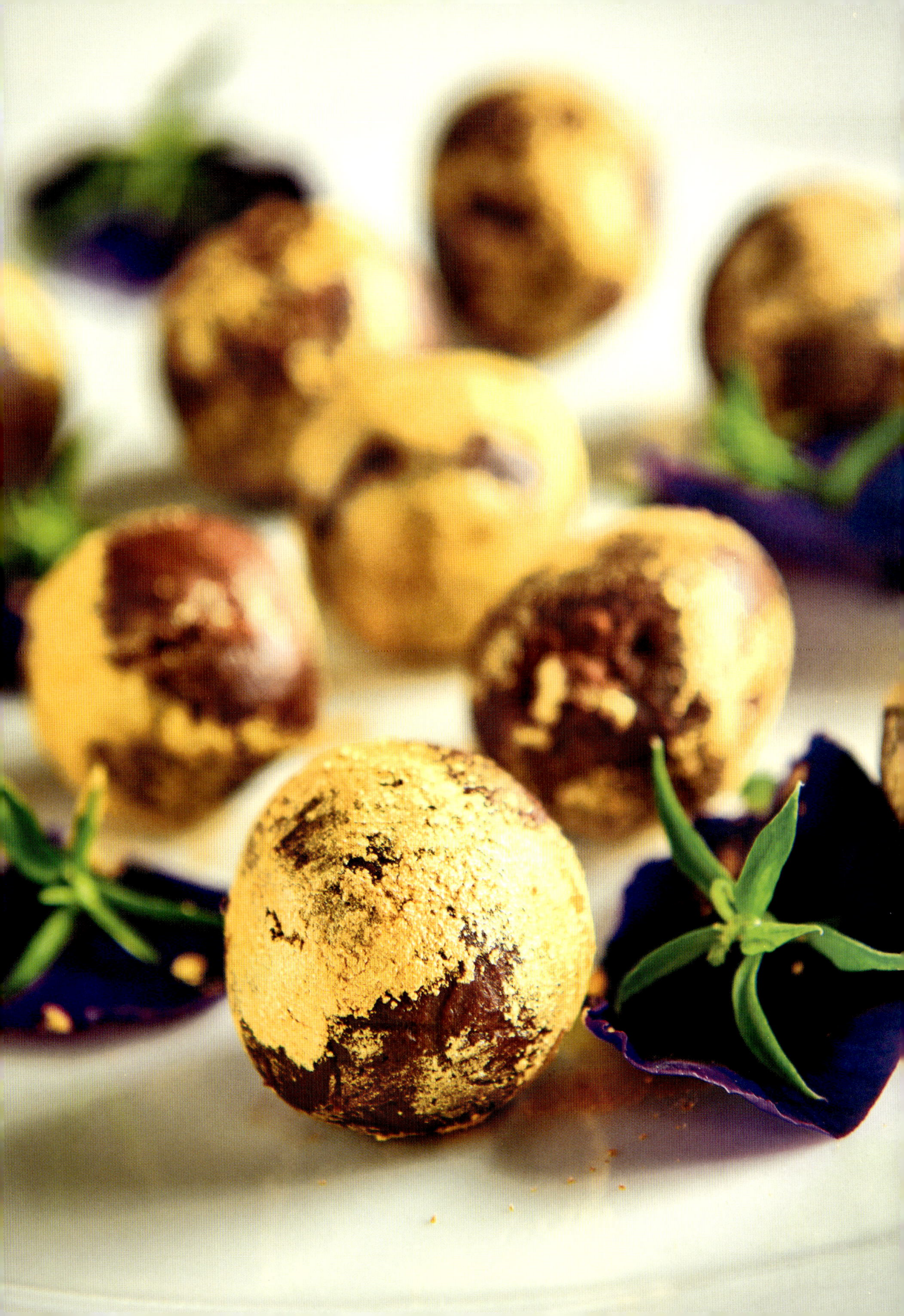

Chocolate Macaroons

INGREDIENTS:
Makes 18 macaroons

30g cocoa powder
100g ground almonds
3 medium free range egg whites
125g icing sugar

For the chocolate ganache
50g dark chocolate, melted
50g milk chocolate, melted
25g salted butter, melted
5g vanilla paste
20ml double cream

METHOD:

Sieve the cocoa powder and combine it with the ground almonds and ensure that the two ingredients are mixed together well.

In a separate bowl, whisk the egg whites to stiff peaks. Whisk in the icing sugar to form a meringue mixture.

Take a large shallow baking tray and line with greaseproof paper. Have a piping bag prepared with a plain nozzle, and a large metal spoon. Using the spoon, gently fold the almonds and cocoa into the meringue mixture until all the dry ingredients are mixed in completely.

Carefully fill the piping bag and pipe the macaroons to 3cm diameter onto the tray, leaving enough room between for them to double in size. Bake in the oven at 160°C for approximately 14 minutes, or until they can be peeled from the greaseproof paper. Leave to cool.

For the chocolate ganache, place all the ingredients into a thick-bottomed pan and heat gently until melted, stirring gently to mix. Remove from the pan and cool.

Once cool, place the mixture in a piping bag with a plain nozzle and pipe the ganache on the flat side of one macaroon before sandwiching two macaroons together and serving.

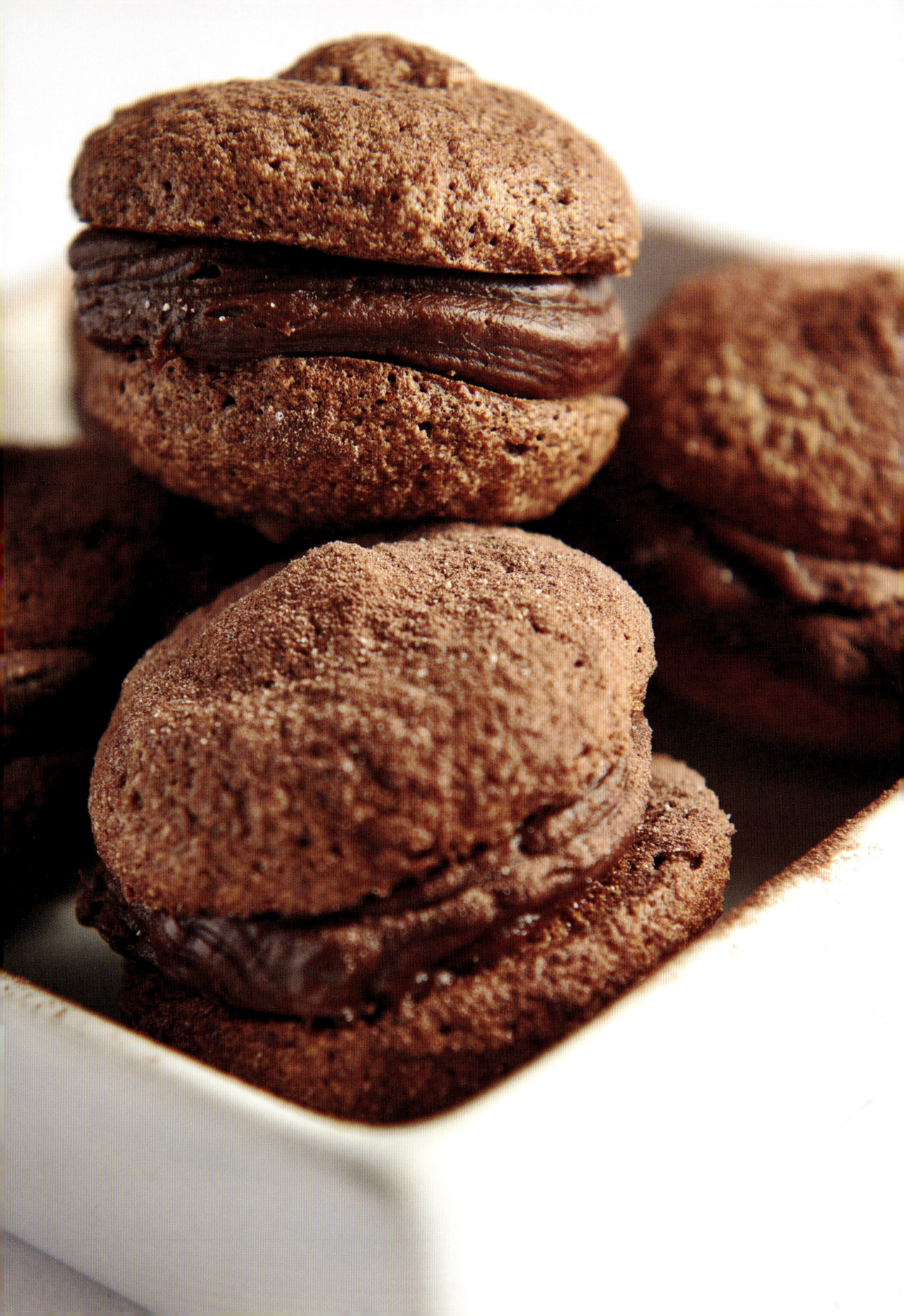

Florentines

INGREDIENTS:
Makes 18 florentines

75g dark chocolate
15g butter
40g golden caster sugar
35ml double cream
25g broken hazelnuts
50g flaked almonds
25g whole candied peel, chopped
25g glacé cherries, chopped
10g plain flour

METHOD:

Place the dark chocolate in a heat proof bowl and melt over a pan of hot water. Leave to one side and keep warm.

In a separate pan, melt the butter. Add the caster sugar, double cream, hazelnuts, 25g almonds, candied peel and glacé cherries. Stir together well over a low heat. Add the flour to bind and remove from the pan into a bowl to cool.

On a large greased baking tray place four teaspoons of the florentine mixture, leaving enough room for them to double in diameter. Bake in the oven at 180°C for 6 minutes, or until golden. Place onto a cooling wire and brush or drizzle with the melted chocolate (you may wish to mark the chocolate surface of the florentine before it sets cold with a wavy pattern with a fork), and sprinkle with a few toasted flaked almonds. Repeat the process with the rest of the mixture and serve within 24 hours.

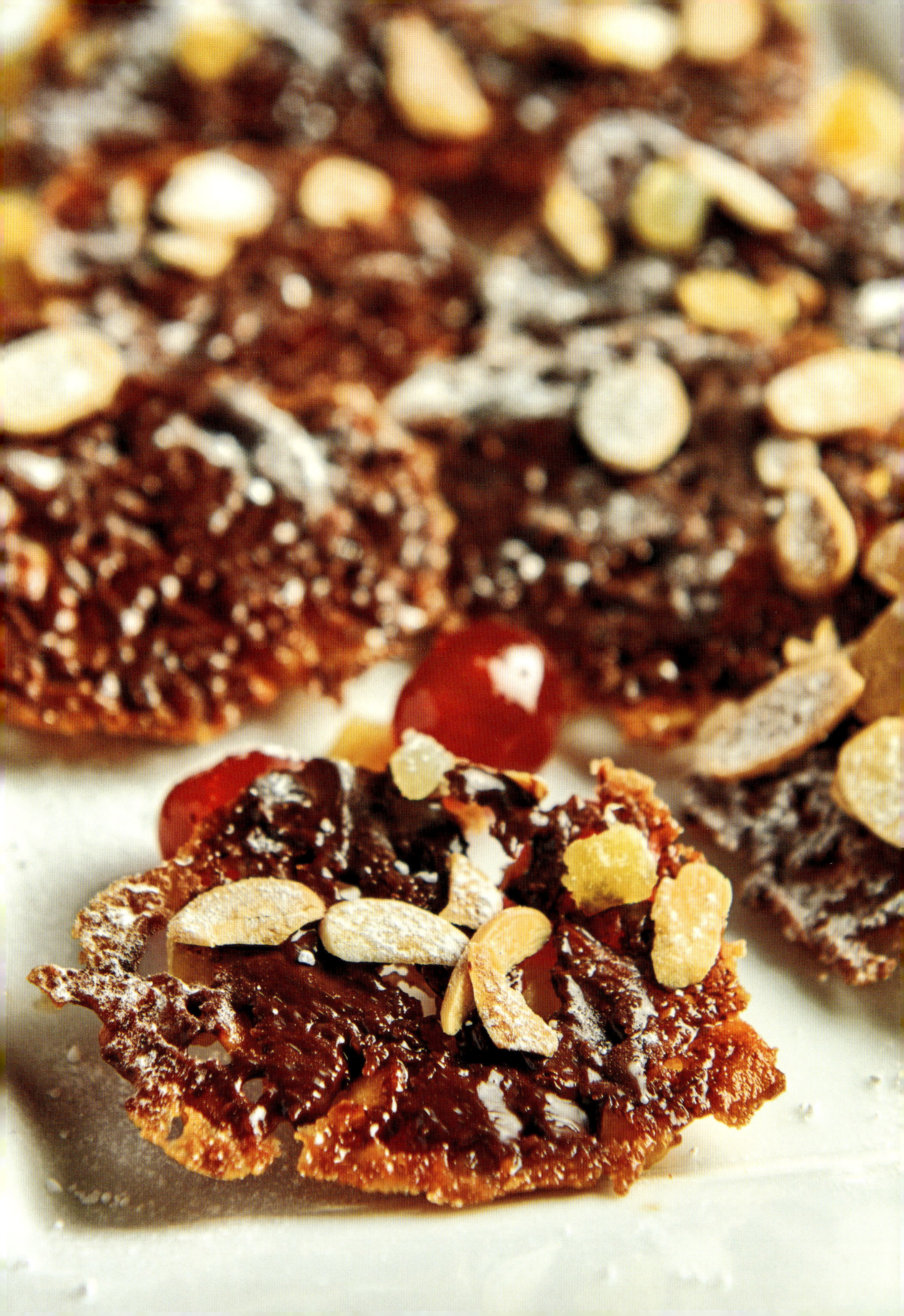

Hazelnut Pralines

INGREDIENTS:
Makes 18 pralines

200g caster sugar
200ml water
5ml rapeseed oil
100g toasted nibbed hazelnuts

METHOD:

Place the caster sugar and water in a thick-bottomed saucepan and bring to the boil on a medium heat.

While the sugar and water are boiling, line a small shallow baking tray with foil and brush with the rapeseed oil.

When the water has evaporated and you are left with a caramel sugar syrup, sprinkle the hazelnuts into the syrup and stir well with a metal spoon.

Pour the contents of the pan onto the oiled tray and spread as thinly as possible while the mixture is hot. Allow the praline mixture to cool in the tray completely.

Using a small toffee hammer (or similar), break the praline into small pieces and serve with your chosen dessert or as a petit four.

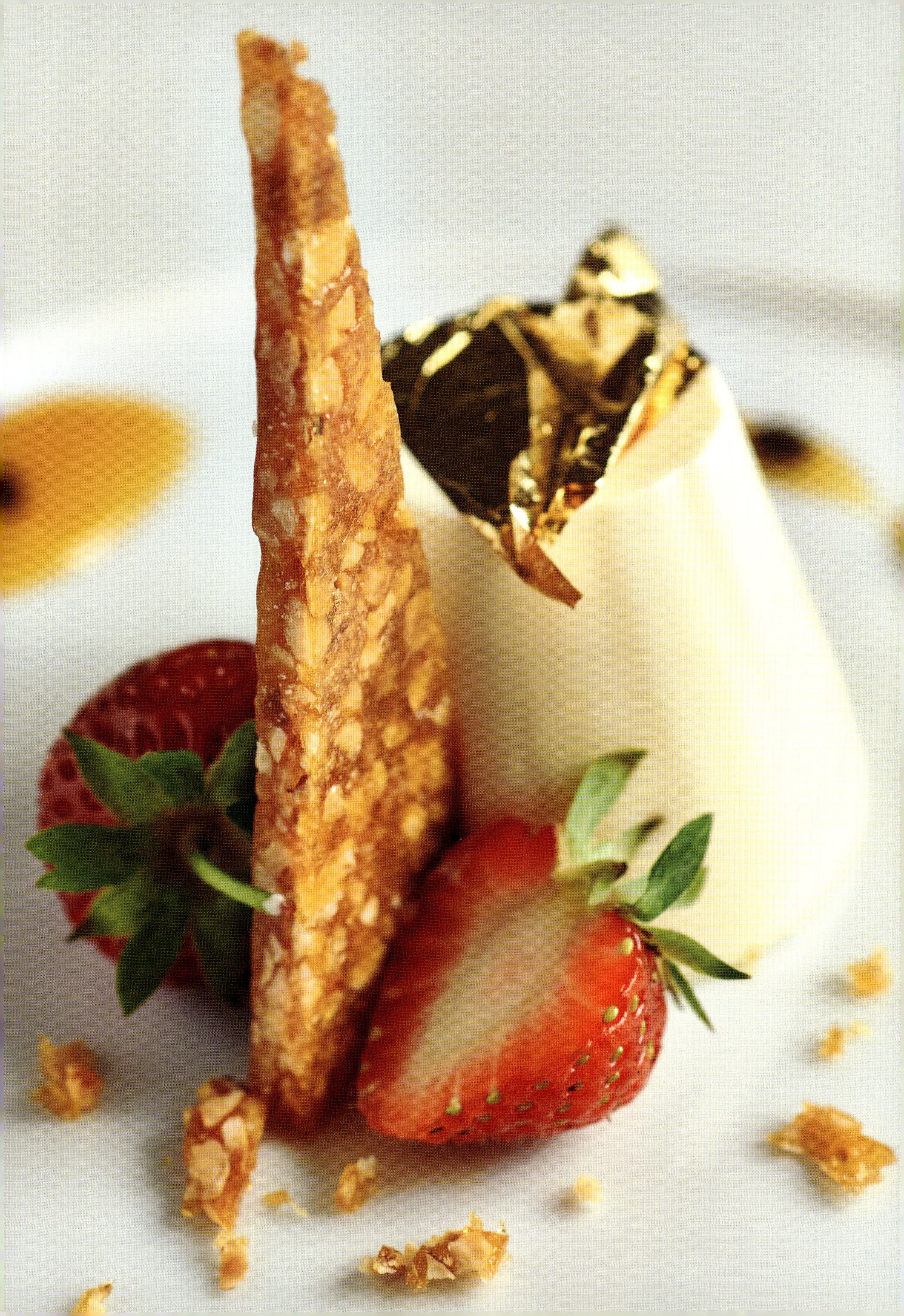

Caramel Creations

INGREDIENTS:
Makes 8 caramel cages, 8 spirals and 1 x 20cm disk of cinder toffee

200g caster sugar
150ml water
rapeseed oil
2g bicarbonate of soda

METHOD:

Place the sugar and water in a small thick-bottomed sauté pan. Bring to the boil on a medium heat.

To make a sugar cage, while the pan is boiling prepare a metal ladle or small glass bowl by applying a thin film of rapeseed oil. Using a dessertspoon, stir the boiling sugar syrup occasionally. When all the water has evaporated from the pan, reduce to a low heat and allow the sugar syrup to continue cooking until a caramel colour is reached.

Remove the pan from the heat and place on a cooling wire and allow it to cook until a golden syrup consistency is reached. Using a dessertspoon, gather some of the caramel sugar and holding the spoon in a downward position, allow the sugar to flow as one continuous thread as you weave back and forth and across, over and around your ladle or bowl to create a sugar cage. Gently cup the sugar cage into the palm of your hand and twist to carefully remove the ladle or bowl.

To make a sugar spiral, lightly oil a long metal sharpening steel and using the same process with the dessertspoon, wind the sugar thread around the steel until a spiral is formed.

To make cinder toffee, foil and lightly grease a shallow baking tray. Return the caramel sugar to a medium to low heat until it becomes a loose syrup again. Add the bicarbonate of soda and whisk vigorously for 5 seconds, then immediately pour onto the greased tray. Allow to cool. Once cold, using a small toffee hammer or similar break into small pieces and serve either plain or coated in chocolate.

These caramel creations make perfect decorations for desserts and the cinder toffee makes a great treat to serve with coffee.

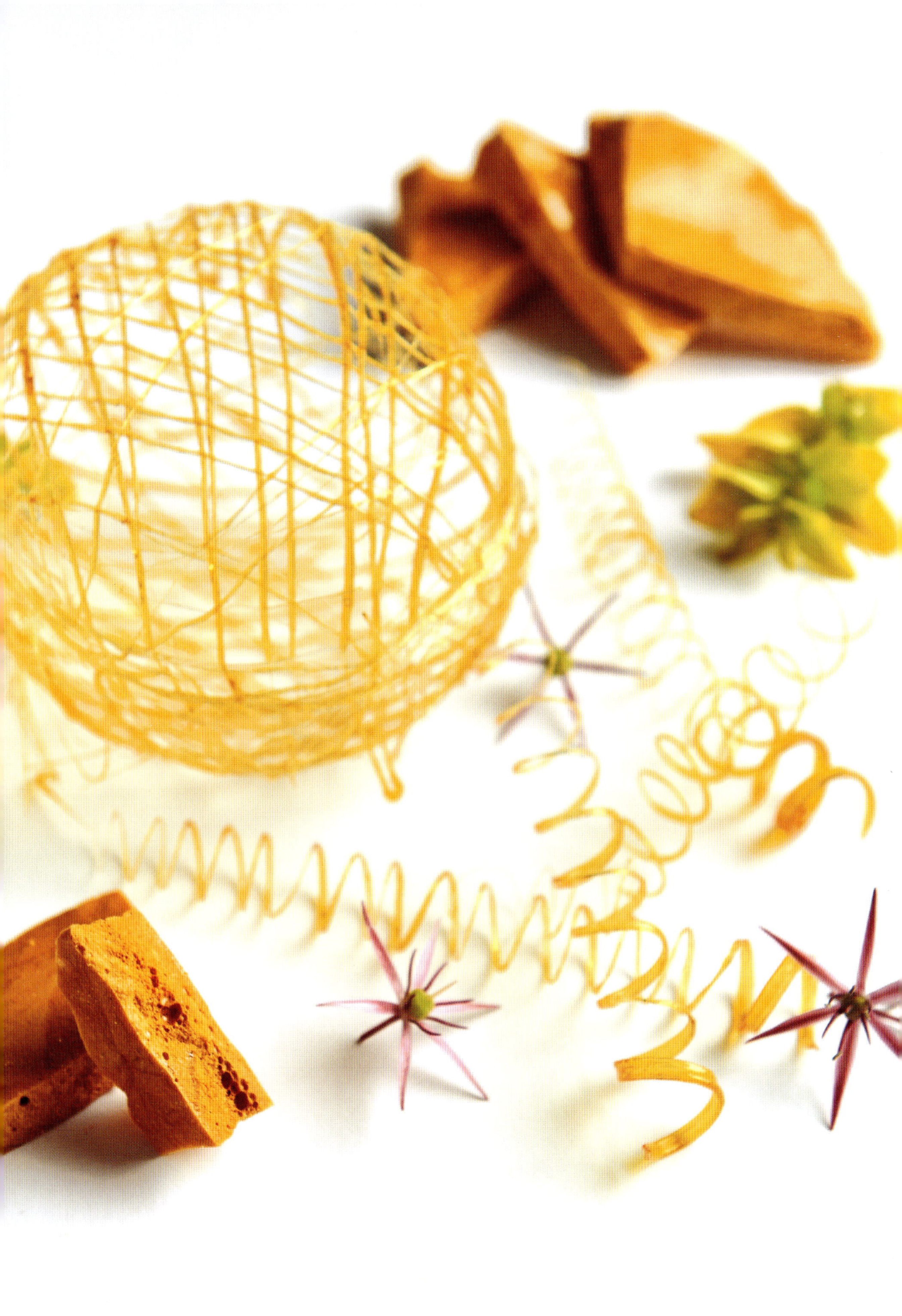

Rich Butter Fudge

INGREDIENTS:

Makes 24 cubes when it's cut

50g golden syrup
120ml water
100g caster sugar
100g salted butter
10g vanilla paste
300g clotted cream

METHOD:

Line a shallow baking tray or small loaf tin with greaseproof paper.

In a thick-bottomed pan, add the golden syrup, water, caster sugar, butter and vanilla. Heat until dissolved, stirring gently to mix. Over the heat, stir in the clotted cream until a typical fudge colour is reached, and the temperature on your sugar thermometer reaches 115°C. Pour the mixture into your prepared tray and cool.

Once cool, refrigerate for 1 hour. Cut the fudge into cubes and serve with coffee.

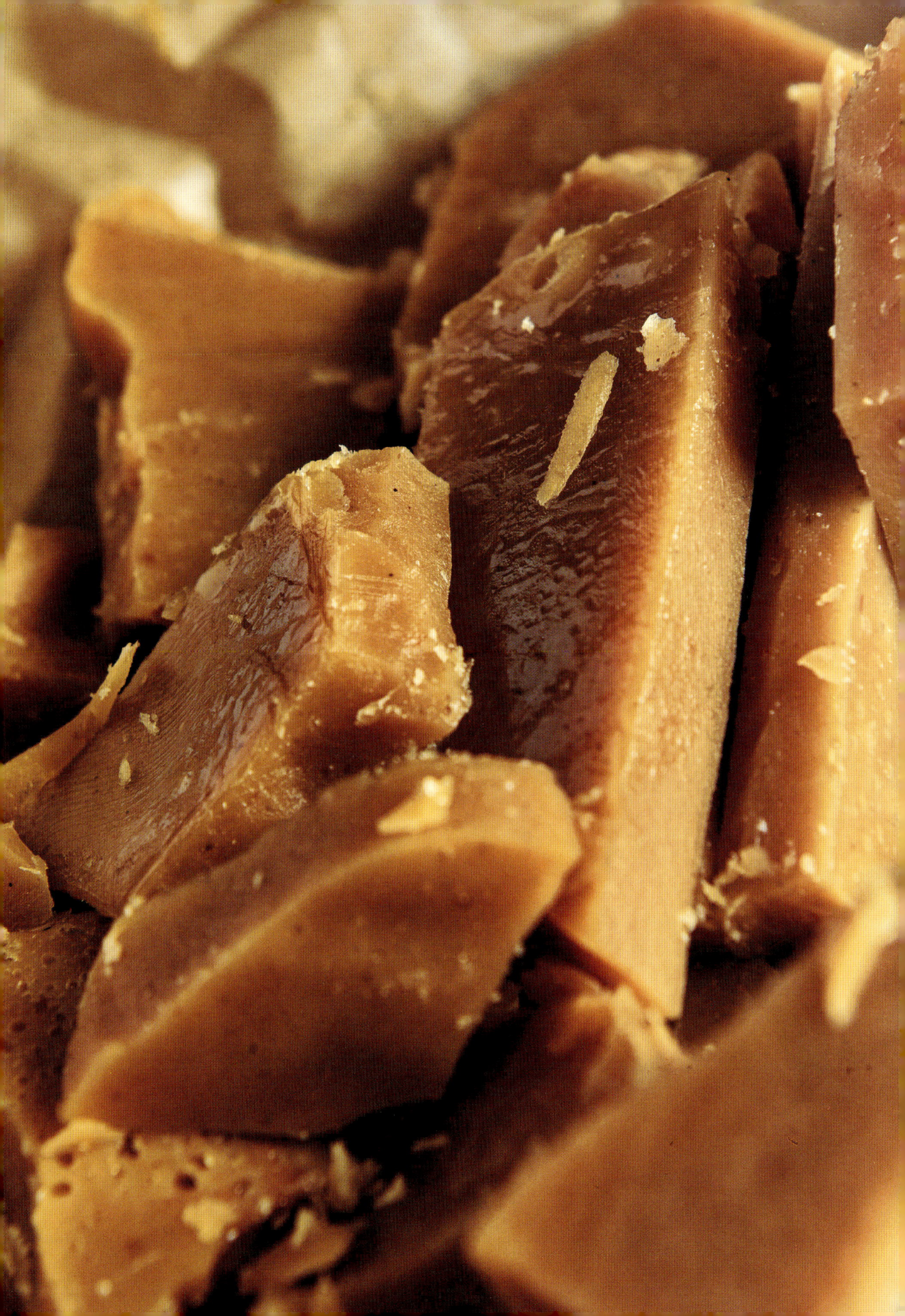

THE WORLD MIGHT HAVE MOVED ON WITH TECHNOLOGY AND ONLINE SHOPPING, BUT IT'S NOT ALWAYS PROGRESS WHEN IT COMES TO CHOOSING YOUR LOAF.
I'M NOWHERE NEAR TO DRAWING MY PENSION YET, BUT I CAN STILL REMEMBER THE DAYS OF JIM THE BREAD MAN TURNING UP IN HIS TRUSTY BREAD VAN.

Breads

BRIOCHE.148
TOMATO AND PARMESAN CIABATTA.150

Sweet Doughs

DEVONSHIRE SPLITS.152
DOUGHNUTS.154
HOT CROSS BUNS.156

Jim would come along each morning to our house, open up the back door of his van and there was the finest display of freshly baked bread loaves, buns and mouthwatering fresh cream cakes on wooden racks.

The smell of fresh-baked goods and the flour-dusted wooden bread trays made you feel as though you were standing in a fully operational bakery at 4am in the morning. We were one of the first deliveries of the day. A van-full of bread straight from the baker's oven: I was in baker's heaven!

There was another feature in Jim's bread van that, as a young boy of five or six, amazed me. Before he handed us our chosen breads and cakes, Jim would wash his hands in a tiny sink located in the front of his van. I could never understand how he could get hot running water in the front of his van!

The days of the bread van may be long gone but the memories will always live on.

NB.
BREADS & SWEET DOUGHS

CHAPTER 9

Brioche

INGREDIENTS:
Makes 1 loaf or 8 individual buns

7g fresh or dried yeast
20ml whole milk
15g caster sugar
150g plain flour
pinch of salt
2 whole free range eggs, beaten
140g butter, softened

For the egg wash
1 egg yolk, beaten
pinch of salt
10ml whole milk

METHOD:

Dissolve the yeast in the milk with the sugar. Sieve the flour into a large bowl with a pinch of salt. Using a small butter knife add the liquid to the flour and stir until absorbed. Add the eggs, one at a time, mixing continuously until a firm dough is formed. Remove from the bowl and knead on a floured surface for 3 minutes.

Spread the dough out, cover with the softened butter, fold and continue kneading for 1 minute. Divide the dough into the required number of portions or place in a greased loaf tin and egg wash. Allow to double in size.

Bake in the oven at 180°C until golden brown and the bottom sounds hollow when tapped.

Allow to cool before serving.

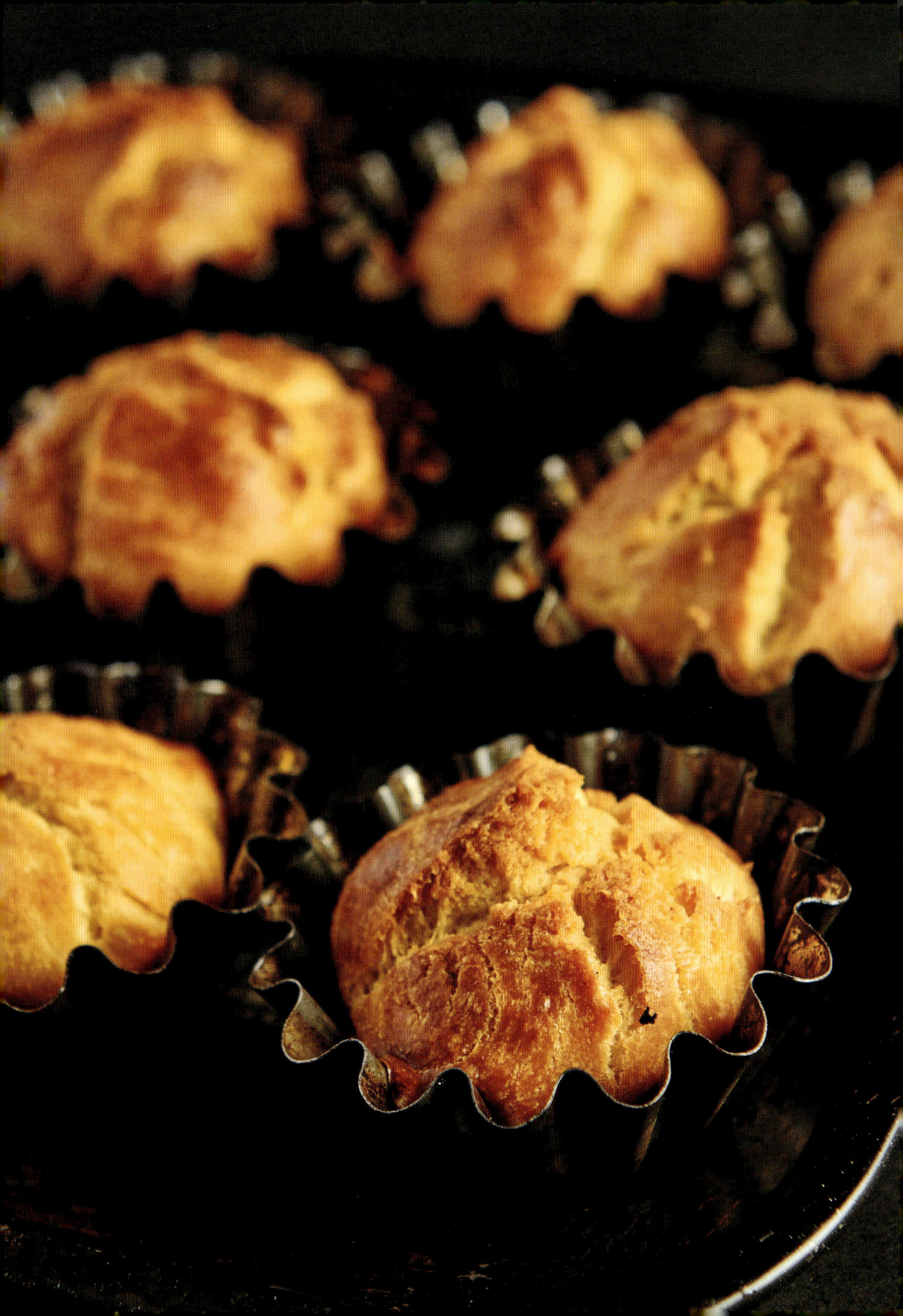

Tomato and Parmesan Ciabatta

INGREDIENTS:
Makes 1 loaf

300g strong white bread flour
pinch of salt
5g fresh or dried yeast
200ml water
150g sundried tomatoes, chopped
1 small sprig of fresh basil, chopped
20ml milk, for glaze
80g grated parmesan

METHOD:

Sieve the flour into a large bowl and add the salt. Place the yeast into the water and stir until dissolved. Make a well in the centre of the flour and pour in the liquid, chopped tomatoes and basil. Using a small butter knife, stir the ingredients to form a bread dough.

Turn the dough out onto a floured surface and knead for 3 minutes. Form into a ball and stretch lengthwise onto a lightly greased baking tray. Brush with the milk followed by a liberal sprinkling of parmesan.

Allow the loaf to prove until doubled in size. Bake in the oven at 180°C until golden brown, and the bottom sounds hollow when tapped.

Allow the ciabatta to cool before serving with any of your favourite pasta recipes.

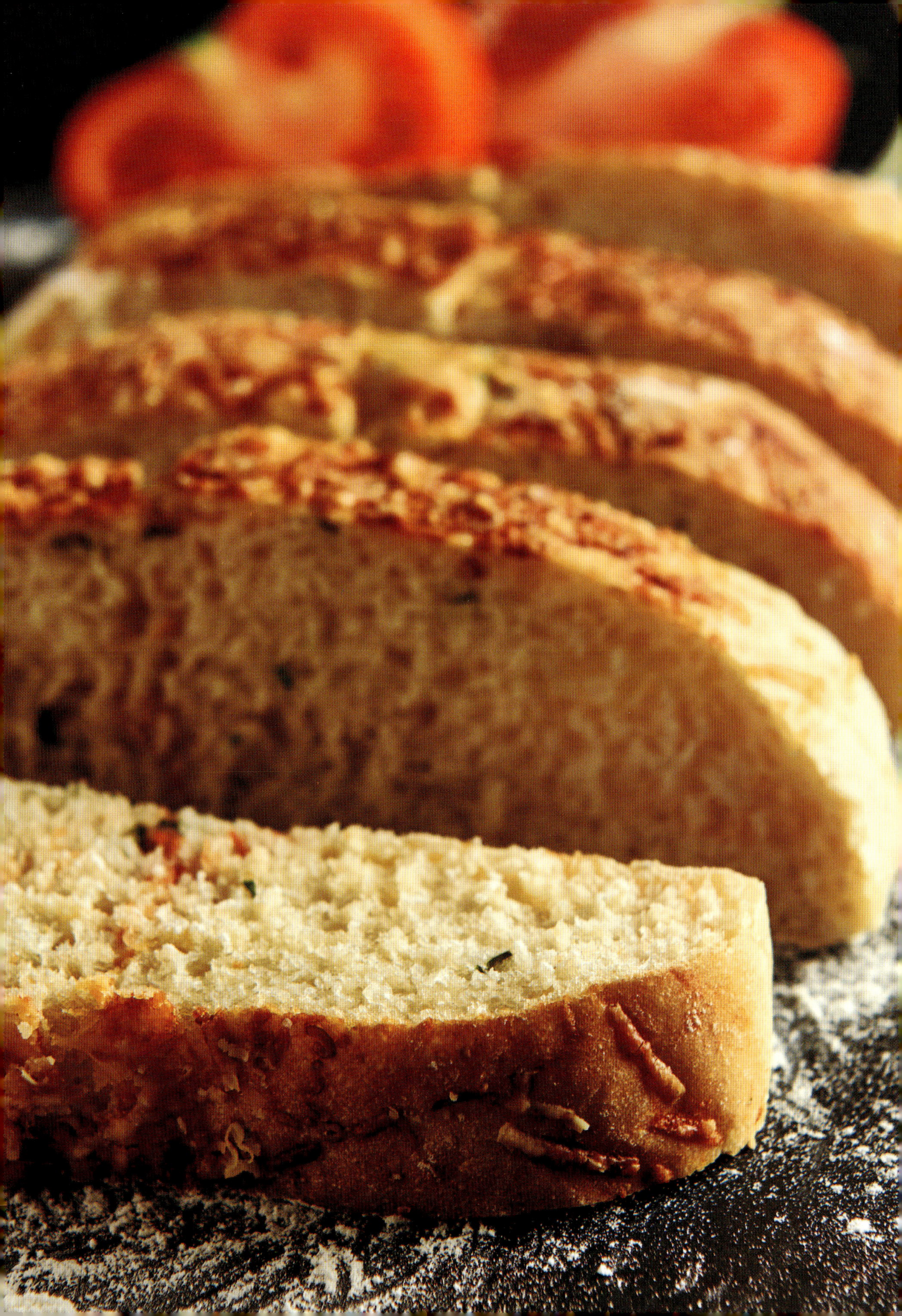

Devonshire Splits

INGREDIENTS:
Makes 12 splits

500g strong white bread flour
pinch of salt
25g golden caster sugar
10g fresh or dried yeast
25g unsalted butter, melted
300ml whole milk
15g icing sugar, for dusting

For the egg wash
1 whole free range egg
1g salt

To fill
whipped or clotted cream
strawberry jam

METHOD:

Sieve the flour into a large bowl with the salt.

Place the sugar, yeast, melted butter and milk into a jug and stir until dissolved. Make a well in the centre of the flour and pour two-thirds of the liquid into the centre. Stir with a small butter knife to start forming the dough. Continue stirring while adding more liquid if required to reach a soft but firm consistency.

Cover the dough with a damp towel or cling film. Prove until doubled in size. Divide the dough into 8 portions, roll into rounds and place onto a greased baking tray. Egg wash the dough balls and leave to double in size again before baking at 180°C until golden brown, and the bottoms sound hollow when tapped.

Once cooled, slice at a slant to form a hinge, fill with jam and cream and dust with icing sugar.

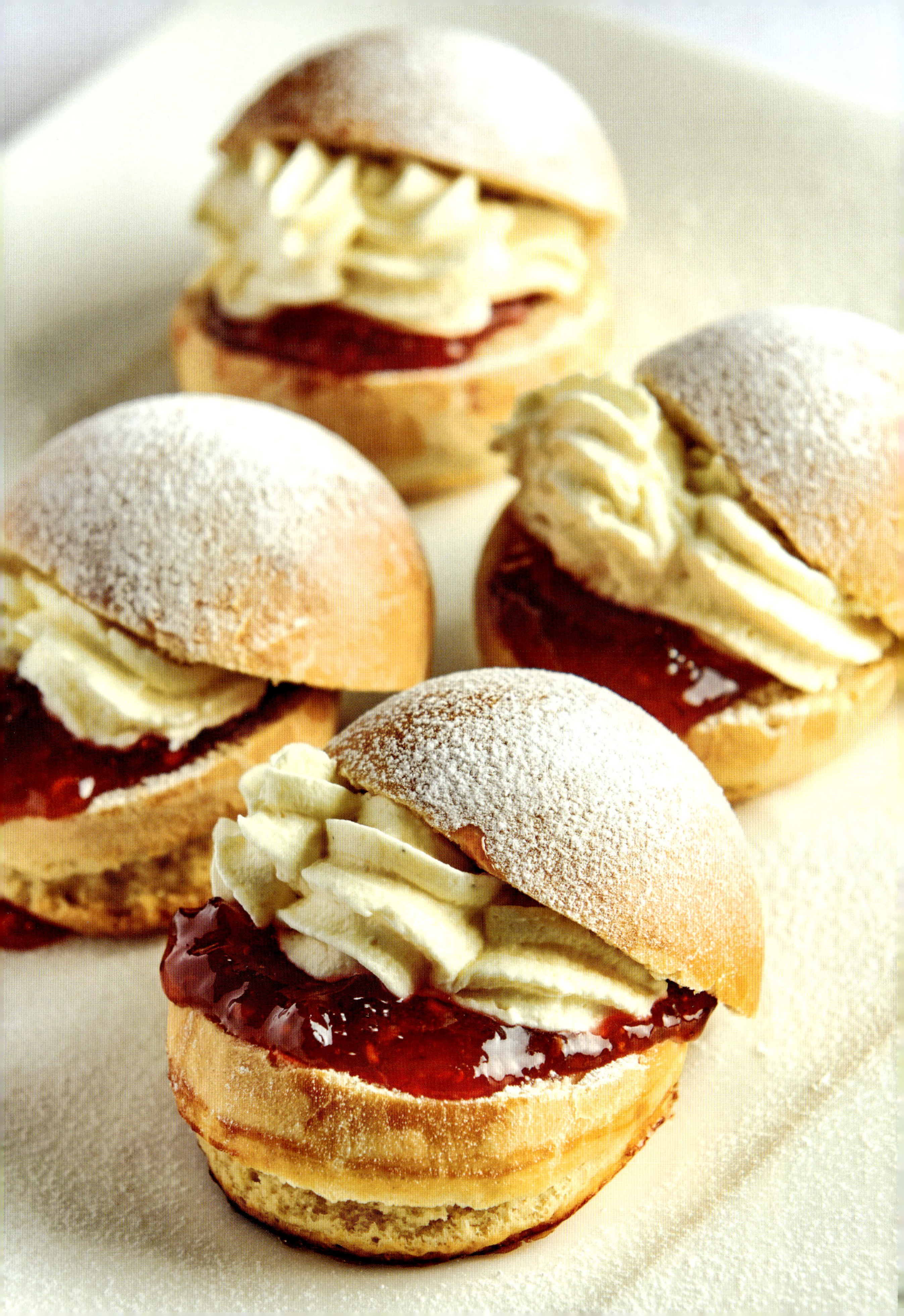

Doughnuts

INGREDIENTS:
Makes 12 doughnuts

320g plain flour
pinch of salt
7g dried yeast
30ml water
170ml whole milk
50g caster sugar
1 large whole free range egg
35g butter
1 litre sunflower oil for frying
vanilla sugar (sugar infused with vanilla pods)
raspberry jam

METHOD:

Sift the flour into a large bowl and add the salt.

Dissolve the yeast with the water, milk, sugar and egg and leave to one side.

Rub the butter into the flour and form a well in the centre. Pour the liquid into the well and using a small butter knife mix together to form a stiff batter. Cover with cling film or a damp towel and leave to rest for 1 hour.

Place the sunflower oil in a large saucepan and heat to 180°C. Using an ice cream scoop or similar, scoop the doughnut batter into the oil and cook for approximately 4 minutes until golden brown. Drain on kitchen paper before rolling in vanilla caster sugar. Serve warm with raspberry jam.

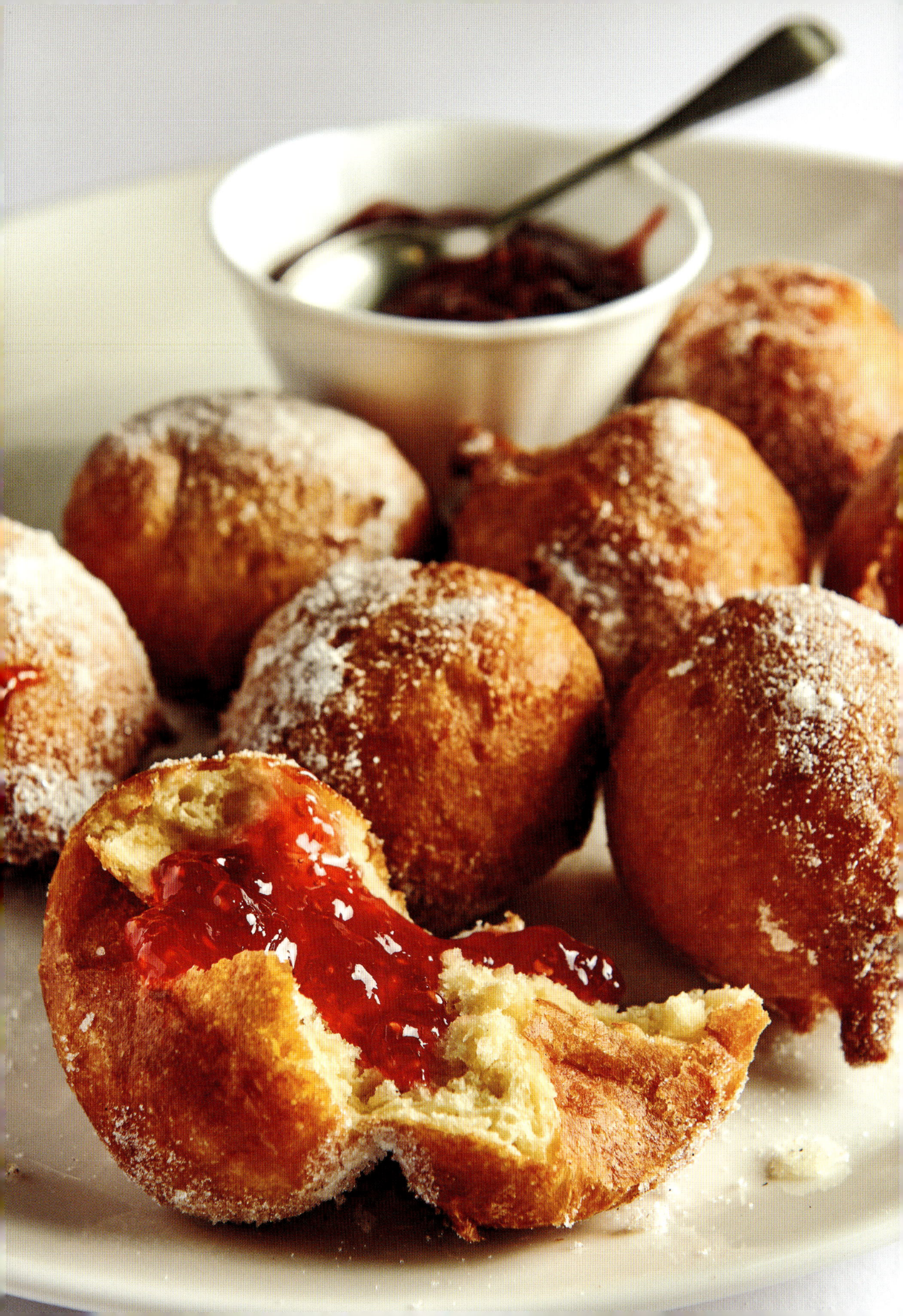

Hot Cross Buns

INGREDIENTS:
Makes 12 buns

For the dough
225g strong white bread flour
6g dried yeast
75ml whole milk
1 large whole free range egg
10g soft brown sugar
25g butter, melted
pinch of salt
2g ground cloves
2g ground cinnamon
2g ground nutmeg
2g ground ginger
80g mixed dried fruit
zest of 1 orange

For the egg wash
1 large whole free range egg
pinch of salt

For the top
50g plain flour
15g caster sugar
30ml whole milk

For the sticky sugar glaze
20ml whole milk
20g caster sugar

METHOD:

Sieve the flour into a large bowl. Dissolve the yeast in the milk and add the egg, sugar and butter. Leave to one side.

Add the salt, cloves, cinnamon, nutmeg and ginger into the flour and mix well, followed by the mixed fruit and orange zest. Make a well in the centre of the flour mixture, add the liquid and stir to create a firm dough.

Place the dough on a lightly floured surface and knead for 3 minutes. Divide into the required number of buns, roll into rounds and place onto a lightly greased baking tray. Egg-wash the buns and allow them to prove until doubled in size.

For the top, mix the plain flour, caster sugar and milk into a loose batter. Once the buns have doubled in size, pipe a cross on them with the batter. Bake in the oven at 170°C until golden brown, and the bottom sounds hollow when tapped.

While the buns are baking, place the glazing milk and sugar in a pan and heat until the sugar has dissolved. Once the buns are cooked, glaze them with the sugar solution while they are still hot and allow to cool.

Serve with lashings of butter.

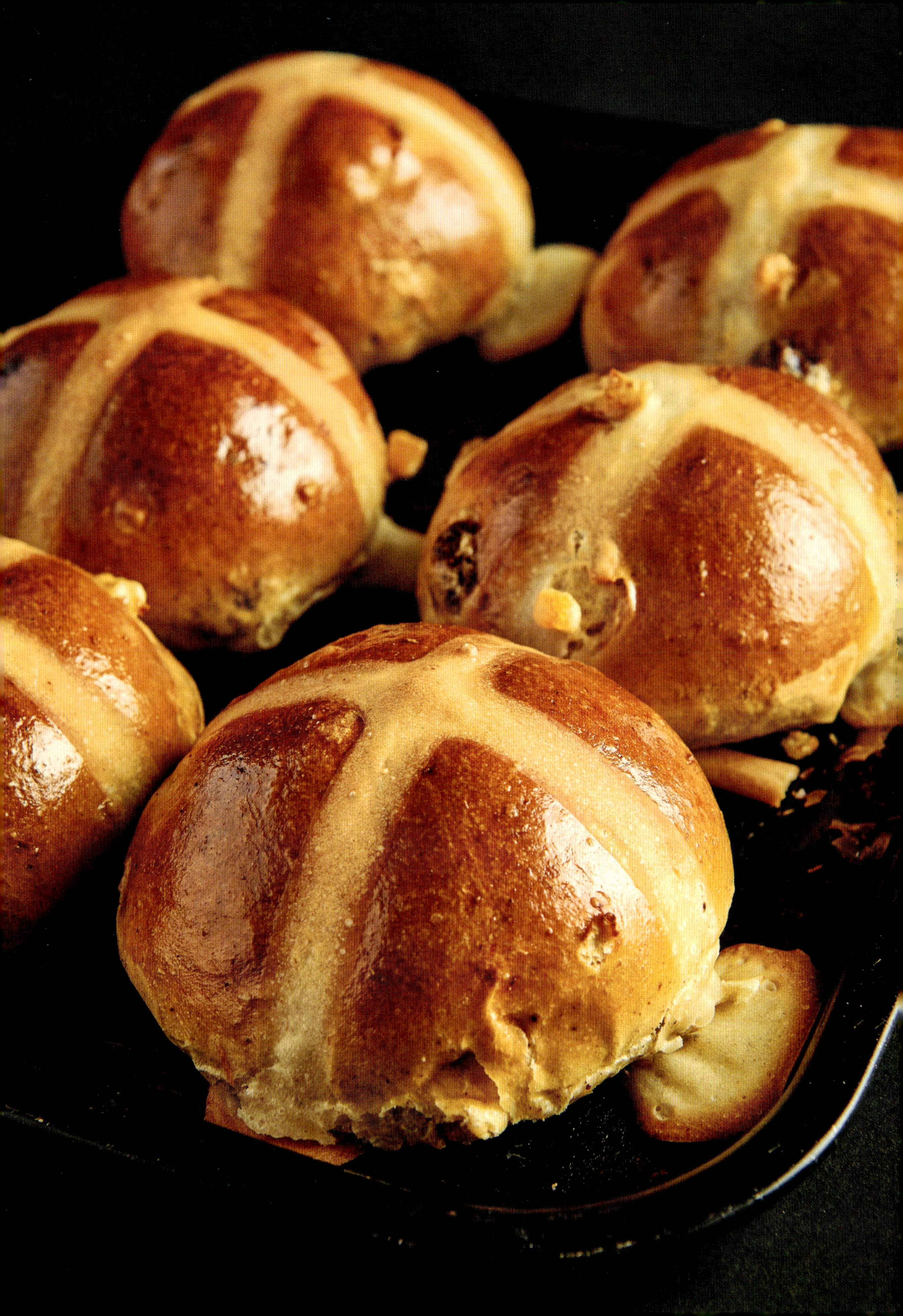

WE ALL ENJOY GETTING INTO THE KITCHEN AT THE WEEKEND AND CREATING GREAT FOOD FOR FAMILY AND FRIENDS; BUT DO YOU EVER GET NERVOUS WHEN YOU'RE COOKING TO IMPRESS? BEING A CHEF IS ONE THING; BEING AN ENTERTAINER IS ANOTHER. WE USUALLY SEPARATE SUCH WORDS AND PROFESSIONS, ASSOCIATING THE LATTER WITH COMEDIANS, CLOWNS AND CONJURERS – CERTAINLY NOT CHEFS!

Something for the Weekend

BLINIS AND BELUGA CAVIAR.160
CROQUE MONSIEUR.162
EGGS BENEDICT.164
FILLET STEAK WITH QUAIL EGGS AND BLACK SUMMER TRUFFLES.166
WELSH RAREBIT.168

The very first cookery demonstration that I did was at a small food festival, in a marquee tucked away in a corner with a six-foot trestle table and a camping stove, a washing-up bowl and an audience of about 12.

That was difficult enough, so you can imagine my nerves when I was invited to do a cookery demonstration in front of 600 serious foodies at one of the country's biggest food festivals of the time, the Melton Mowbray Food Festival. Now that was a game-changer for me.

With a 45-minute slot allocated, the pressure was on. I was there to promote and sell my newly produced dinner party cookery DVDs. I spent weeks practising my recipes to time and used my family as guinea pigs. I almost rehearsed word-for-word what I would say during my demonstration as I couldn't afford to get this one wrong.

Saying that I was a bag of nerves would be an understatement, especially when I discovered on the morning that I'd be demonstrating in between some award-winning local chefs, master bakers and celebrity chefs Clarissa Dickson Wright and Jean-Christophe Novelli.

My nerves were already in tatters as I waited, not helped by a packed cookery theatre of mainly starry-eyed women waiting for Jean-Christophe. Then an announcement was made: he was stuck in traffic on the motorway; it would be another hour before he appeared.

So I too had an extended wait for my slot to begin – it was like having an extra hour in the dentist's waiting room! Jean-Christophe arrived and with his demonstration done, I was sure that the packed audience would make a mass exodus, having been there for almost two hours already.

But no: kind and generous as ever, Jean-Christophe asked the audience to stay and watch me, telling them I was going to put on a fantastic show. He didn't know me from Adam! Beads of sweat were trickling down my face; I felt like a rabbit would with the headlights of a car hurtling towards it at 60 miles an hour!

My demonstration was over and around 95% of the audience was still there: a victorious occasion for me. I'd done it and kept them all there and entertained while I cooked! Even the man himself, Jean-Christophe, was impressed: I was invited to deliver a course at his world famous Novelli Academy. That certainly wasn't on the cards when I woke up that morning. A great friendship had begun.

NB.
SOMETHING FOR THE WEEKEND

CHAPTER 10

Blinis and Beluga Caviar

INGREDIENTS:
Makes 24 blinis

4g dried yeast
100ml whole milk, room temperature
100g plain flour, sifted
1 free range egg yolk
1 free range egg white, whisked to
  a stiff peak
pinch of salt and white pepper
25g unsalted butter
50ml rapeseed oil
50g Beluga caviar or similar
1 small bunch of fresh parsley, chopped

METHOD:

Combine the yeast, 50ml of the whole milk and 25g of the flour in a small bowl to make a batter.

In a separate bowl, add the remaining flour, milk, egg yolk, salt and pepper and mix together.

Leave both batters to rest. After 1 hour, combine them and gently fold in the egg white.

Heat the butter and rapeseed oil in a sauté pan on a medium heat and using a dessertspoon or very small ladle place the blini batter into the pan and fry on both sides until lightly golden and cooked. Remove from the pan and cool. Repeat the process for the required number of servings.

Serve the blinis with Beluga caviar and parsley.

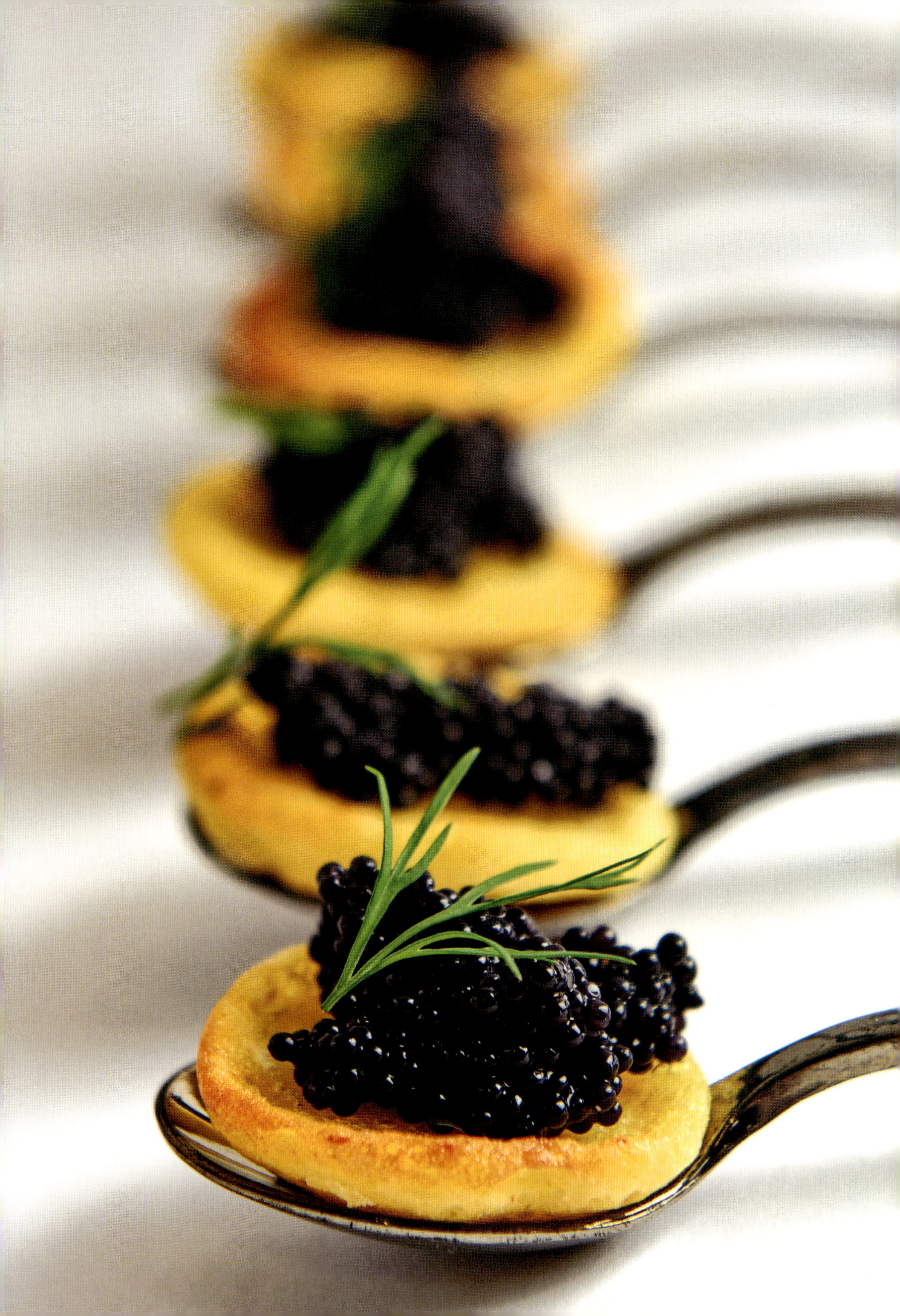

Croque Monsieur

INGREDIENTS:
Makes 4

150ml béchamel sauce, see page 234
30g French mustard
fresh grated nutmeg
1 small bunch of fresh parsley, chopped
pinch of salt and ground black pepper
200g Gruyère cheese, finely grated
8 thick-cut brioche slices, toasted
4 slices thick cut cooked ham hock

METHOD:

Combine the béchamel sauce with the mustard, nutmeg, parsley, salt and pepper and half of the cheese.

Sandwich the mixture between the slices of toasted brioche. Place on a greased baking tray and sprinkle with the remaining cheese. Bake in the oven at 180°C, or until the cheese has melted and turned golden.

Serve freshly baked and warm on their own or with seasonal salad.

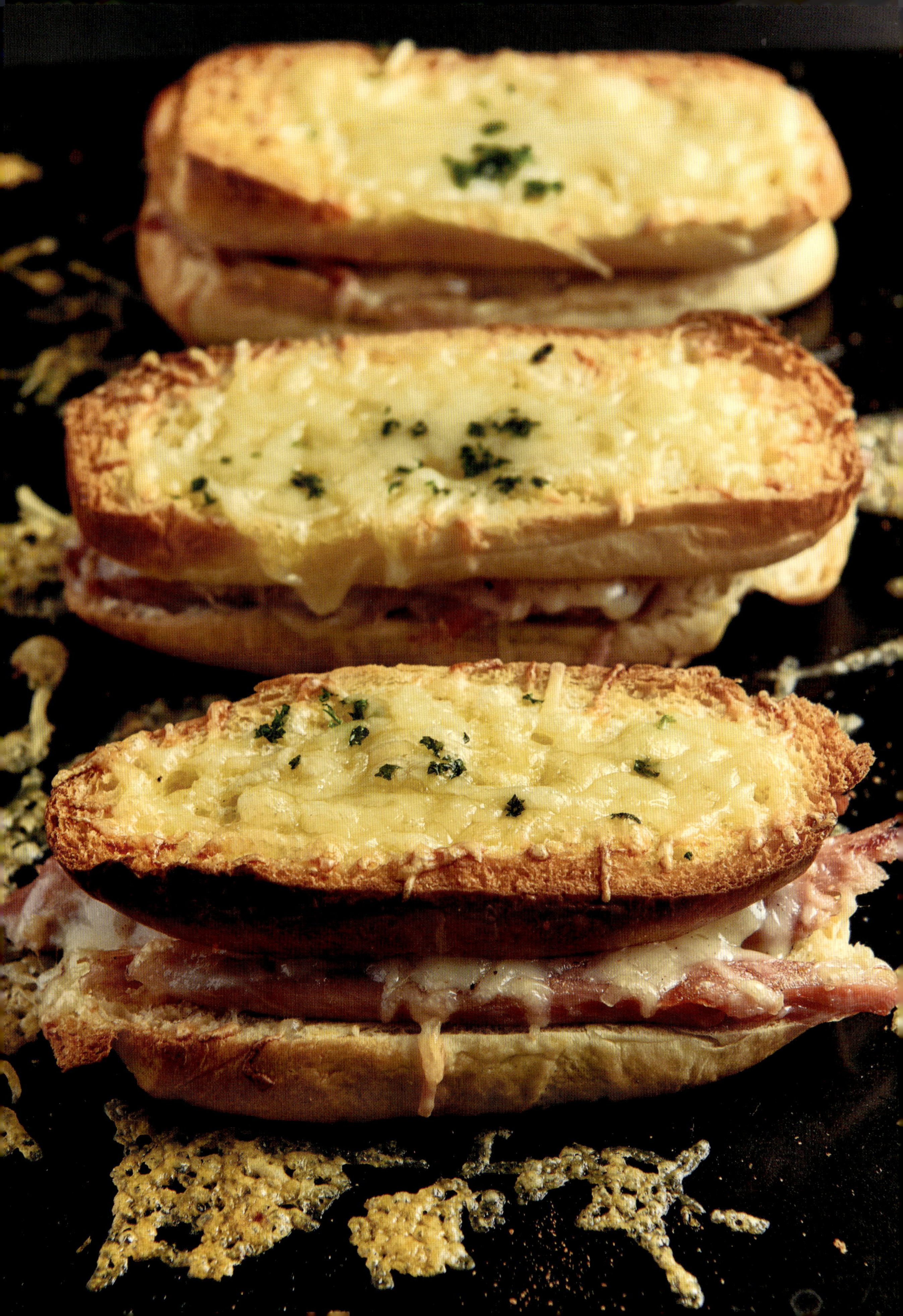

Eggs Benedict

INGREDIENTS:
Makes 4

100ml white wine vinegar
pinch of salt
4 large free range eggs
120g spinach, steamed
4 slices boiled ham hock
4 thick-cut round slices of toasted brioche, see page 148
150ml hollandaise sauce, see page 240
pinch of smoked paprika
1 small sprigs of fresh parsley

METHOD:

Take a medium-sized saucepan, half-fill with cold water and add the white wine vinegar and a pinch of salt. Place on the heat to simmer.

Once the water is gently simmering, use a whisk to make a swirling vortex in the pan. While the water is spinning, crack 1 egg into the centre and poach for just over 3 minutes. Repeat the process with the remaining eggs. When each eggs are poached, remove from the pan and drain on kitchen paper.

While the eggs are poaching place the cooked spinach and ham on the 4 slices of brioche and warm gently in the oven for 5 minutes at 180°C. Place a poached egg on top of the ham and spinach, coat with hollandaise sauce, and sprinkle with paprika and parsley.

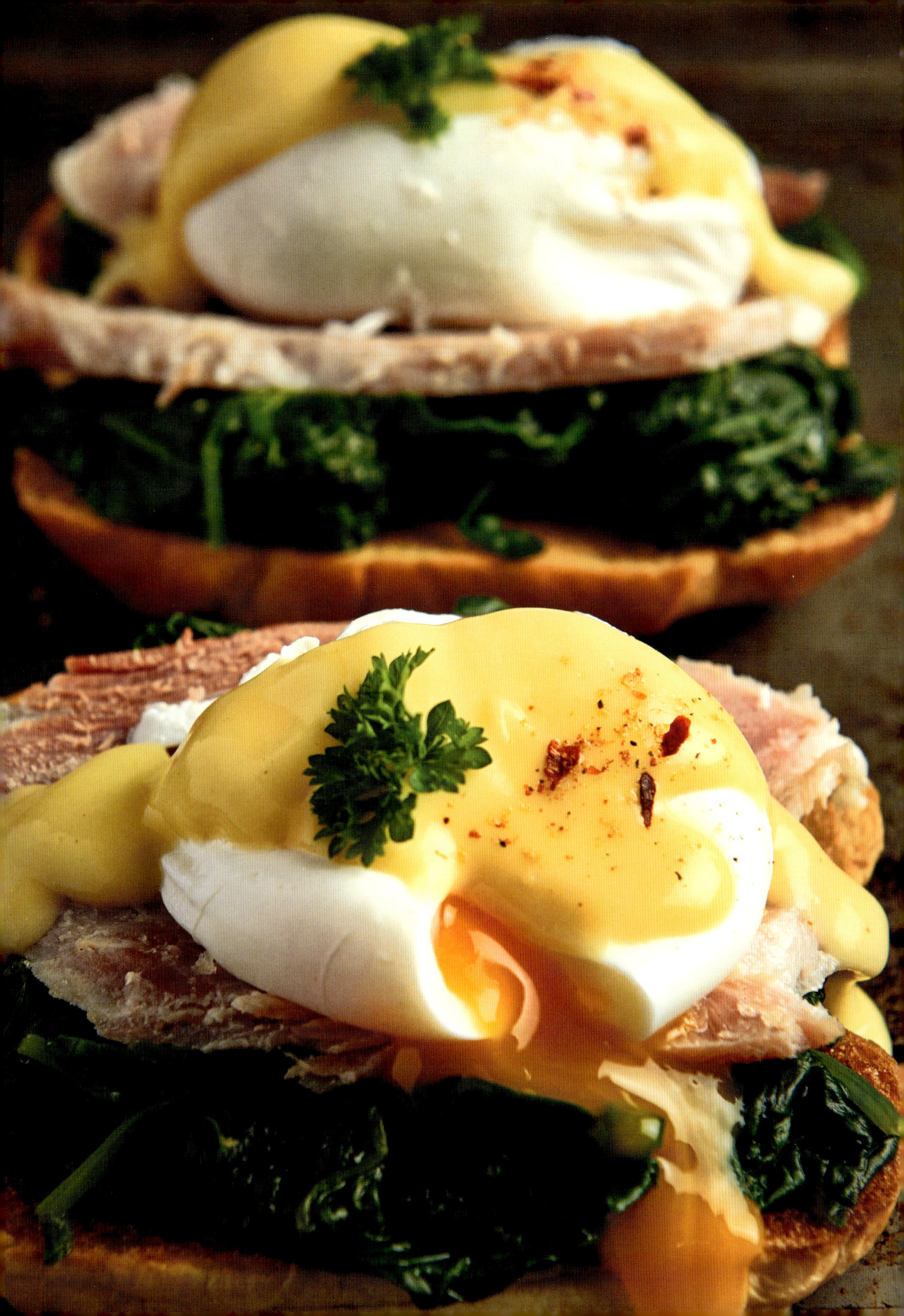

Fillet Steak with Quail Eggs and Black Summer Truffles

INGREDIENTS:
Serves 4

100ml rapeseed oil
4 x 170g fillet steaks
pinch of salt and ground black pepper
2 small sprigs of fresh thyme
4 quail eggs
1 medium black summer truffle
50g unsalted butter
50g tomberries or small cherry tomatoes

METHOD:

Take a large thick-bottomed sauté pan, add 50ml of rapeseed oil and place on a medium heat.

On a chopping board, season the fillet steaks with salt and pepper and a sprinkling of thyme.

In a separate small sauté pan, add the remaining rapeseed oil and place on a medium heat.

To cook the fillet steaks, place them into the large, hot sauté pan. Cover with a lid and cook for 2 minutes on a medium heat.

While the steaks are cooking, snip the pointed end of the quail eggs off with a pair of scissors, pour the eggs into the small hot sauté pan then reduce the heat to low.

While the eggs are cooking turn the steaks and continue cooking for a further 2 minutes without the lid.

Place the fried eggs on top of the steaks in the pan, with a thin slice of black summer truffle and a sprig of fresh thyme on top. Just before serving, add the unsalted butter to the steak pan and allow to foam. Remove the steaks from the pan and allow to rest for 1 minute.

While resting, heat the tomatoes in the foaming butter and serve with the steaks.

Serve as a miniature portion as hot canapés or with chunky chips and seasonal vegetables or salad.

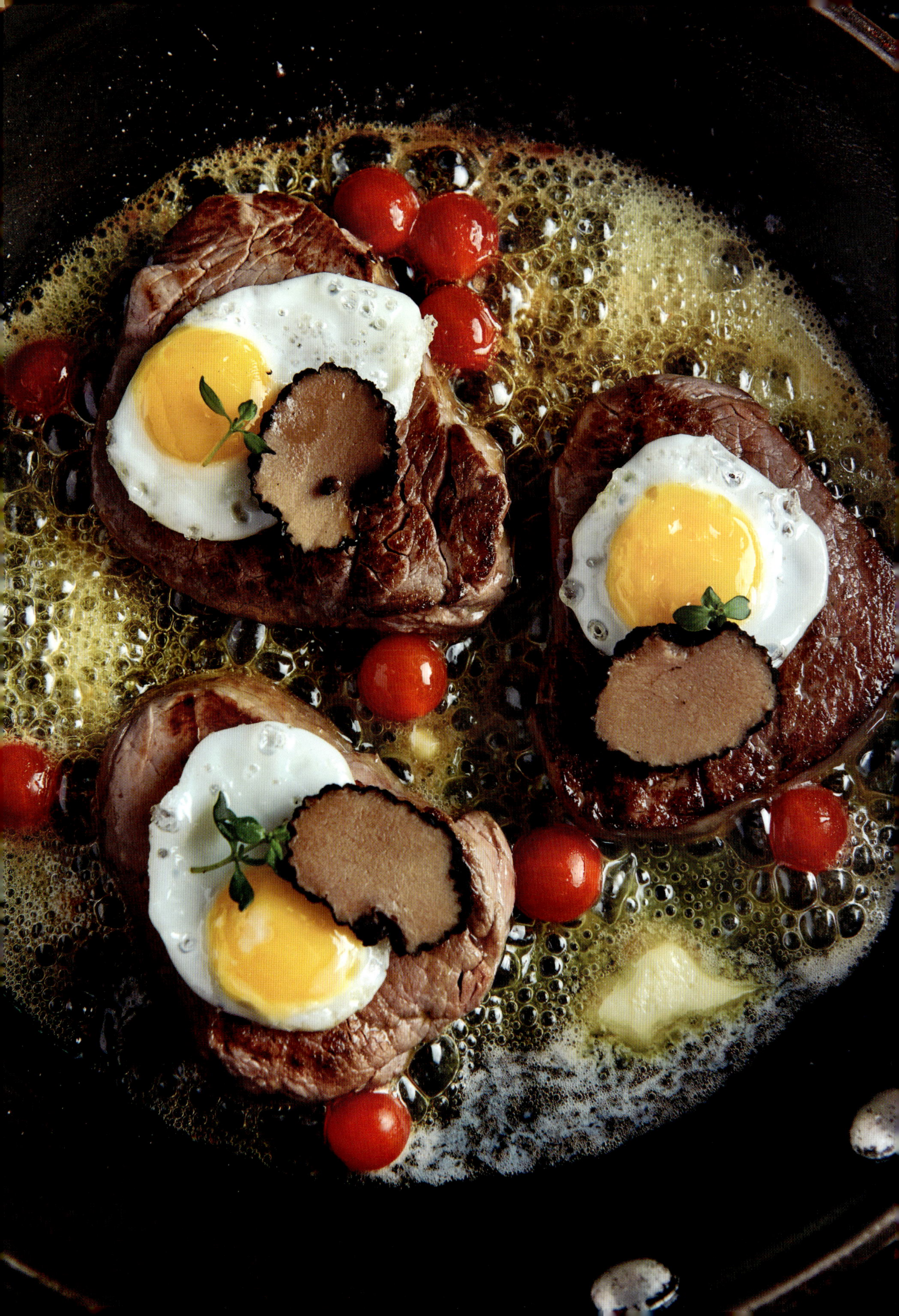

Welsh Rarebit

INGREDIENTS:

Serves 4

8 thick-cut slices of white bloomer loaf
200ml béchamel sauce, see page 234
50ml dark ale
20g English mustard powder
20ml Worcestershire sauce
2 free range egg yolks
pinch of salt and ground black pepper
200g strong cheddar, grated

METHOD:

Toast the bread slices on both sides and put to one side.

In a bowl, combine the béchamel sauce, dark ale, mustard, Worcestershire sauce, egg yolks, seasoning and half of the cheese. Using a palette knife or dessertspoon, spread the mixture on the toast followed by a sprinkling of the remaining cheese.

Place the Welsh rarebit on a baking tray and grill until the cheese is bubbling and golden.

Serve hot straight from the grill with a sprinkling of parsley and seasonal salad.

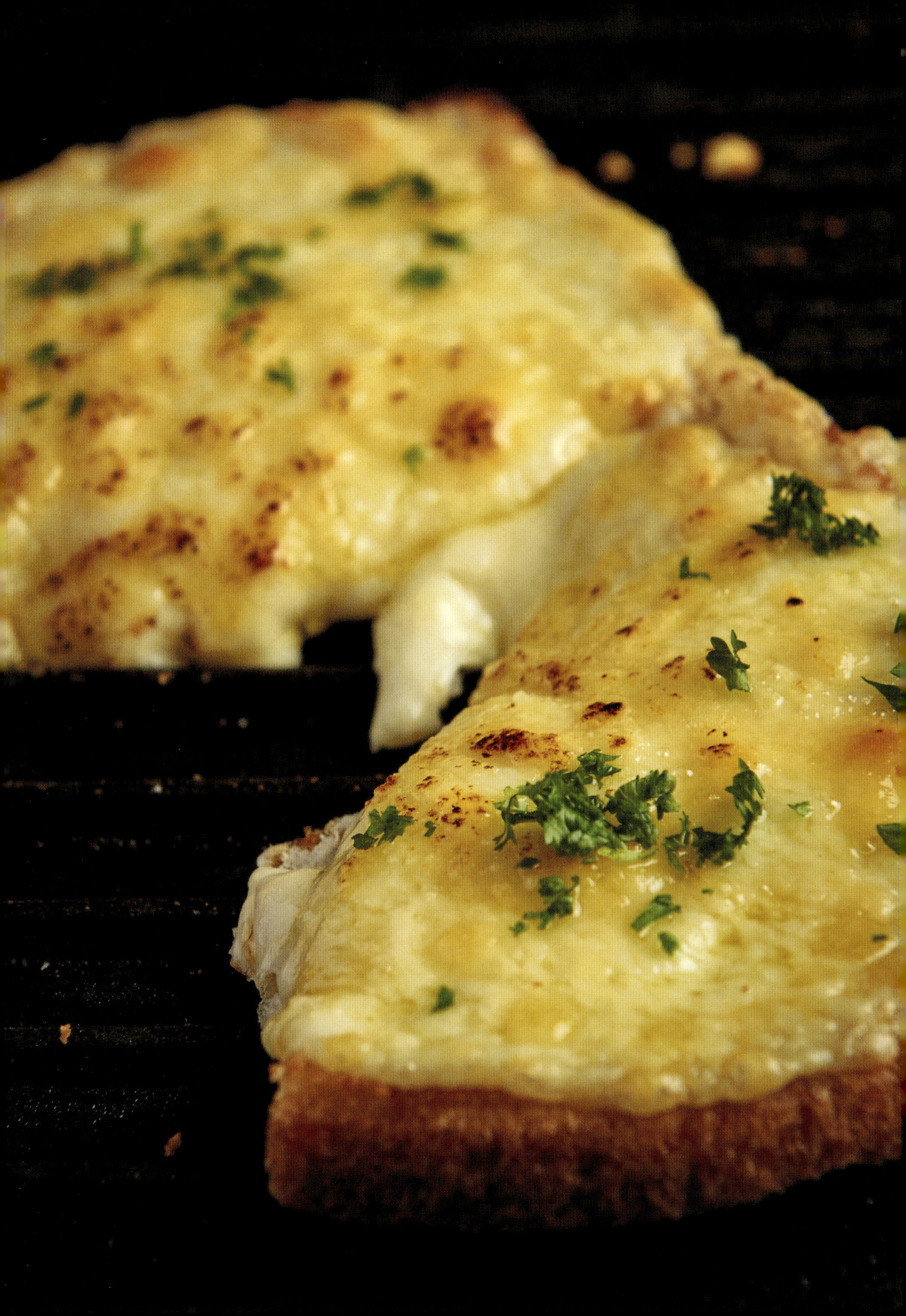

ANYONE WHO HAS A SHOTGUN LICENCE AS I HAVE WILL KNOW THAT THE CHANGING SEASONS BRING AN ABUNDANCE OF DIFFERENT FOOD THROUGHOUT THE YEAR AND TO BE INVITED ONTO A HIGH BIRD GAME SHOOT OR A GROUND GAME SHOOT IS QUITE SOMETHING: JUST GETTING INTO A SYNDICATE SHOOT CAN SOMETIMES BE HARDER THAN GETTING YOUR NAME ON THE GOLF COURSE MEMBERSHIP LIST FOR CONSIDERATION.

Spring

ASPARAGUS TART WITH HOLLANDAISE SAUCE.172
RHUBARB, GINGER AND TEA TIRAMISU.174

Summer

CHICKEN AND BACON CLUB SANDWICH.176
SPICED SUMMER BERRY PUDDING.178

Autumn

BAKED SALMON COULIBIAC.180
PEAR BELLE HÉLÈNE.182

Winter

BEEF STEW AND DUMPLINGS.184
BAKED APPLE AND ALMOND TART.186

I tried for the golf course membership once and there was a 15-year waiting list. It probably didn't help my application when they saw me: a spotty-faced 20-something who turned up at the club in a Fiat Panda – what a (golf) balls-up that was! The shotgun application took priority from there on.

To shoot something on the first walking drive of the morning of a ground game shoot isn't always the best plan, as I found out the hard way. My aim for the day was to shoot a hare or two: the classic recipe for jugged hare was on my mind.

Off we set into the wet and muddy fields, our wellies quickly gaining pounds in weight from the clinging clay mud. Then suddenly, with a running hare to my forward right and no shots from my fellow guns, the hare was mine and in my sights. A pull of the trigger and down it went: impressed 'well dones' came from down the line. Not a bad start, I thought, being my first shot of the morning.

With no gun dog to my heel or game bag over my shoulder I then had to carry the hare – about the weight of a small lamb, I'd say – until lunchtime. So, lesson number one: unless you have a gun dog, game bag or can afford your own personal loader and game carrier, never shoot a hare before lunch. Leave it for the next gun – they all did, and that gun was me.

While we're talking of shooting, here's a new option for you: rainbow trout shooting, with an air rifle. One of my brothers in his wisdom decided we would both go for a discreet walk down to a local freshwater stream not far from where we lived to try and shoot a rainbow trout for tea. Shooting a fish – it seemed like a great plan as we stood leaning over the bridge looking into the stream to choose our dinners. The trout were abundant, like lobsters in a tank. Within a minute or two a trout was shot.

What I hadn't bargained for was what came next. I was the lucky one who had to wade into the stream, knee deep in my best Wrangler jeans and shoes to catch the trout before it floated further down stream. It was a cracking shot but if we do it again – can we take waders and a net? It was a very wet and squelchy walk home. The poached rainbow trout was delicious though.

NB.
SEASONAL FAVOURITES

CHAPTER 11

Asparagus Tart with Hollandaise Sauce

INGREDIENTS:
Serves 4

200g shortcrust pastry, see page 228
1 whole free range egg and pinch
    of salt for the egg wash
6 small shallots, finely diced
pinch of salt and ground black pepper
1 small bunch of fresh parsley, chopped
1 bunch fresh asparagus, trimmed
25g butter, melted
100ml hollandaise sauce, see page 240
5g smoked paprika

METHOD:

Divide the pastry into 4 portions and roll each piece to a 14cm square, around 1cm thick. Egg wash the left and right side and fold in the edges by 1cm to form 2 raised sides.

Sprinkle the shallots down the centre of the pastry along with the seasoning and fresh chopped parsley.

Trim the asparagus to the length of the pastry and blanch in boiling salted water for 1 minute. Drain and refresh in cold water.

Lay the asparagus on top of the pastry and shallots. Brush the asparagus with melted butter and egg wash the pastry edges.

Bake the tarts in the oven at 180°C until the pastry is golden, approximately 12 minutes. Serve with the hollandaise sauce and a sprinkling of paprika.

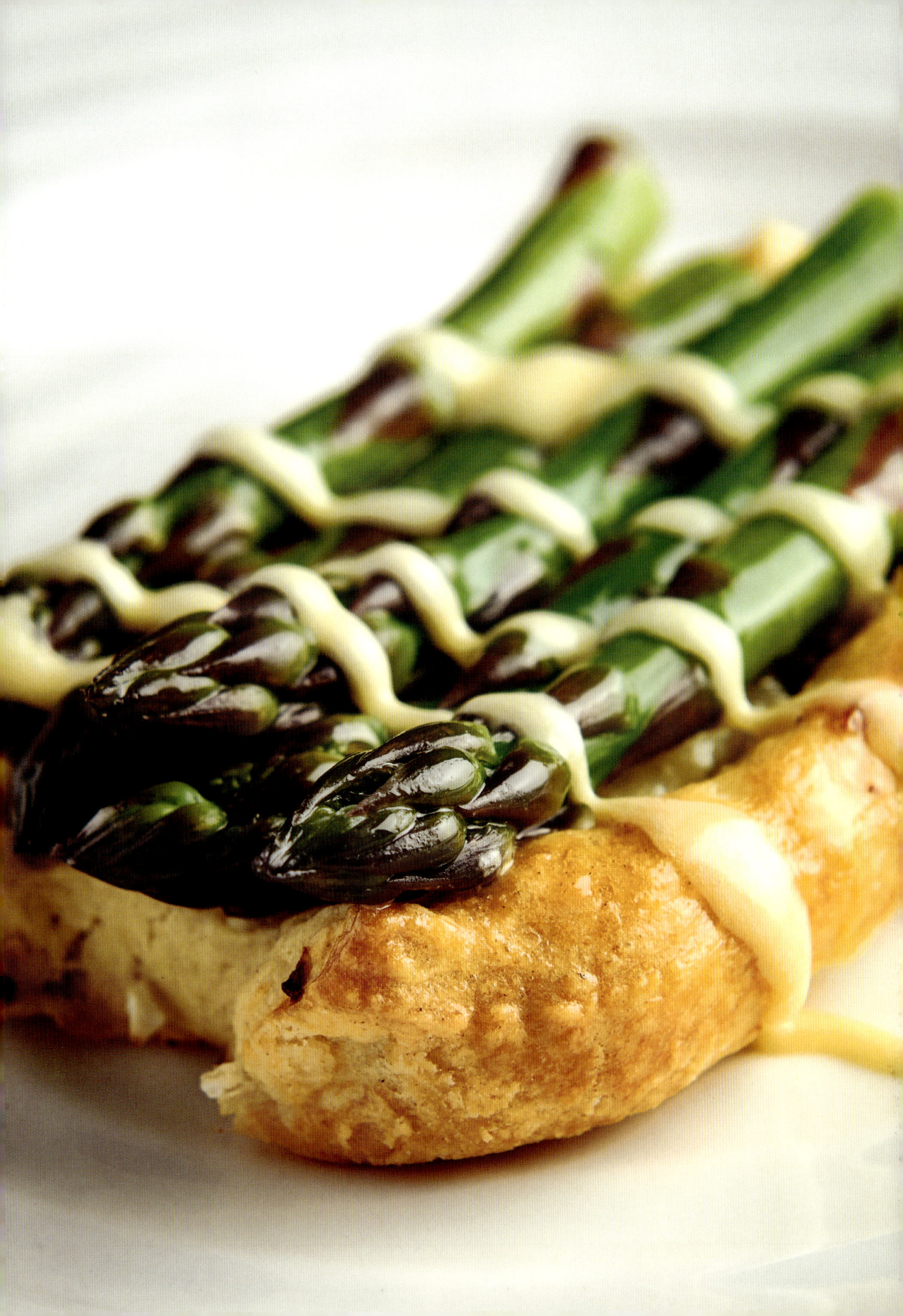

Rhubarb, Ginger and Tea Tiramisu

INGREDIENTS:
Serves 4

16 sponge fingers
30ml Marsala
100ml cold strong English breakfast tea
100g mascarpone cheese
30g fresh ginger, peeled and grated
10g caster sugar
4 free range egg whites, whisked
150g stewed rhubarb

For the zabaglione
4 free range egg yolks
5g vanilla paste
50g caster sugar
70ml Marsala

For the cocoa topping
40g cocoa powder and 40g icing sugar sieved together

METHOD:

Break the sponge fingers into small pieces and place them in the bottom of a serving dish or glasses. Add 30ml Marsala to the cold tea, stir and pour over the broken fingers to soak.

For the zabaglione, in a separate bowl place the egg yolks, vanilla paste, sugar and Marsala. Place over a pan of hot water and whisk until the mixture becomes lighter, creamy and to a ribbon stage. Remove from the heat and cool, stirring occasionally.

In a separate large bowl, combine the mascarpone cheese and grated ginger with 10g caster sugar.

Using a large metal spoon or spatula, fold the zabaglione sabayon into the mixture, then gently fold in the whisked egg whites. Place the complete mix over the soaked biscuits and level the surface with a palette knife.

Dust the surface with the cocoa topping and refrigerate for 2 hours before serving.

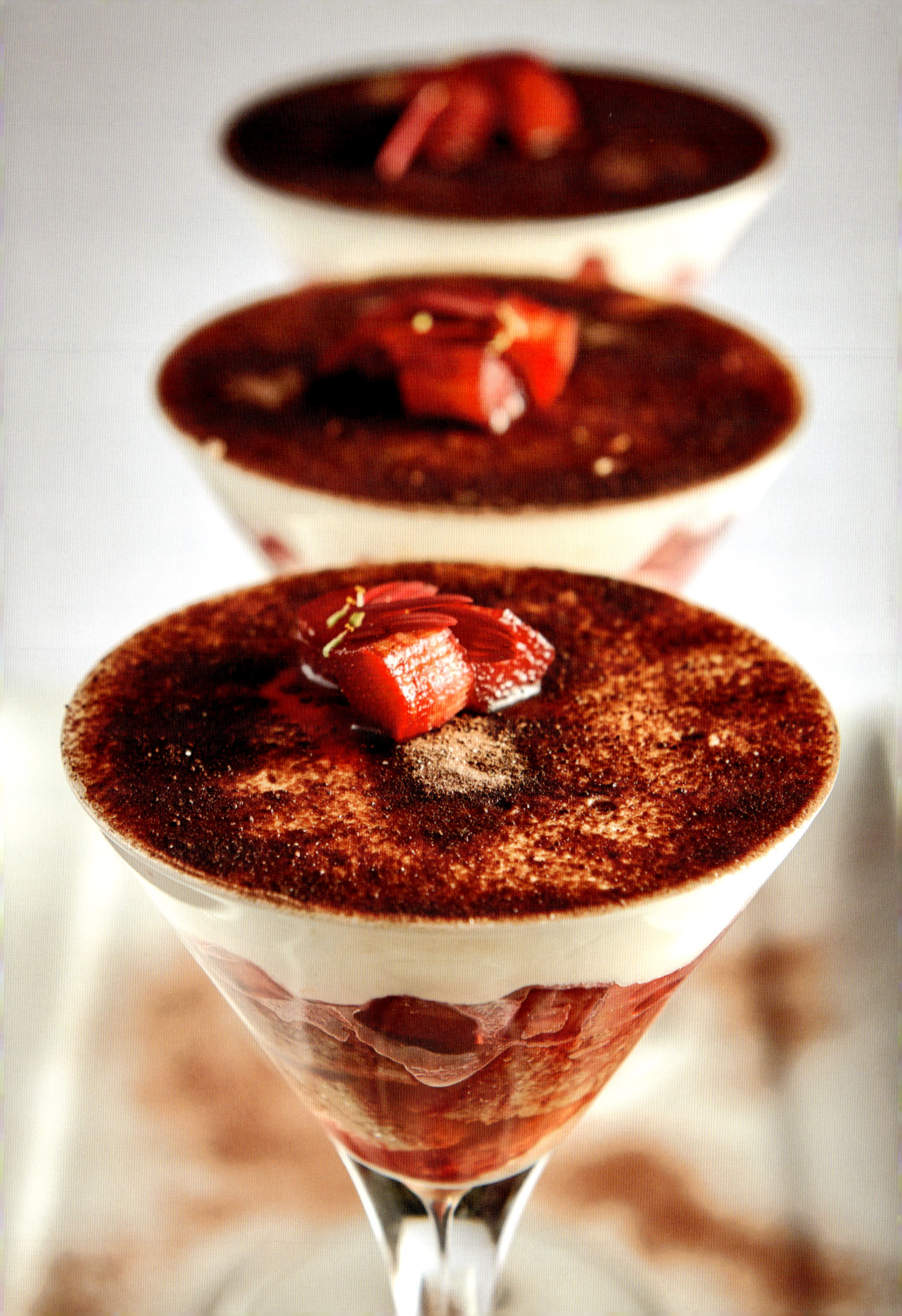

Chicken and Bacon Club Sandwich

INGREDIENTS:

Serves 4

12 slices of bloomer loaf bread, toasted
200ml mayonnaise
1/2 a head iceberg lettuce, washed and finely shredded
ground black pepper
4 sun-ripened vine tomatoes
1/4 of a cucumber, peeled, sliced and lightly salted
4 whole cooked roast chicken breasts, sliced
1 small bunch of fresh basil, picked leaves
8 rashers smoked bacon, grilled until crispy
16 club sandwich skewers
4 small sprigs of parsley

METHOD:

Take a slice of toast and spread with a little mayonnaise, followed by a sprinkling of iceburg lettuce, a pinch of black pepper, 2 thin slices of tomato and 3 slices of the salted cucumber.

Add half of one sliced chicken breast to the stack followed by another slice of toast. Spread mayonnaise on the top followed by more iceberg lettuce, tomatoes, cucumber, basil and the remaining chicken.

Lay the bacon on top of the chicken and top with a final slice of toast spread with mayonnaise. If halving the sandwich, secure with 2 skewers. Repeat the process for the other 3 sandwiches.

Finish with a fresh sprig of parsley.

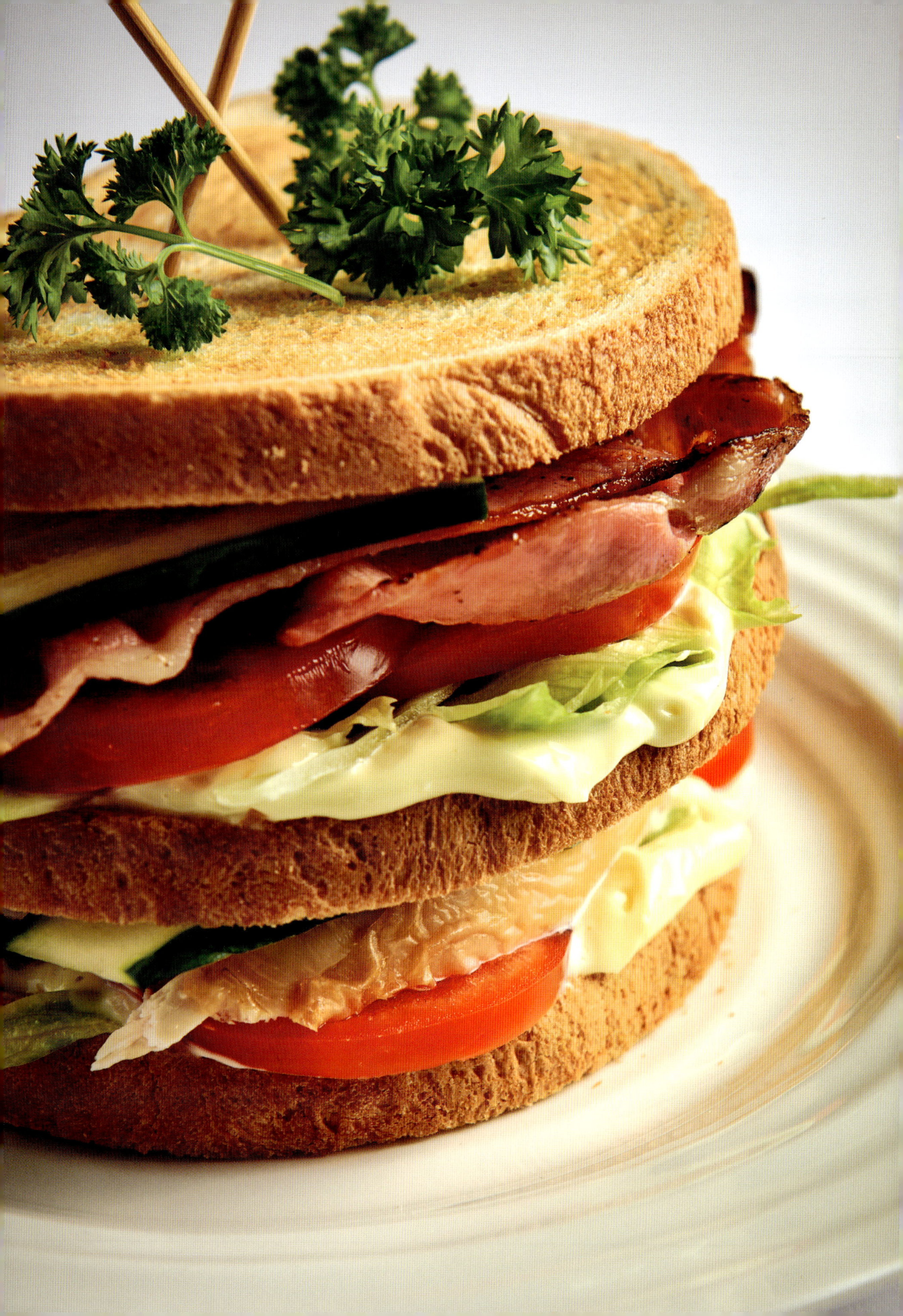

Spiced Summer Berry Pudding

INGREDIENTS:
Serves 4

400g raspberries
200g strawberries
100g redcurrants
2 Braeburn apples, peeled, cored and grated
1 large orange, zest and juiced
60g caster sugar
2 star anise
1 cinnamon stick
1 vanilla pod and seeds
4g leaf gelatine, softened in cold water
8 slices of brioche, thinly sliced, see page 148
100ml cream, whipped or clotted
sprig of mint

METHOD:

Wash and hull all the berries and place into a thick-bottomed pan along with the grated apples, zest and juice of the orange, caster sugar, star anise, cinnamon and vanilla. Place on a medium heat to allow the sugar to dissolve and the spices to infuse, stirring occasionally. Remove from the heat but leave in the pan.

While the berry mixture is still hot, add the softened gelatine and gently stir to disperse. Place the mixture into a clean bowl and set to one side.

Cut the brioche slices to size to fit a pudding basin or 4 small moulds. Dip each slice into the berry mixture to soak, then line your basin or moulds. Remove the star anise and cinnamon sticks from the mixture.

Spoon the mixture into the lined moulds and finish with a final disc of soaked bread on top. Cover with cling film and refrigerate for 3 hours or overnight.

To serve the pudding, dip the basin or moulds into hot water and with a gentle shake remove the pudding and place on a serving dish with clotted cream and a sprig of mint.

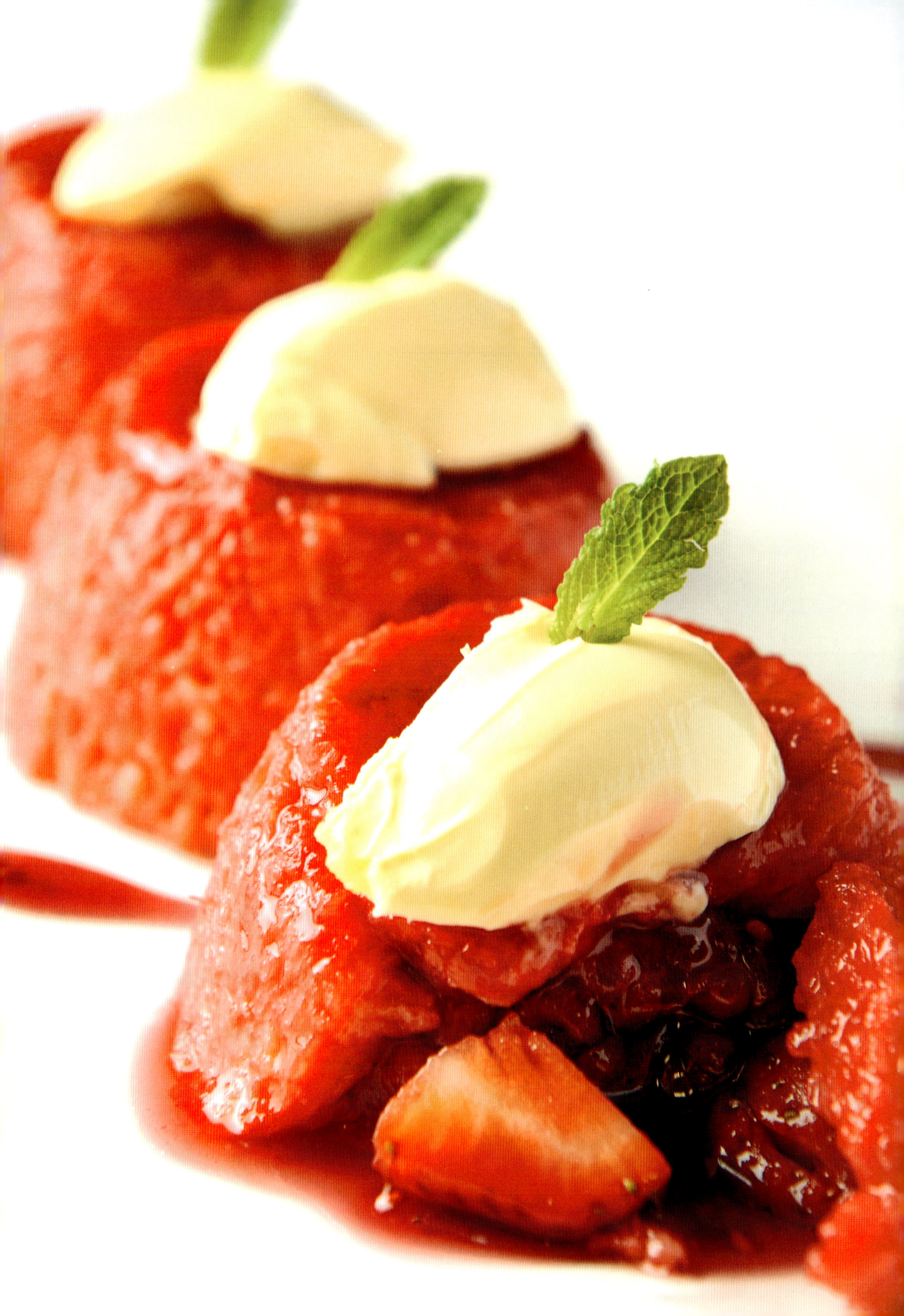

Baked Salmon Coulibiac

INGREDIENTS:
Serves 4

400g puff pastry, see page 226
100g long grain rice, cooked and chilled
200g chestnut mushrooms, sliced, sautéed and chilled
4 spring onions, trimmed and sliced
30g fresh parsley, finely chopped
20g cornflour
pinch of salt and ground black pepper
600g whole salmon fillet, skinned and de-boned
2 hard-boiled eggs, sliced
1 lemon, zest and juice
30g salted butter, melted
1 medium free range egg and pinch of salt for the egg wash

METHOD:

Roll the pastry out to twice the size of the salmon fillet.

Combine the rice, mushrooms, spring onions, parsley, cornflour and seasoning. Using half the mixture make a bed of rice the same size as the salmon fillet in the centre of the pastry. Place the salmon on top of the rice, skin side down. Lay the sliced hard-boiled eggs over the salmon followed by the remaining rice mixture. Zest the lemon over the ingredients, sprinkle with the lemon juice, then drizzle with the melted butter.

Egg wash the pastry and fold each side over the salmon to seal. Trim the excess and egg wash the top. Place onto a greased baking tray, and bake in the oven at 180°C for approximately 35-40 minutes.

Allow to stand for 5 minutes before slicing and serving.

Serve with steamed seasonal vegetables or crisp salad leaves.

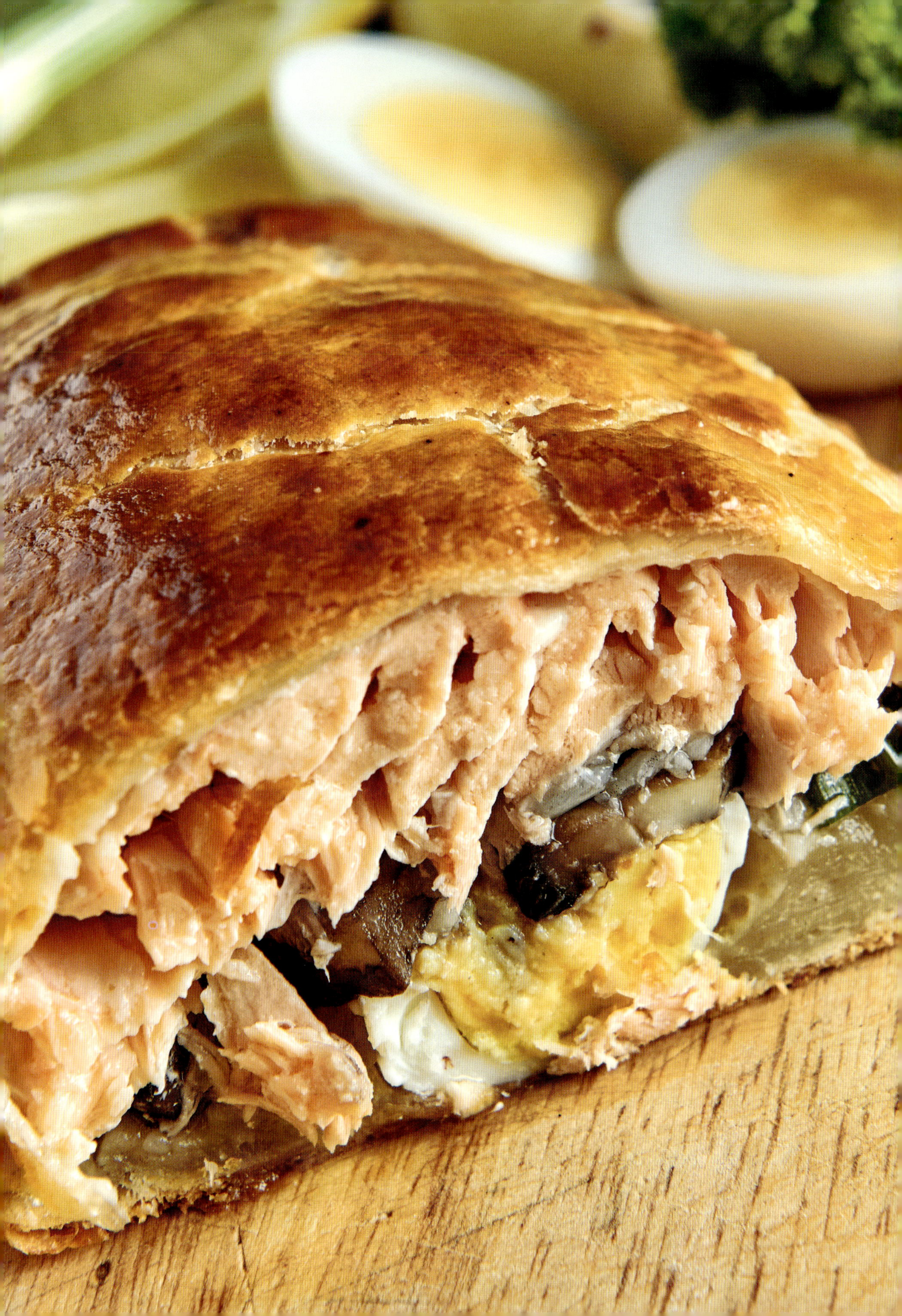

Pears Belle Hélène

INGREDIENTS:
Serves 4

For the pears
4 small Comice pears
200ml water
200g sugar
vanilla pod
cinnamon stick

For the ice cream
250ml double cream
200ml whole milk
2 vanilla pods, seeds scraped out or 10g vanilla paste
4 free range eggs yolks
100g caster sugar

For the chocolate sauce
200ml double cream
300g chocolate (70 per cent cocoa solids), broken into small pieces
30g salted butter
10g vanilla paste

For the Chantilly cream
100ml whipping cream
5g caster sugar
5ml vanilla paste

METHOD:

Peel, half and core the pears and place in a thick-bottomed saucepan with the water, sugar, vanilla and cinnamon stick. Bring to the boil and simmer until the pears are cooked. Remove from the heat and allow to cool with the pears in the syrup. Once cool, remove them from the syrup into a clean bowl, cover with cling film and refrigerate until use.

For the ice cream, place the cream, milk and vanilla into a thick-bottomed saucepan and allow to simmer for 1 minute. Remove from the heat and allow the contents to cool for 10 minutes then sieve into a pouring jug.

In a bowl, whisk the egg yolks and sugar together until the sugar has dissolved. Whisk the milk liquid through the egg mixture and return the recipe to a clean thick-bottomed pan on a medium heat, stirring continuously until the mixture coats the back of a spatula.

Remove the pan from the heat and allow to cool down to 10°C before placing the ice cream mixture into an ice cream machine; churn until frozen.

In a separate pan, put the double cream, chocolate, butter and vanilla paste over a medium heat, and stir continually until all the ingredients have formed a rich chocolate sauce. Remove from the heat and cool.

To make the Chantilly cream, whip all the ingredients together to a piping consistency.

Place a scoop of ice cream followed by 2 pear halves, sliced or whole. Drizzle with the chocolate sauce and serve with Chantilly cream.

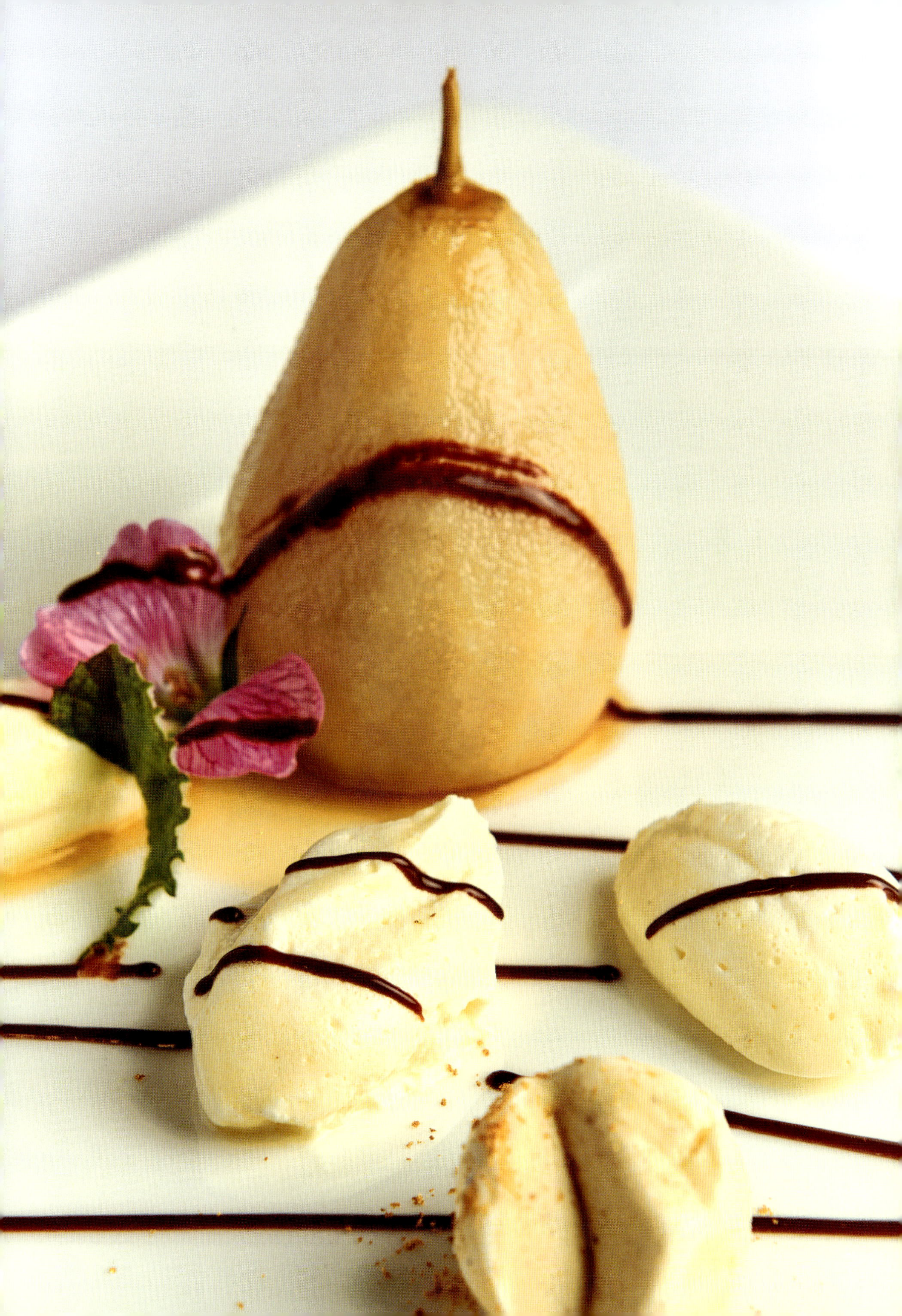

Beef Stew and Dumplings

INGREDIENTS:
Serves 4

For the dumplings
120g self-raising flour
60g shredded beef suet
pinch of salt and ground white pepper
50ml cold water

For the beef stew
20ml rapeseed oil
1 large onion, peeled, quartered and layers separated
800g braising steak, cut into cubes
2 large carrots, peeled, trimmed and diced large
40g plain flour
1 litre beef stock, see page 216
10ml dark soy sauce
10ml Worcestershire sauce
4 bay leaves
1 small bunch of parsley, finely chopped

METHOD:

For the dumplings, sieve the self-raising flour into a mixing bowl and add the beef suet, salt and pepper. Stir the ingredients together while gradually adding the water to form a firm dumpling dough. Once formed, divide into 8 dumplings and leave to one side on a floured tray.

For the beef stew, place a large thick-bottomed saucepan on the heat with the rapeseed oil and fry the onions until golden. Add the cubes of beef and seal until brown on all sides.

Add the carrots and plain flour and stir until all the ingredients are coated. Pour in the beef stock, soy sauce, Worcestershire sauce and bay leaves. Place a lid on the pan and allow it the gently simmer for approximately 1 hour 40 minutes, topping up with beef stock occasionally if required.

Place the dumplings in the beef stew and continue cooking for a further 15-20 minutes with the lid on or until the dumplings are cooked.

Serve the stew in an earthenware dish with chopped parsley.

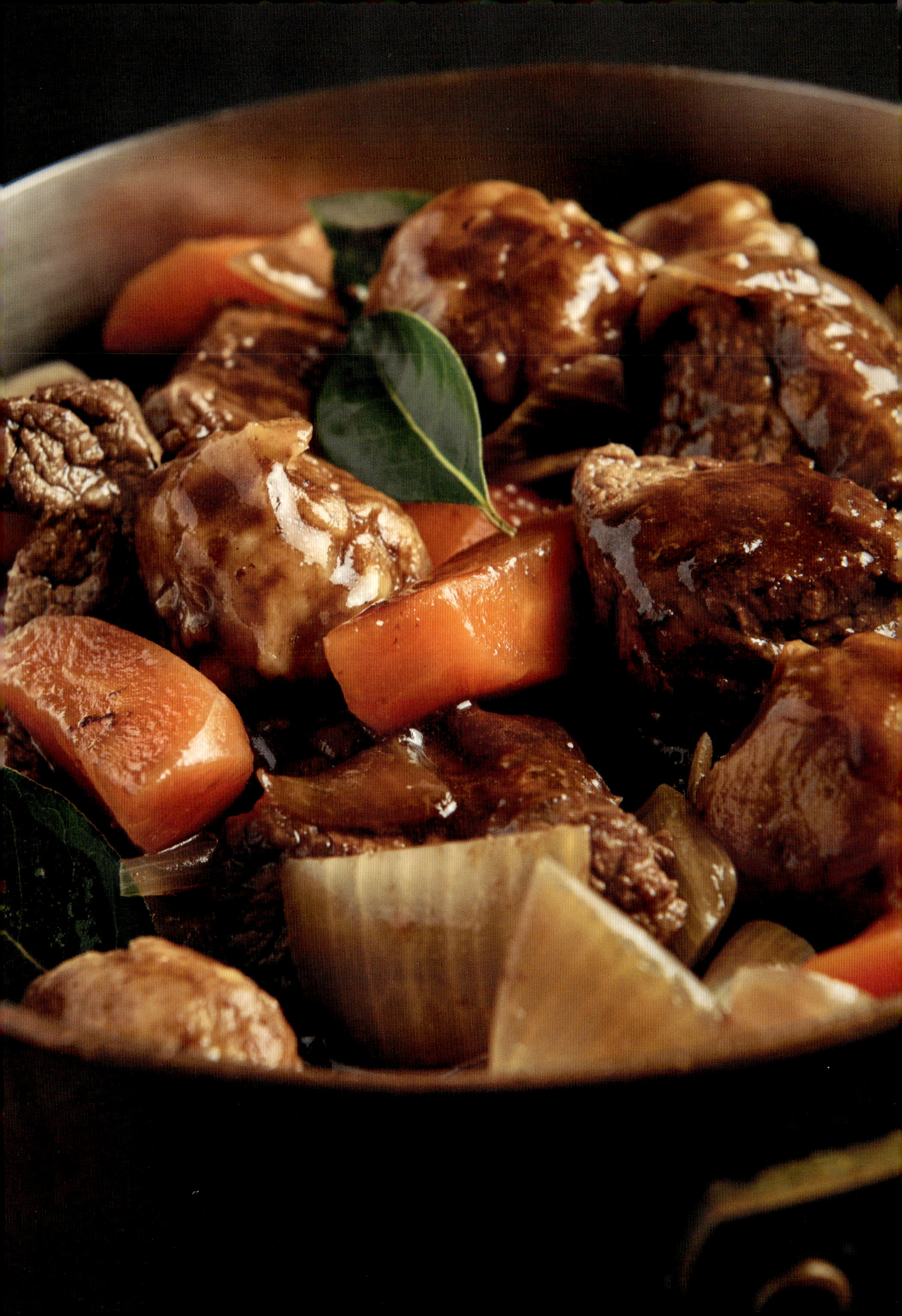

Baked Apple and Almond Tart

INGREDIENTS:

Serves 8

For the frangipane
120g butter, softened
120g caster sugar
5ml almond essence
5g vanilla paste
2 large free range eggs
20g plain flour
120g ground almonds
30g flaked almonds

300g sweet pastry, see page 232
3-4 Braeburn dessert apples, peeled, cored and sliced
30g soft brown sugar

For the apricot glaze
50g apricot jam
100ml water

METHOD:

Line a 7" flan dish or ring with the sweet pastry.

For the frangipane, in a bowl, place the butter, caster sugar, almond essence and vanilla paste. Mix the ingredients together with a spatula until a creamy, light and fluffy consistency is reached. Blend in the eggs, one at a time, followed by the flour and ground almonds. Evenly spread the mixture in the base of the lined flan dish.

Neatly arrange the sliced apples in a fan formation until the surface of the flan dish is completely covered. Sprinkle the apple with the soft brown sugar and flaked almonds. Bake the tart in the oven at 180°C until the pastry is golden and the apples are cooked, approximately 30 minutes.

For the apricot glaze, place the water and jam in a small saucepan and bring to the boil until the liquid coats the back of a spoon.

Once cooked, brush the hot apple tart with the apricot glaze and serve warm.

Serve with a quenelle of clotted cream or vanilla custard.

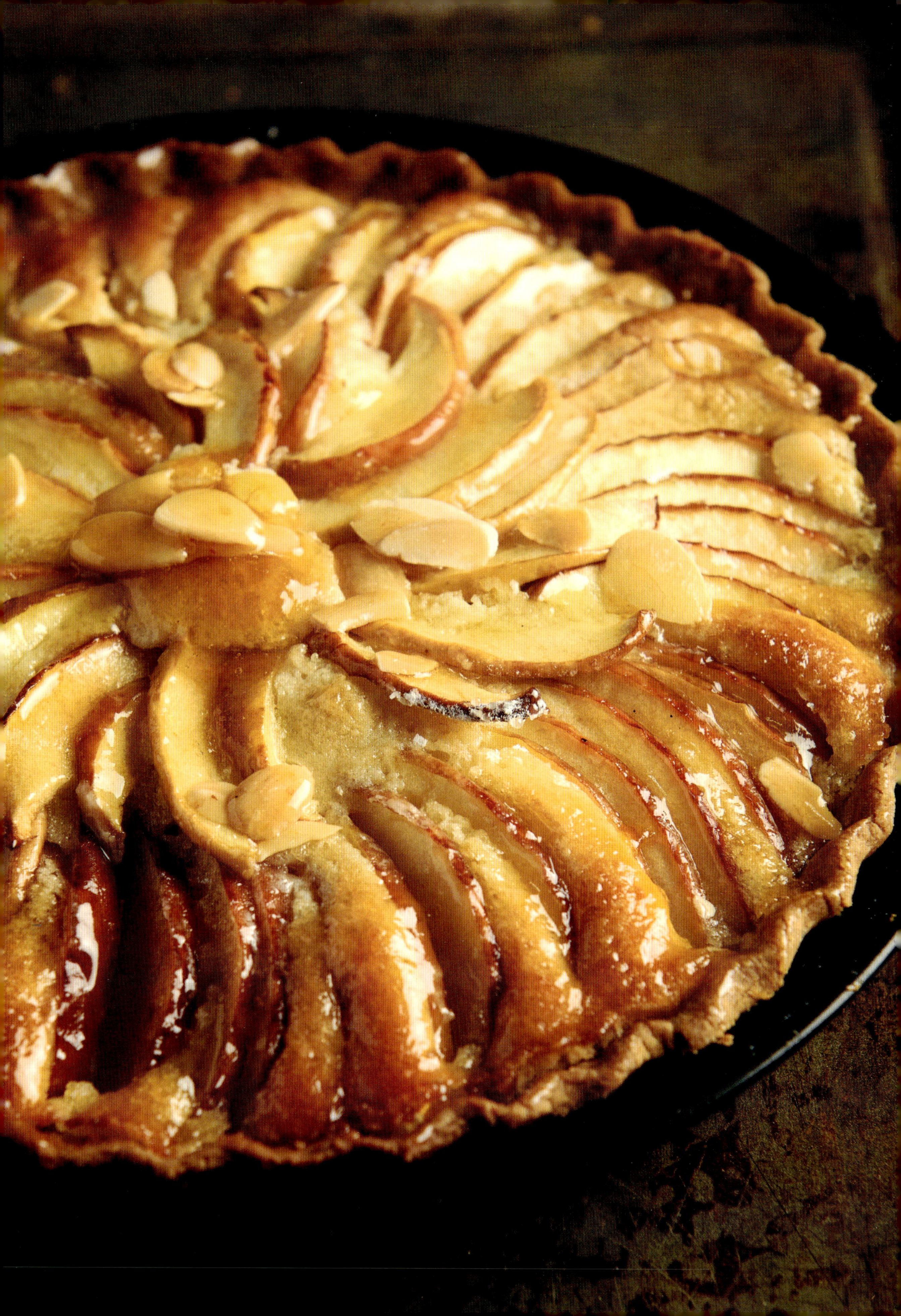

ONE DAY MRS B WAS SUFFERING FROM A MILD VERSION OF FEMALE MAN 'FLU, SO I THOUGHT I'D CHEER HER UP. OFF I TROTTED TO THE KITCHEN TO MAKE AND BAKE A DOZEN SCONES. I WAS WELL PREPARED AND HAD BOUGHT THE CLOTTED CREAM AND STRAWBERRY JAM THE DAY BEFORE. WITH THE SCONES BAKING, I HAD JUST ENOUGH TIME FOR THE FIRST LAWN CUT OF THE YEAR. FRESHLY BAKED AND ONTO THE COOLING WIRE: BY 'ECK! GRANDMA BROWN WOULD HAVE BEEN PROUD.

Afternoon Tea

CHOCOLATE ÉCLAIRS.190
FRUIT BARQUETTES.192
LEMON TART.194
RICH PORT FRUIT CAKE.196
SCONES.198
STRAWBERRY CHOUX SWANS.200

With a newly refurbished lounge, a brand new suite including some 'oh-so-comfy' rocker recliner chairs and a bright and almost spring-like-looking conservatory, I just needed a suited and booted pianist to tickle the ivories for the perfect Sunday afternoon tea effect.

Problem is we don't have a baby grand piano, nor a pianist, so I opted for the Bose Sound Link, my iPhone and good old YouTube app for a music search.

After a quick search for some afternoon tea piano music I found the perfect selection.

Bluetooth connected, gentle background music playing, tea and scones served: perfect. Mrs B was starting to feel better already.

"That's lovely music, what is it?" she asked.

Being the sophisticated person that I am, I replied that it was a fine selection of chopping piano music.

"Chopping piano music?" Mrs B repeated.

"Yes," I said. "It's good isn't it?"

"Chopping piano?" she repeated again.

"Yes." I took my iPhone to show her the YouTube chopping piano music for herself.

"Oh, yes," Mrs B said. "You mean 'Chopin'."

No, I replied, if it was pronounced like that it would have been spelled 'showpan'.

I think we can safely say that I won't be reading any auto-cues any time soon.

Bloody 'chopping' piano music. Still, it cheered Mrs B up – mission accomplished I'd say.

NB.
AFTERNOON TEA

CHAPTER 12

Chocolate Éclairs

INGREDIENTS:
Makes 8

For the éclair finger
200g choux pastry, see page 222

For the chocolate coating
100g 70% dark chocolate
10g salted butter
30ml double cream

To drizzle
50g white chocolate, melted

Chantilly cream
200ml whipping cream
10g caster sugar
5ml vanilla paste

METHOD:

Grease a baking tray and using a piping bag, with a 15mm plain nozzle, filled with choux pastry mixture, pipe lengths onto the tray, 10cm long and spaced 10cm apart. Sprinkle a liberal quantity of cold water over the piped éclairs and the tray then bake in the oven at 180°C for approximately 15 minutes or until the éclairs have risen and turned light golden brown. Cool on a rack.

For the chocolate coating, take a small thick-bottomed saucepan and melt the chocolate, butter and double cream gently over a low heat.

For the Chantilly cream, whip all the ingredients together to a piping consistency.

When the éclairs are cold, slice in half lengthways and pipe the Chantilly cream along the centre of the base. Dip the top of the éclair in the chocolate coating and drizzle with the melted white chocolate. Gently place the chocolate topped section on top of the cream.

Keep chilled until serving.

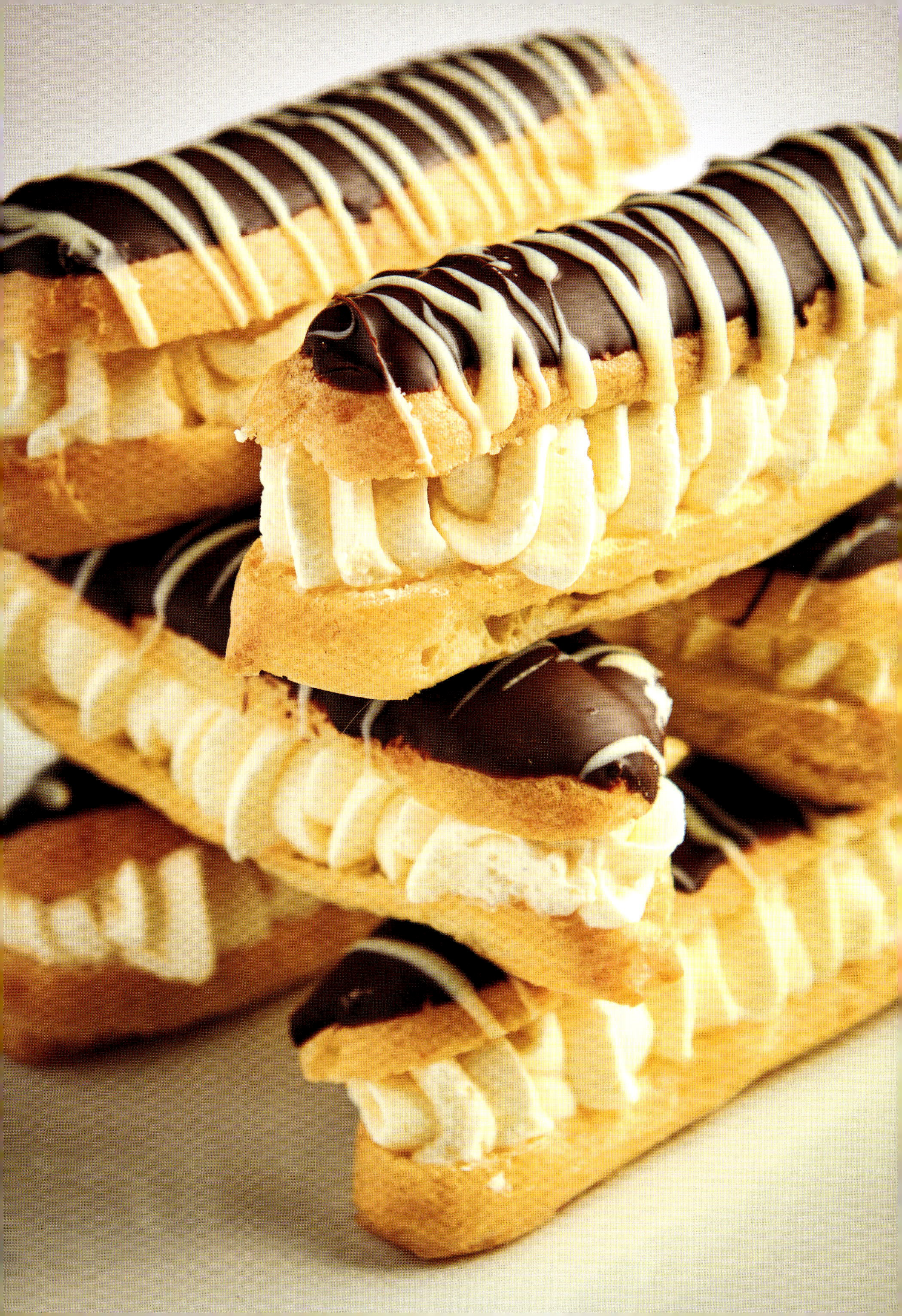

Fruit Barquettes

INGREDIENTS:
Serves 4

For the barquette cases
180g sweet pastry, see page 232

Chantilly cream for the filling
200ml whipping cream
10g caster sugar
5ml vanilla paste

To finish the barquettes
50g apricot jam
100ml water
selection of fresh raspberries, strawberries, cherries, mango and kiwi fruit

METHOD:

Roll out the sweet pastry on a lightly floured surface and line barquette moulds or tartlet tins. Insert a small piece of greaseproof paper and some baking beans into each mould or tin and bake blind at 180°C for 6 minutes. Remove the greaseproof and baking beans and continue baking for a further 4 minutes or until the pastry is light golden brown. Leave to cool.

To make the Chantilly cream, whip all the ingredients together to a piping consistency.

In a small thick-bottomed saucepan, melt the apricot jam with the water and leave to one side to cool.

Using a piping bag fitted with a 1cm star nozzle, neatly fill the barquettes with the Chantilly cream.

Decorate with your selection of fruits and brush the fruits with the cooled jam.

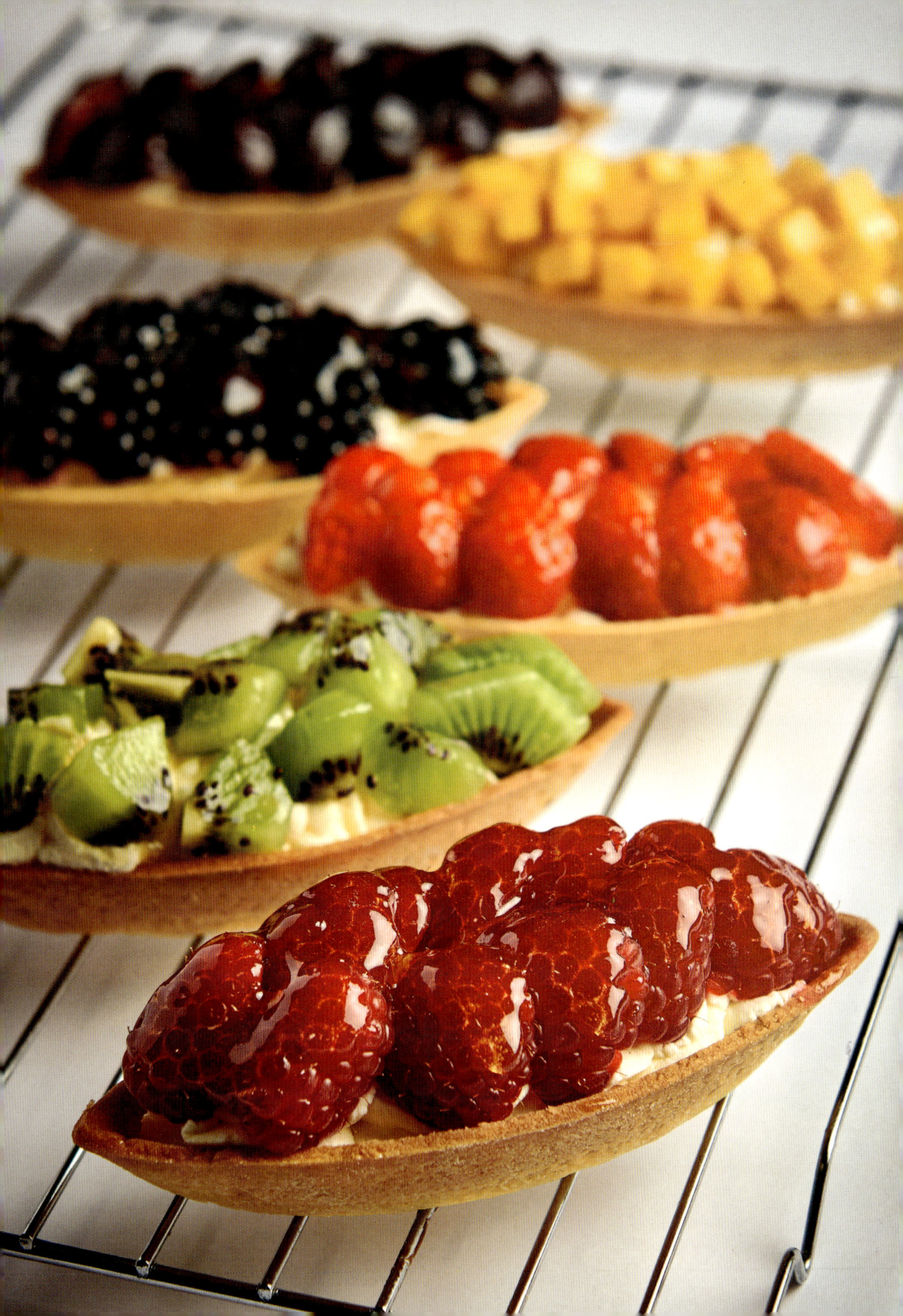

Lemon Tart

INGREDIENTS:
Serves 4

For the case
180g sweet pastry, see page 232

For the filling
120g caster sugar
120ml double cream
6 medium free-range eggs
2 egg yolks
60ml freshly squeezed lemon juice
1 lemon, finely zested

METHOD:

Roll out the sweet pastry on a lightly floured surface and line a small flan ring or dish, approximately 18cm in diameter.

Cut a circle of greaseproof paper 22cm in diameter. Place it inside the lined flan ring and fill with baking beans. Bake the flan case blind in the oven at 180°C for 8-10 minutes. Remove the baking beans and greaseproof and continue baking for a further 5 minutes or until the base is light golden brown. Leave to cool.

In a bowl, mix the sugar, double cream, eggs, egg yolks and lemon juice together and strain into a pouring jug. Pour the mixture into the baked flan case and carefully zest 1 lemon over the tart.

Reduce the oven temperature to 170°C and bake the tart for approximately 15-20 minutes or until the filling has a firm wobble.

Cool completely, and refrigerate for 2 hours before serving sliced with your favourite vanilla ice cream.

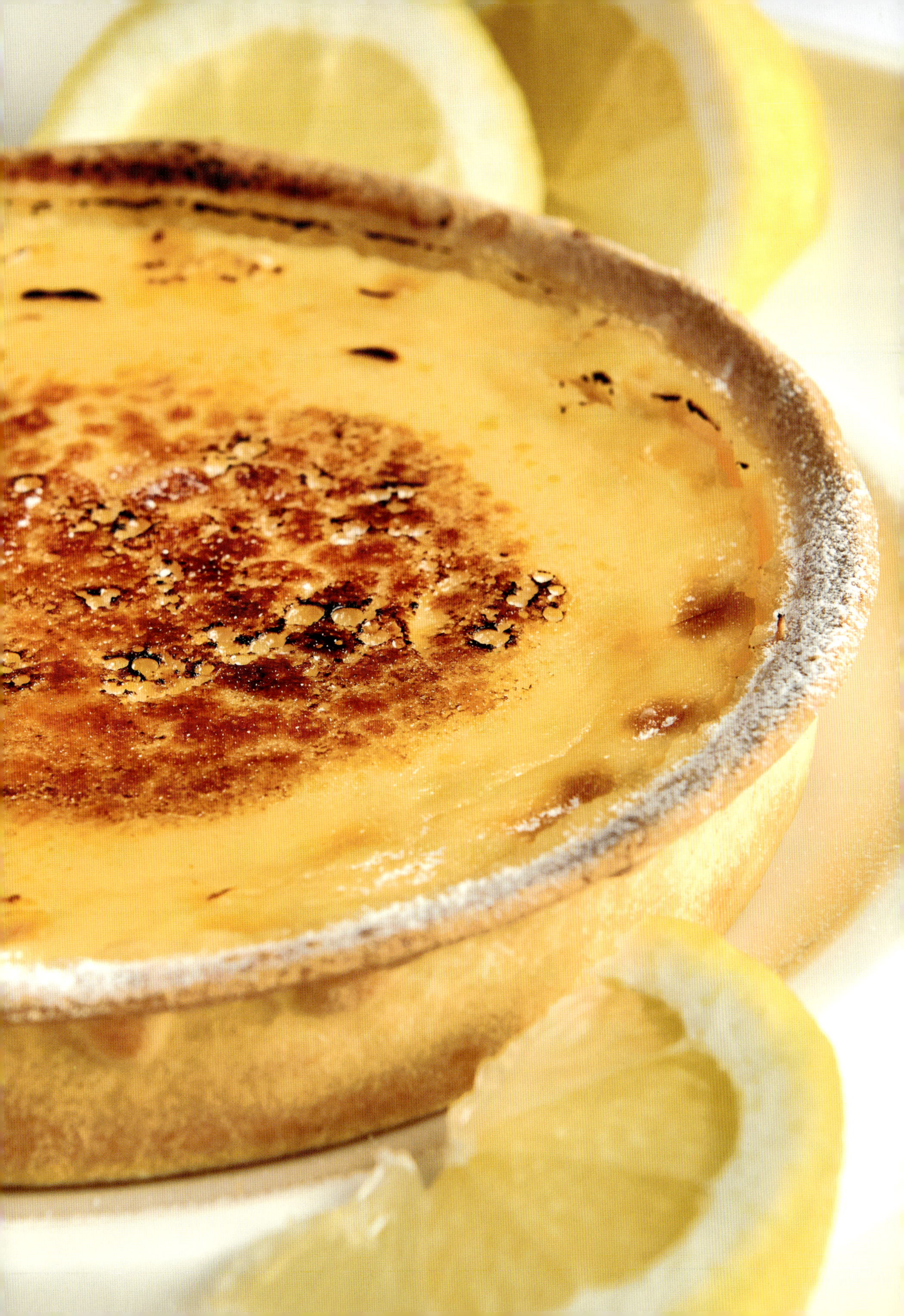

Rich Port Fruit Cake

INGREDIENTS:
Makes a 20cm cake

60g butter
50g soft dark brown sugar
1 medium free range egg
170g plain white flour
5g baking powder
10g ground mixed spice
180g luxury mixed dried fruit
80g dates, destoned and chopped
100ml whole milk
1/2 orange, grated zest
1/2 lemon, grated zest
200ml port

METHOD:

Using greaseproof paper, line a 20cm loaf tin.

In a large mixing bowl, cream the butter and soft dark brown sugar together and add the egg.

Sieve the flour into the bowl with the baking powder and add the mixed spice, dried fruits, dates, milk, orange zest and lemon zest. Mix well together. Add 100ml port and spoon the mixture into the lined loaf tin.

Bake at 170°C for approximately 60-90 minutes. Test the cake is baked by inserting a skewer; if it comes out clean, the cake is done.

Cool in the tin. Once cold, leaving the cake in the tin, drizzle over the rest of the port, then wrap in cling film.

Leave for 2 days in the fridge before serving sliced either on its own or with your favourite crumbly cheese.

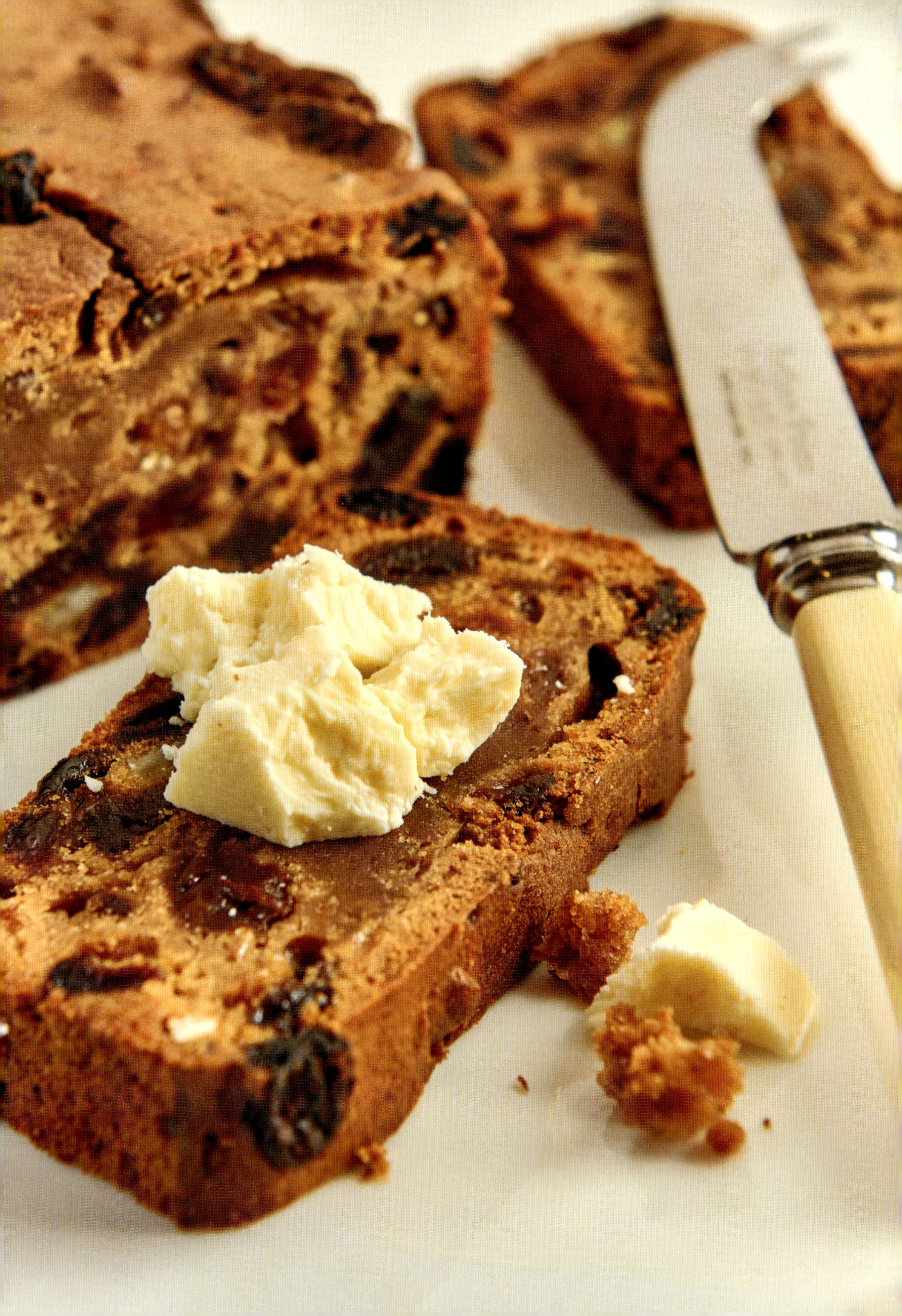

Scones

INGREDIENTS:
Makes 8 scones

300g self-raising flour
50g salted butter, cubed
80g sultanas (optional)
150ml whole milk
60g golden syrup
5ml vanilla paste
1 free range egg and pinch of salt
    for the egg wash
50g caster sugar

To serve with the scones
150g clotted cream
100g strawberry jam

METHOD:

Sieve the flour into a large bowl. Rub the butter into the flour to crumb stage then add the sultanas and mix well.

In a pouring jug, add the milk, golden syrup and vanilla paste and mix well. Make a well in the centre of the flour and whilst stirring, gradually add the liquid until all the ingredients start to form a firm scone dough, (be careful not over-knead the dough at this stage).

Turn the dough onto a lightly floured surface and by hand, shape the dough to between 4-6cm in depth. Using a fluted cutter, cut the scones out and place them onto a greased baking tray upside down.

Egg wash the scones and sprinkle with sugar.

Bake in the oven at 180°C for approximately 10-12 minutes until golden brown, and the bottoms sound hollow when tapped.

Serve warm with strawberry jam and clotted cream.

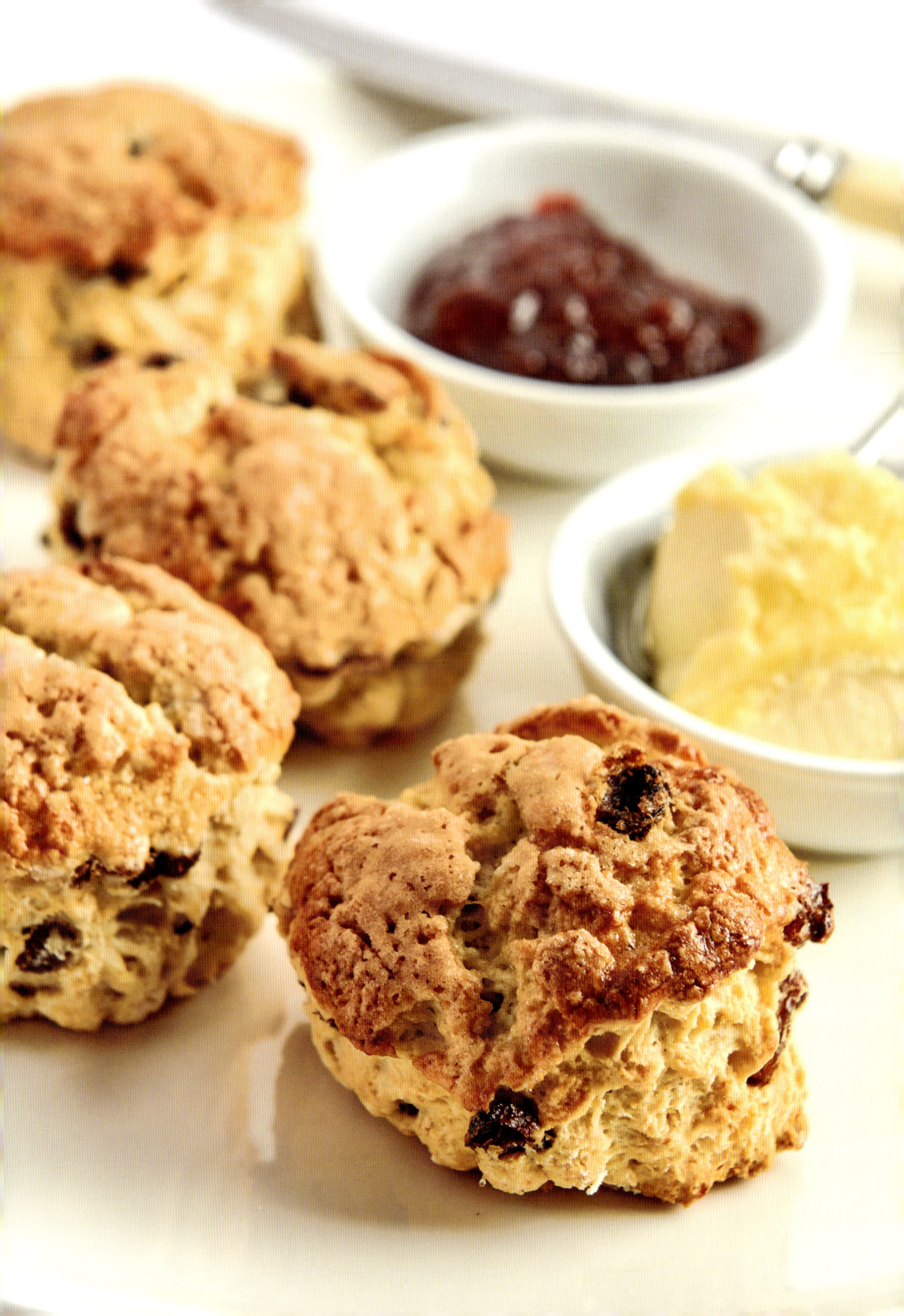

Strawberry Choux Swans

INGREDIENTS:
Makes 4 swans

For the swans
180g choux pastry, see page 222
50g dark chocolate, melted

Chantilly cream for the filling
200ml whipping cream
10g caster sugar
5ml vanilla paste

To finish the swans
4 large fresh strawberries, washed, hulled and sliced
20g icing sugar

METHOD:

Using a piping bag fitted with a 15mm star nozzle, pipe shallow ovals of choux pastry onto a greased baking tray – these will be the bodies of the swans. Sprinkle a liberal amount of cold water over both the tray and the piped choux pastry and bake in the oven at 180°C for 14-16 minutes or until they have puffed up and turned golden brown all over. Cool on a rack.

Using a piping bag fitted with a 5mm plain nozzle, pipe elongated S shapes onto a greased baking tray – these will be the swans' necks. Bake in the oven at 180°C for 14-16 minutes or until they have puffed up and turned golden brown all over. Cool on a rack and once cold, dip the tip of one end of each neck in melted chocolate to make a beak. Leave the necks to one side until the chocolate has set.

To make the Chantilly cream, whip the cream, sugar and vanilla together to a stiff peak consistency. Gently fold in the pastry cream.

Slice the main bodies of the swans in half horizontally and fill the base by piping the Chantilly cream mixture using a piping bag fitted with a 1cm star nozzle. Slice the top section of the body in half vertically to create the swans' wings.

Assemble the swan by placing the neck in one end of the cream. Insert the wings at an angle leaving room down the centre for the sliced strawberries to create a fantail. Dust with icing sugar.

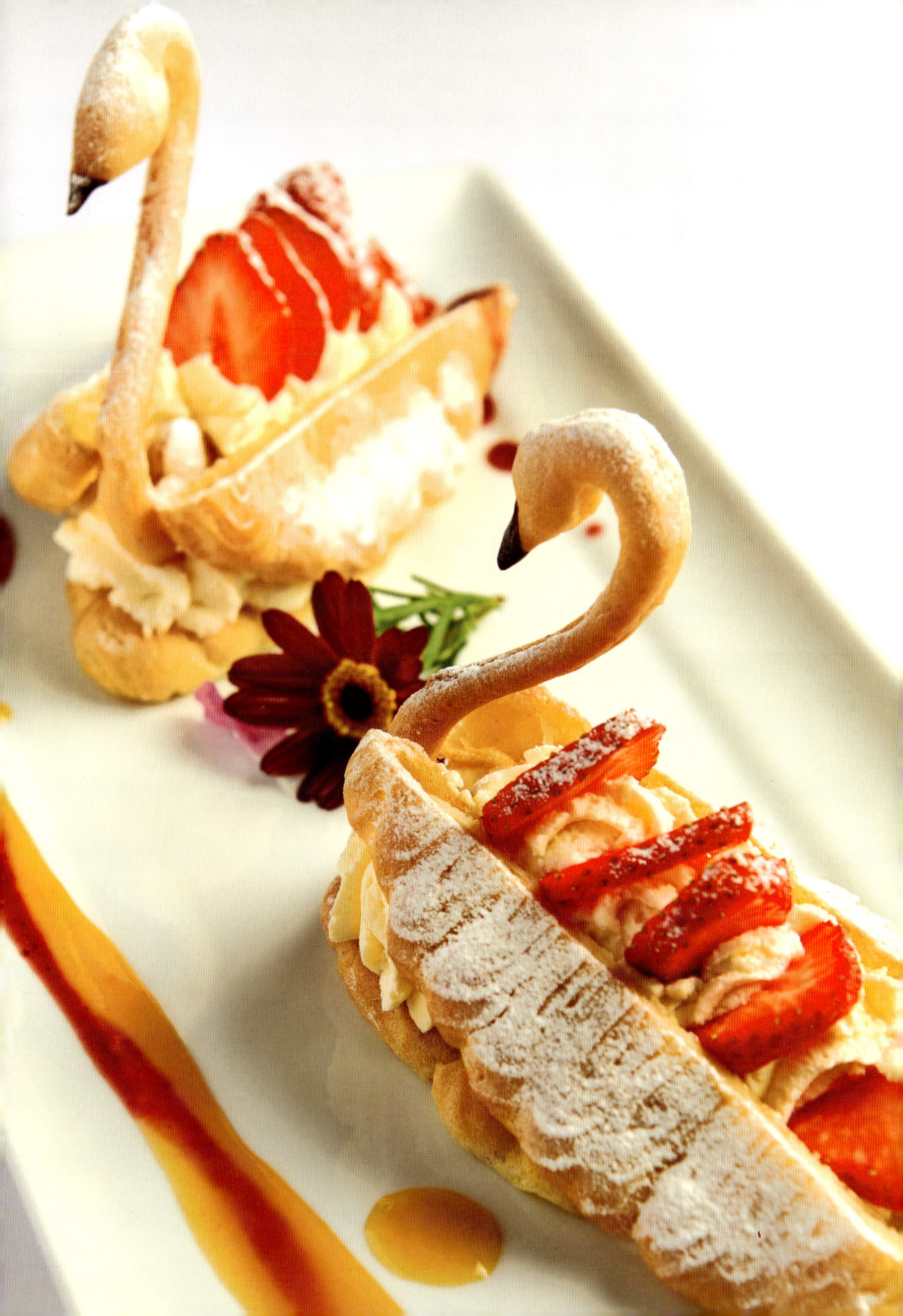

WHEN IT COMES TO FOOD - BRUNCH, LUNCH, DINNER, CALL IT WHAT YOU WILL - FOR SOME PEOPLE IT'S JUST FUEL. SOME ARE HAPPY WITH THEIR LUNCHTIME PACK-UP. BUT FOR OTHERS, DINING IS A CHANCE TO SAVOUR THE DEDICATION AND CRAFTSMANSHIP OF SOME OF THE BEST CHEFS IN THE WORLD.

Ultimate Dinner

SMOKED HADDOCK & GRUYÈRE CHEESE TARTS.204
HAM HOCK TERRINE.206
LOBSTER BISQUE WITH STEAMED MUSSELS.208
BEEF WELLINGTON.210
CRÈME BRÛLÉE.212

One of my earliest memories of being invited for lunch would be when I was about four years old. Mr Dunn, our gardener, would always take his lunch in his shed: whitewashed and pebble-dashed, no door, a corrugated roof and a window with more cobwebs than you'd find at a Spiderman convention.

For Mr Dunn, an all-weather gardener, lunch was just as you'd expect: a rusty old Oxo tin, tied with string and filled with doorstop sandwiches, an apple or an orange, a chunky slice of Mrs Dunn's rich fruit cake and a flask of tea, always tea, with tea leaves in.

Sometimes Mr Dunn would also have a jam tart and a packet of crisps with the blue sachet of salt in his pack-up: he would always insist they were mine.

I would have loved to invite Mr Dunn to try my ultimate dinner, so this chapter is dedicated to him.

NB.
ULTIMATE DINNER

CHAPTER 13

Smoked Haddock and Gruyère Cheese Tarts

INGREDIENTS:

Makes 18 canapés or an 18cm tart

200g shortcrust pastry, see page 228
6 small shallots, peeled and finely diced
100g smoked haddock, skinned, de-boned and diced
50g Gruyère cheese, finely grated
1 small bunch of fresh curly parsley, finely chopped
2 medium free range eggs
100ml double cream
pinch of salt and ground black pepper
5g paprika

METHOD:

On a lightly floured surface, roll out the pastry to 2-3mm thickness. Using a fluted cutter, cut 12 discs and line a tartlet tray.

Sprinkle a small amount of the shallots in the base of each tartlet along with the smoked haddock, cheese and some of the parsley.

In a bowl, add the eggs, double cream, salt, pepper and whisk and strain into a pouring jug. Fill the tarts.

Bake in at 180°C, for approximately 12 minutes or until the tarts are golden. Once cooked, sprinkle with the remaining parsley, a dusting of paprika and serve either warm or cold as a canapé or a starter.

These are a great addition to a summer's picnic.

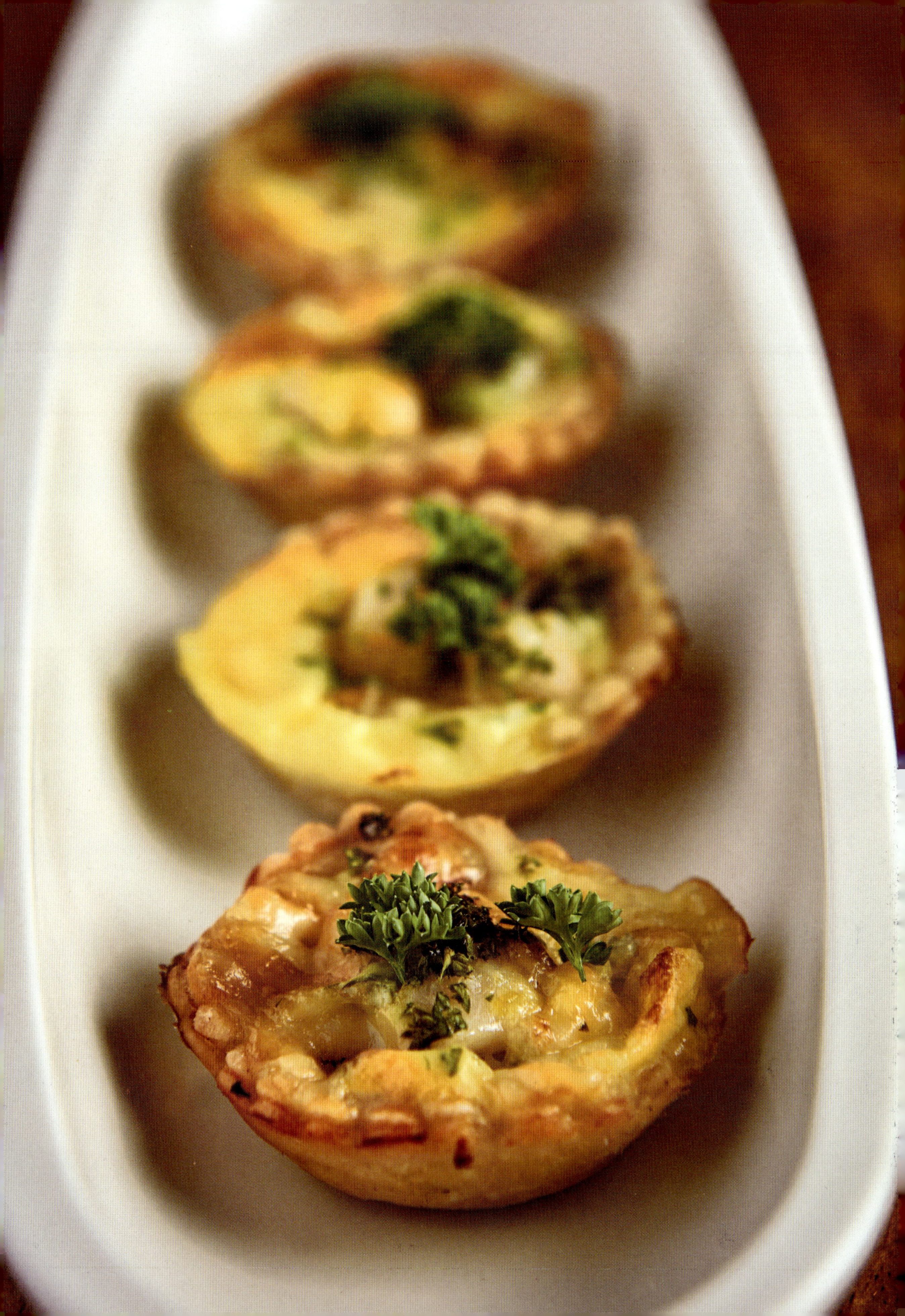

Ham Hock Terrine

INGREDIENTS:

Serves 4

500g ham hock, uncooked, off the bone and diced
8 Chantenay carrots, washed, peeled and diced
2 celery sticks, string removed and diced
8 shallots, peeled, trimmed and diced
a small bunch of freshly-picked basil leaves
4 bay leaves
2g leaf gelatine, soaked in cold water
pinch of freshly ground black pepper
15ml rapeseed oil
1 tsp English mustard

METHOD:

Place all the prepared ingredients, except the gelatine, into a large thick bottomed saucepan and cover with cold water to 5cm above the ingredients.

Bring to the boil and allow to gently simmer until the cooking liquid has reduced to the level of the ingredients.

Remove the pan from the heat. Squeeze the water from the gelatine and stir into the hot ingredients. Allow to cool to 10°C.

Drain the cooking liquid into a pouring jug and place the ingredients into a suitable terrine dish or dishes. Carefully flood the terrine with the cooking liquid to cover the ingredients, wrap with cling film and refrigerate for 24 hours. To serve the terrine, dip the dish in a bowl of hot water and turn out onto a chopping board. Slice with a hot knife to serve, cleaning the knife between each slice.

Serve the slices of terrine cold with seasonal salad or additional cooked and chilled carrots and celery. Drizzle with rapeseed oil mixed with the mustard.

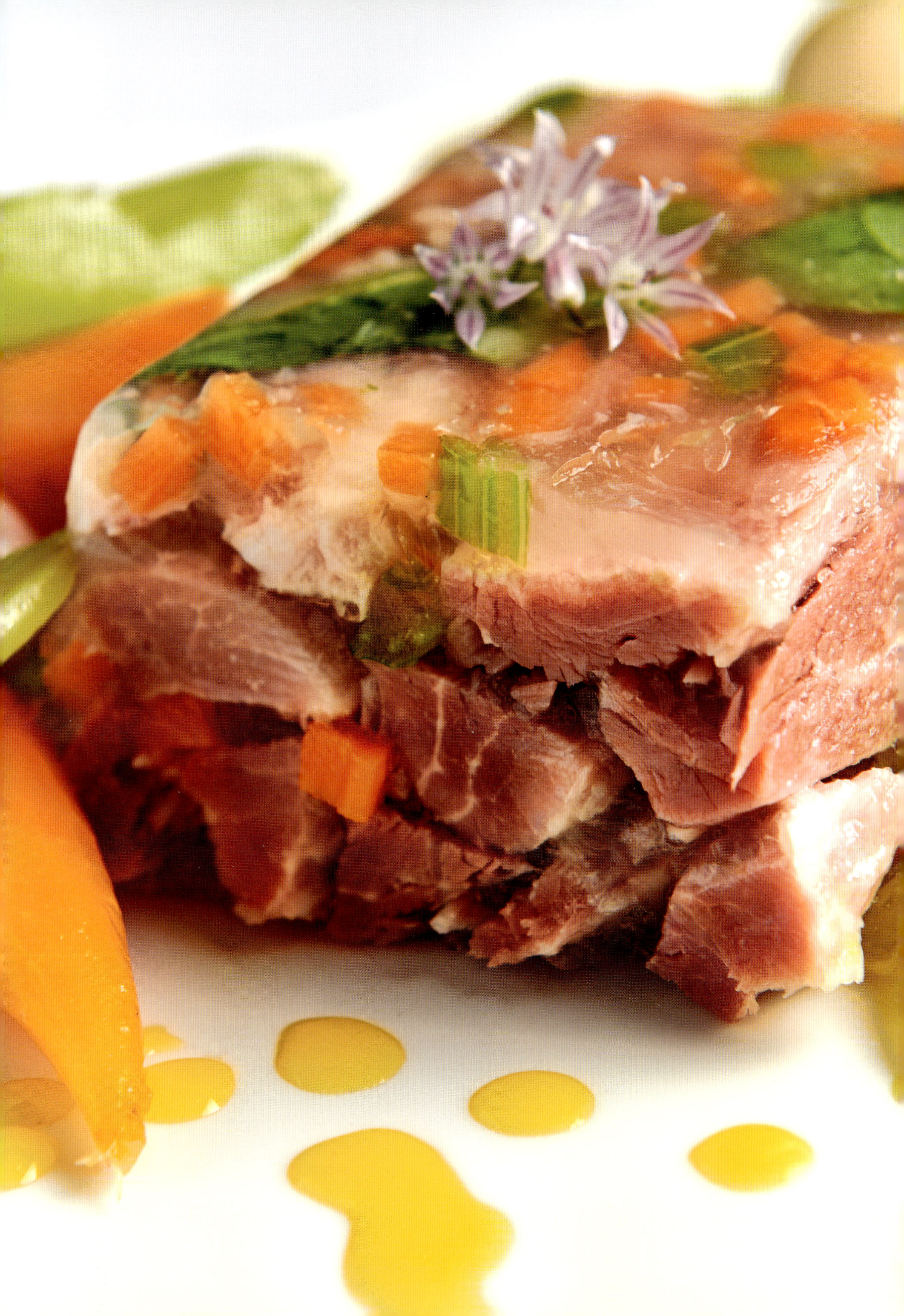

Lobster Bisque with Steamed Mussels

INGREDIENTS:
Serves 4

2 whole cooked lobsters
15ml rapeseed oil
2 celery sticks, washed, trimmed and quartered
2 medium carrots, washed trimmed and quartered
1 onion, peeled, trimmed and quartered
1 leek, washed, trimmed and quartered
4 bay leaves
a small bunch of fresh parsley stalks
1 garlic clove, crushed
150ml brandy
60g tomato purée
100g arborio rice or 200g potato, washed, peeled and diced small
200ml fish stock, see page 220
pinch of salt and ground black pepper
100ml double cream
150ml dry white wine
20g salted butter
1kg live mussels, scrubbed and de-bearded

To serve
50mls double cream
4 sprigs of dill

METHOD:

Cut the lobsters in half lengthways. Crack the claws and remove the meat, saving the shell. Remove the tail meat and save the shell. Wash the claw and tail meat under running cold water, remove and discard the entrail from the tail meat (waste tract, this is a long thin pocket that runs the length of the tail meat and may be dark in colour). Refrigerate the meat for later.

Place a large thick bottomed saucepan on a medium heat and add the rapeseed oil followed by all the shell and debris, celery, carrots, onion, leek, bay leaves, parsley stalks and garlic, and sweat with a lid on for 5 minutes.

Remove the lid, add the brandy and ignite with a naked flame to burn off the alcohol. Add the tomato purée and potato or rice. Stir well to coat all the ingredients. Add sufficient fish stock to cover all the ingredients; if necessary add some water. Bring the bisque to a simmer and allow to cook for approximately 1 hour, stirring occasionally.

Strain the bisque through a sieve into a clean pan and reduce the quantity by half on a medium heat. Check for seasoning, add the double cream.

Place a separate pan on a medium heat and add the white wine and butter. Place the mussels in a colander and shake; any that stay open must be discarded. Pull the beards from the remaining mussels and once the wine and butter are steaming add the mussels, keeping a lid on the pan for 3 minutes, shaking occasionally. Add the lobster tail and claw meat and continue to steam for a further 2 minutes.

Serve the mussels in their shells, with the lobster tail and claw meat, and pour the lobster bisque into a bowl. Dress with a drizzle of double cream and a fresh sprig of dill.

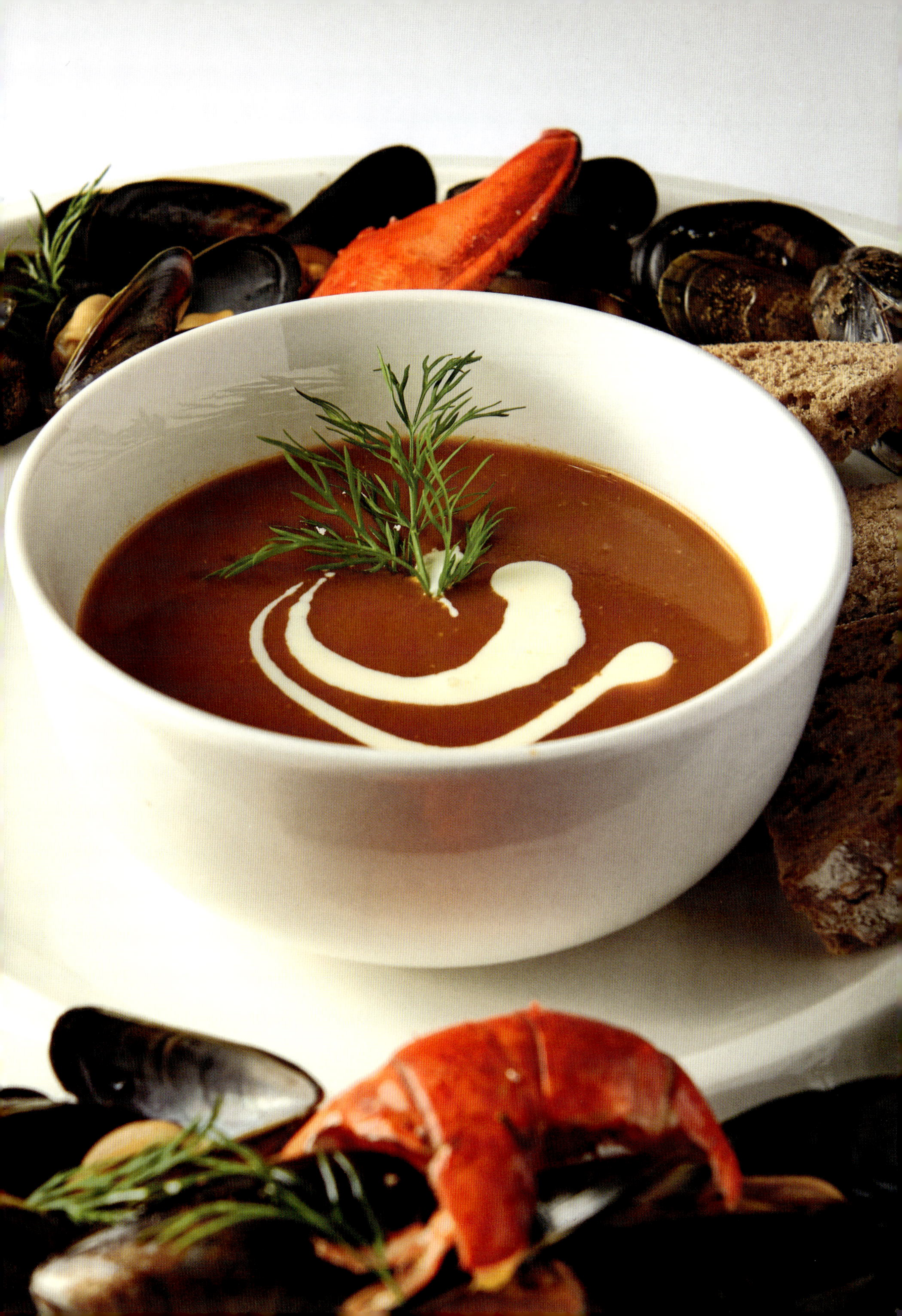

Beef Wellington

INGREDIENTS:
Serves 4

25g butter
1 onion, peeled and finely chopped
200g open flat mushrooms, peeled and roughly chopped
1 small sprig of fresh thyme
1 clove garlic, crushed (optional)
30g fresh curly parsley, finely chopped
30g cornflour
500g shortcrust pastry, see page 228
800g beef fillet, trimmed, seasoned and chilled
salt and ground black pepper
5ml rapeseed oil
1 or 2 very thin pancakes (optional, if using, make the Yorkshire pudding batter on page 86 to make 1 or 2 pancakes)
1 whole free range egg and pinch of salt for the egg wash

METHOD:

Place the butter in a thick-bottomed saucepan and heat. Add the onion, mushrooms, thyme, garlic and parsley and cook on a medium until almost all the moisture has evaporated from the ingredients. Remove from the heat, allow to cool slightly, then place in a food processor. Blend until a smooth pâté consistency is reached. Place the mushroom pâté in a bowl and cool completely before mixing in the cornflour.

Roll out the pastry on a floured surface to twice the size of the beef fillet. Season the beef and seal in a large sauté pan with the rapeseed oil. Leave to cool.

If using pancakes, place these in the centre of the rolled pastry, side by side, slightly overlapping. Spread the mushroom pâté on the pancakes (or pastry) and place the beef fillet on the pâté. Egg wash the pastry edges then fold, wrap and seal the Wellington.

Place the beef Wellington on a greased baking tray, egg wash and bake in the oven at 180°C for approximately 30-35 minutes. Remove from the oven and allow to rest for 5 minutes. Slice and serve.

Serve with seasonal vegetables, potatoes and sprigs of fresh watercress.

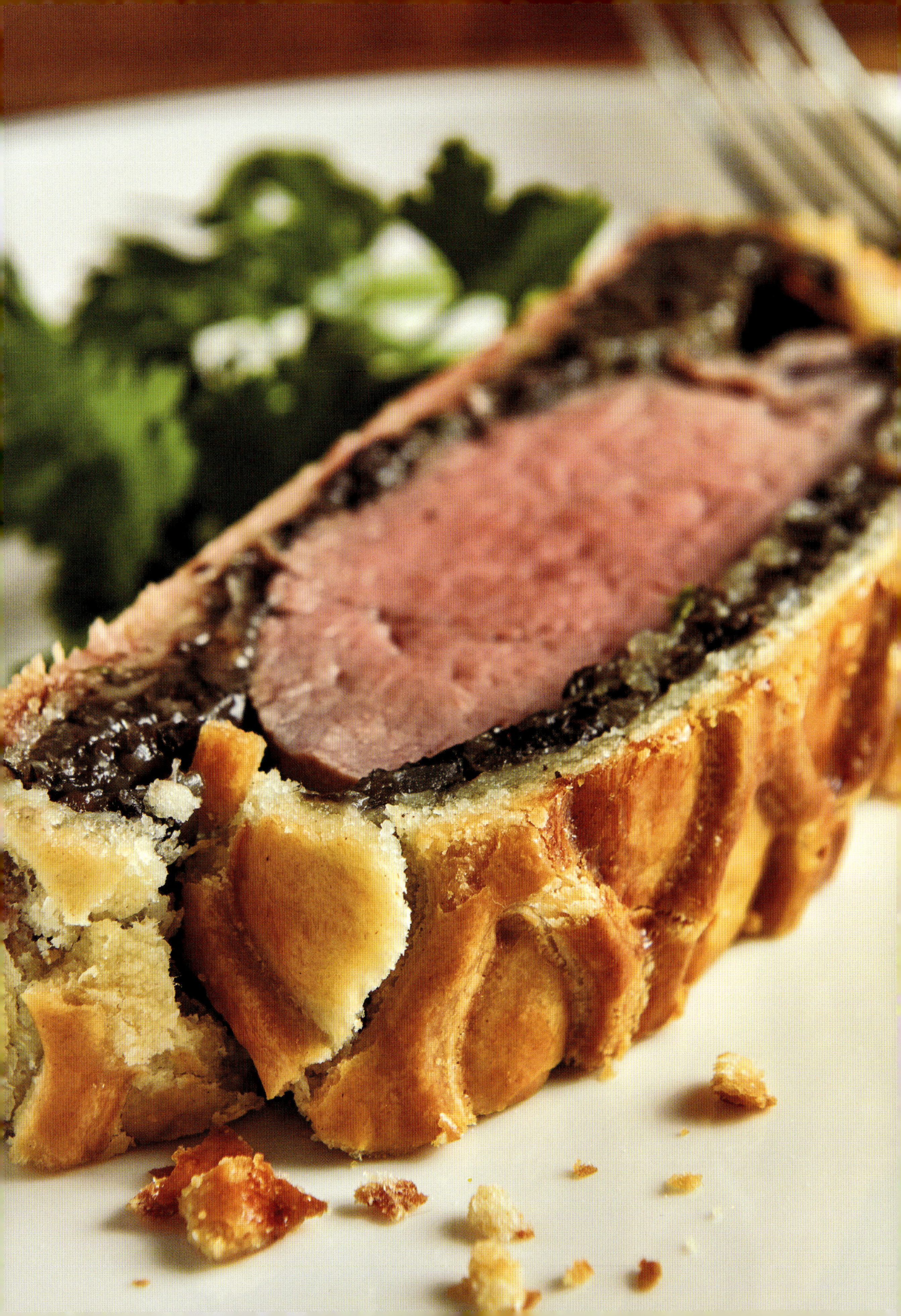

Crème Brûlée

INGREDIENTS:
Serves 4

2 vanilla pods
600ml of double cream
12 large free range egg yolks
40g of vanilla sugar
60g caster sugar

METHOD:

Split the vanilla pods and remove the seeds. Place the seeds and pods in a thick-bottomed saucepan with the cream. Bring to simmering point then remove from the heat.

In a bowl, whisk the egg yolks and vanilla sugar together. Gradually pour in the warm cream and stir well. Strain the brûlée mixture back into a clean thick-bottomed saucepan and place on a medium heat, stirring continuously until the brûlée mixture thickens and coats the back of a spoon. (Do not allow this to boil).

Carefully pour the mixture into your chosen dishes and cool, then refrigerate for 2 hours.

Before serving, sprinkle the crème brûlées with the caster sugar and either place under a very hot grill, or carefully use a blow torch, to caramelise the sugar.

This is great served with fresh raspberries or simply on its own.

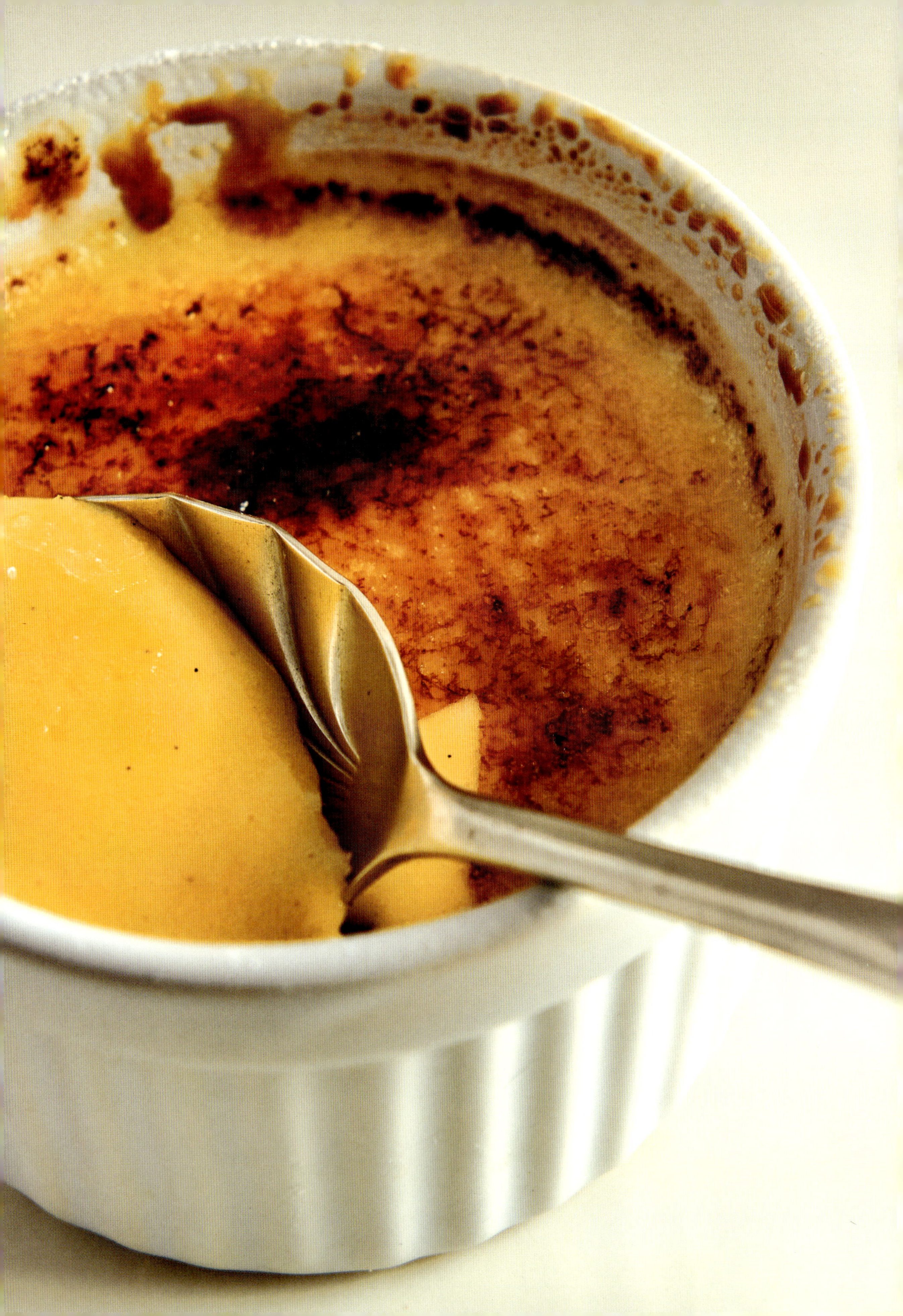

ONE OF MY EARLIEST MEMORIES OF FOOD TAKES ME BACK TO THE DAYS OF JUNIOR SCHOOL, WHEN I WAS AROUND SEVEN. ADMITTEDLY, ACADEMICALLY I WAS NEVER GOING TO BE THE SHARPEST PENCIL IN THE POT. I WAS ONE OF THE SHYEST BOYS IN THE SCHOOL; MAYBE THE SHYEST. BUT MRS HARPER HAD A PLAN FOR ME!

Stocks

BEEF STOCK.216
CHICKEN STOCK.218
FISH STOCK.220

Pastry

CHOUX PASTRY.222
HOT WATER PASTRY.224
PUFF PASTRY.226
SHORTCRUST PASTRY.228
SUET PASTRY.230
SWEET PASTRY.232

Sauces

BÉCHAMEL SAUCE.234
CHICKEN VELOUTÉ SAUCE.236
ESPAÑOLA SAUCE.238
HOLLANDAISE SAUCE.240
MAYONNAISE.242
PASTRY CREAM.244
VANILLA CUSTARD.246

Bakery

ITALIAN MERINGUE.248
WHITE BREAD ROLLS.250

For my very first cookery lesson I remember being taken as part of a special group of about four (I now prefer to think of us as 'a hand-picked, select few promising children') to what I seem to remember was the staff room, where a cooker stood in the corner. I'm guessing it was for the teachers to make their porridge and toast before assembly.

The lesson began: Egg in a Windmill. Two slices of bread fried or toasted to perfection. Then the technical challenge: to crack a hen's egg into the pan and not break the yolk. The pressure was on. I kept my calm and out popped the perfect fried egg with the yolk still intact.

For me it was like getting an A* in maths – overjoyed doesn't even come close to how I was feeling that day!

Pastry cutters were introduced and I nervously but bravely cut the centre out of one of the slices of toast, then into quarters with the bluntest butter knife you've ever seen: the windmill sails.

From Egg in a Windmill to Toad in the Hole, beats being an academic any day I'd say! Thanks, Mrs Harper.

NB.
THE BASICS

CHAPTER 14

Beef Stock

INGREDIENTS:
Makes 1.5 litres

1kg roasted beef bones
2 celery sticks, quartered
2 carrots, peeled and quartered
2 onions, peeled and halved
1 leek, washed, peeled and quartered
4 bay leaves
1 small bunch of fresh parsley
1 small sprig of fresh thyme
3ltr cold water to cover

METHOD:

Place all the ingredients into a large, thick-bottomed pan and cover with water.

Bring to the boil, lower the heat and simmer for 4 hours, topping up the water for the first 2 hours if necessary. After this time, allow to reduce by half.

Remove from the heat and cool.

Strain through a fine sieve into a bowl or storage container and refrigerate or freeze.

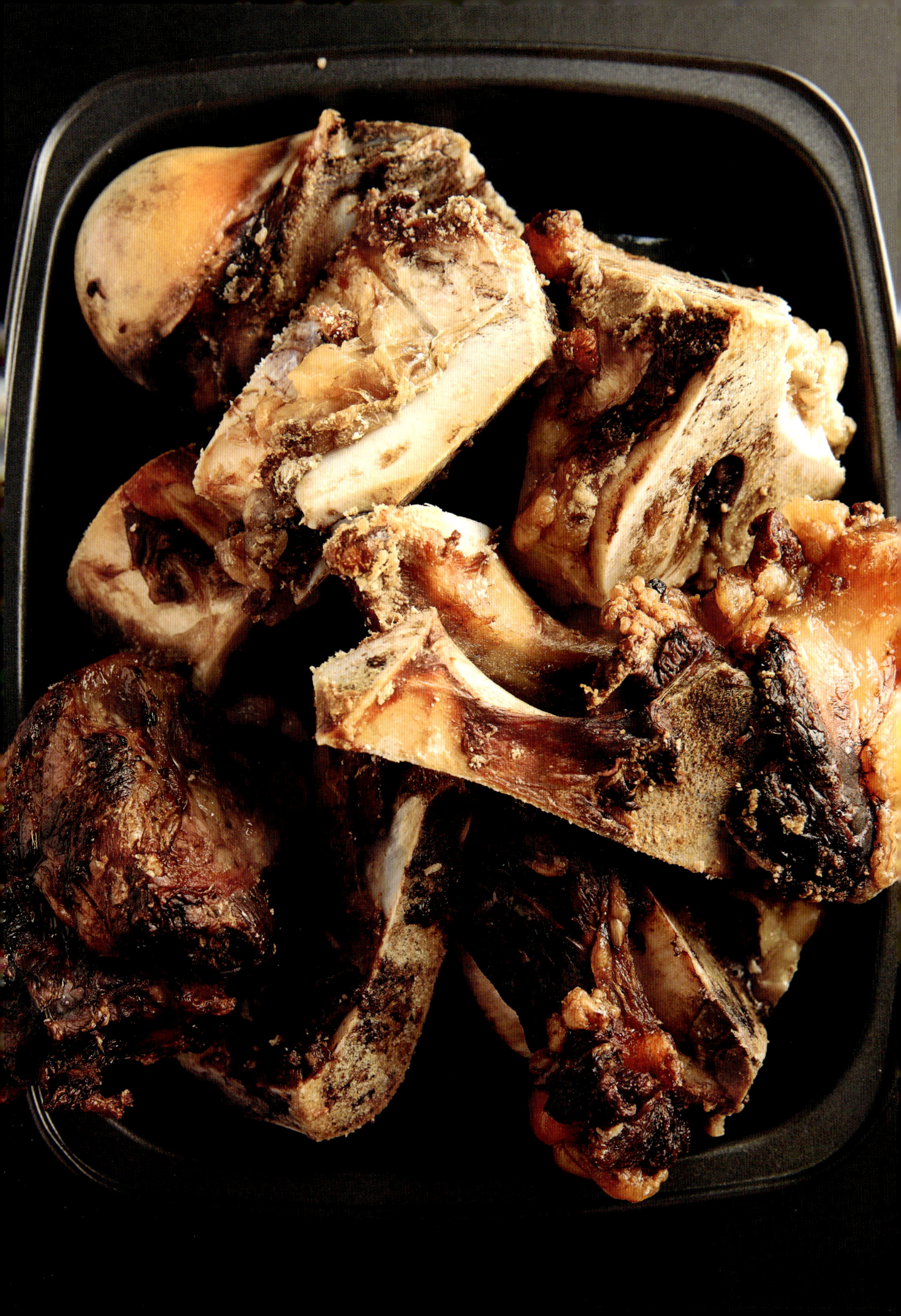

Chicken Stock

INGREDIENTS:
Makes 1.5 litres

1kg roasted chicken carcass
2 celery sticks, quartered
1 large carrot, peeled and quartered
1 large onion, peeled and halved
1 leek, washed, peeled and quartered
4 bay leaves
1 small bunch of fresh parsley
3ltr cold water to cover

METHOD:

Place all the ingredients into a large, thick-bottomed pan and cover with water.

Bring to the boil, then lower the heat and simmer for 2 hours or until it's reduced by half.

Remove from the heat and cool.

Strain through a fine sieve into a bowl or storage container and refrigerate or freeze.

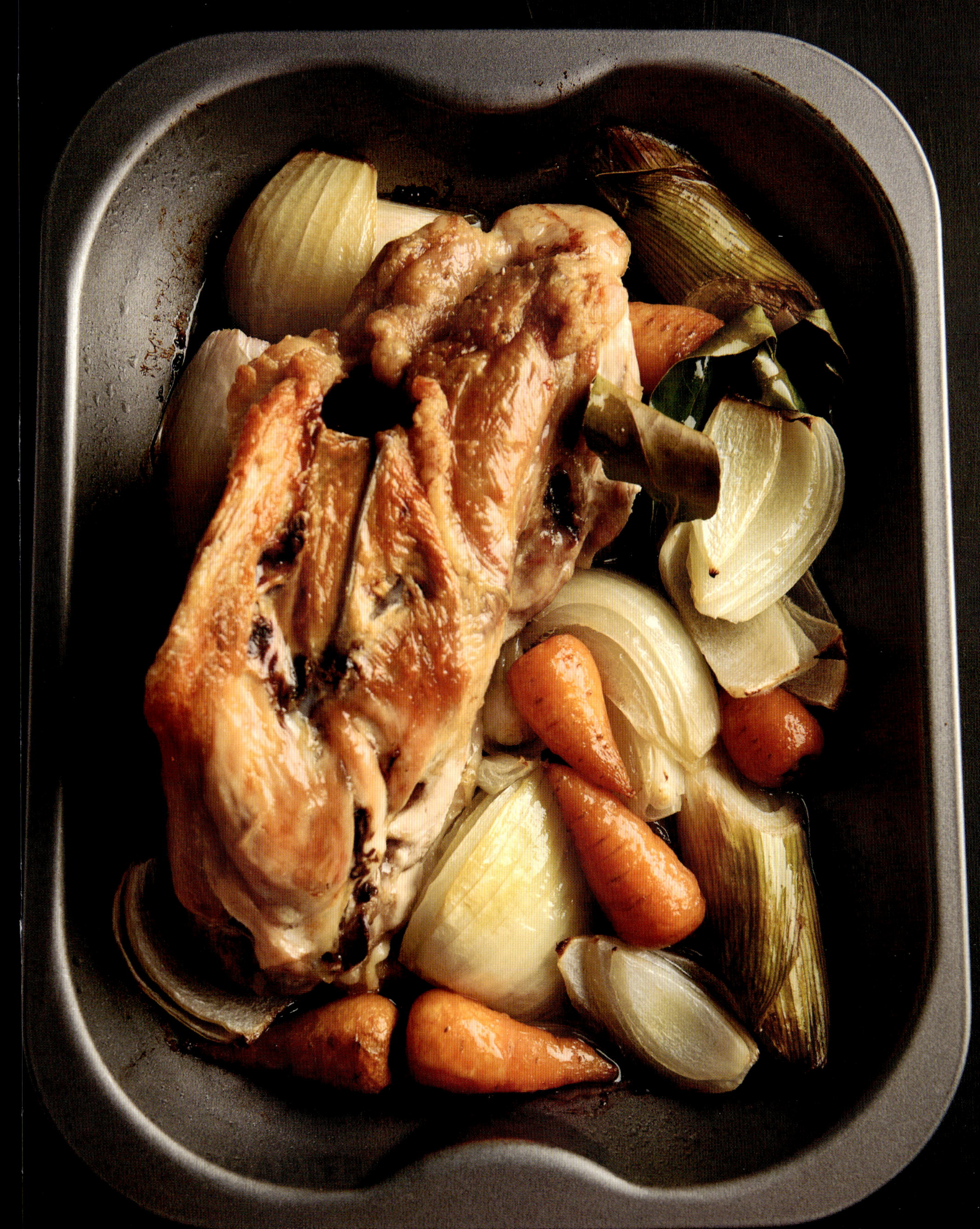

Fish Stock

INGREDIENTS:

Makes 1 litre

1kg plaice or lemon sole bones and skin
1 onion, peeled and quartered
1 stalk celery, roughly chopped
1 leek, washed, peeled and quartered
1 fennel bulb, roughly halved (optional)
4 bay leaves
1 small bunch of fresh parsley
2ltr cold water to cover

METHOD:

Place all the ingredients into a large, thick-bottomed pan and cover with water.

Bring to the boil, lower the heat and simmer for 20 minutes.

Remove from the heat and cool.

Strain through a fine sieve into a bowl or storage container and refrigerate or freeze.

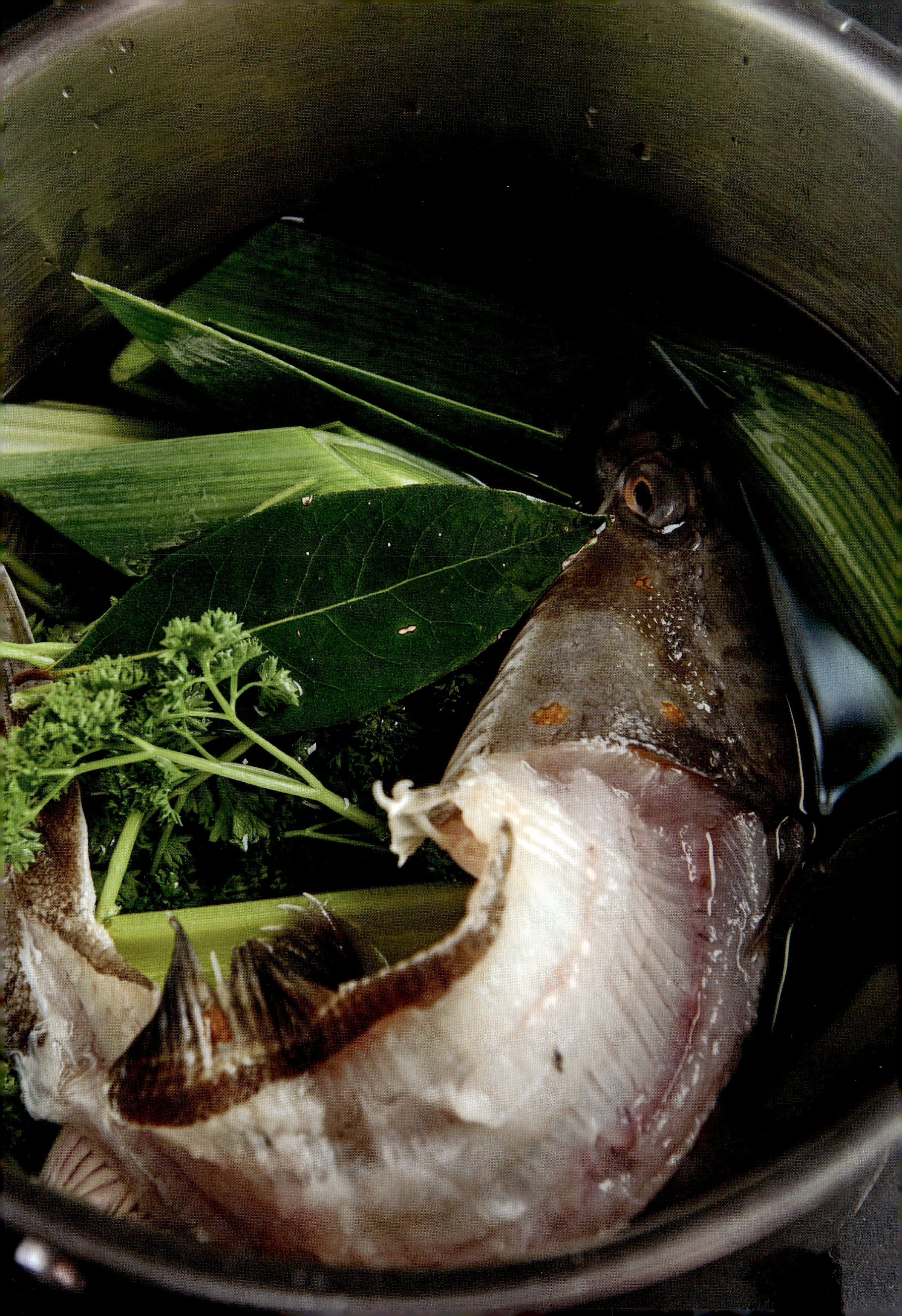

Choux Pastry

INGREDIENTS:
Makes 500g

300ml cold water
100g salted butter
pinch of salt or pinch of caster sugar
 (depending on whether the pastry is
 wanted for a sweet or savoury recipe)
130g strong white flour, sieved
3 whole free range eggs
1 egg white

METHOD:

Place the water, butter, sugar or salt into a thick-bottomed pan.

Place on the heat and bring to the boil.

When just about boiling, add the sieved flour and stir vigorously on a low heat for 1 minute.

Remove the pan from the heat and place the ingredients into a large bowl. Cool for 10 minutes.

Mix in the eggs and egg white, beating vigorously until a smooth silky consistency is reached.

Leave in the bowl and cover with cling film. Refrigerate until needed.

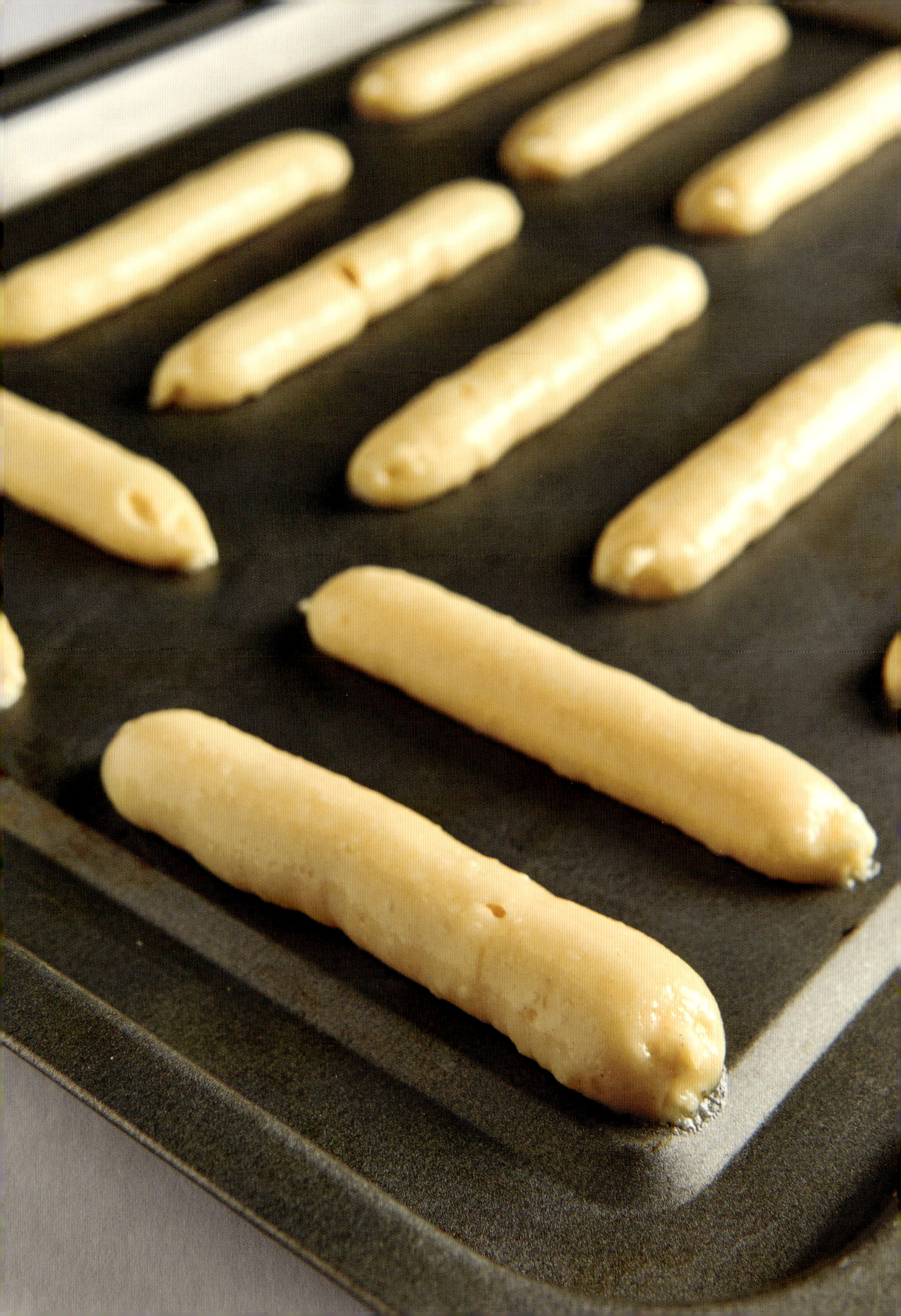

Hot Water Pastry

INGREDIENTS:
Makes 400g

100ml water
pinch of salt
80g lard
225g plain flour
1 whole free range egg

METHOD:

Place the water, salt and lard into a thick-bottomed pan. Place on the heat and bring to a boil.

Sieve the flour into a large bowl.

When the lard, water and salt mixture is boiling add the flour and stir vigorously until a thick paste is formed. Remove from the heat and pour the mixture into a large bowl.

When the mixture is cool enough to handle mix in the egg.

Cool, then wrap in cling film and refrigerate until needed.

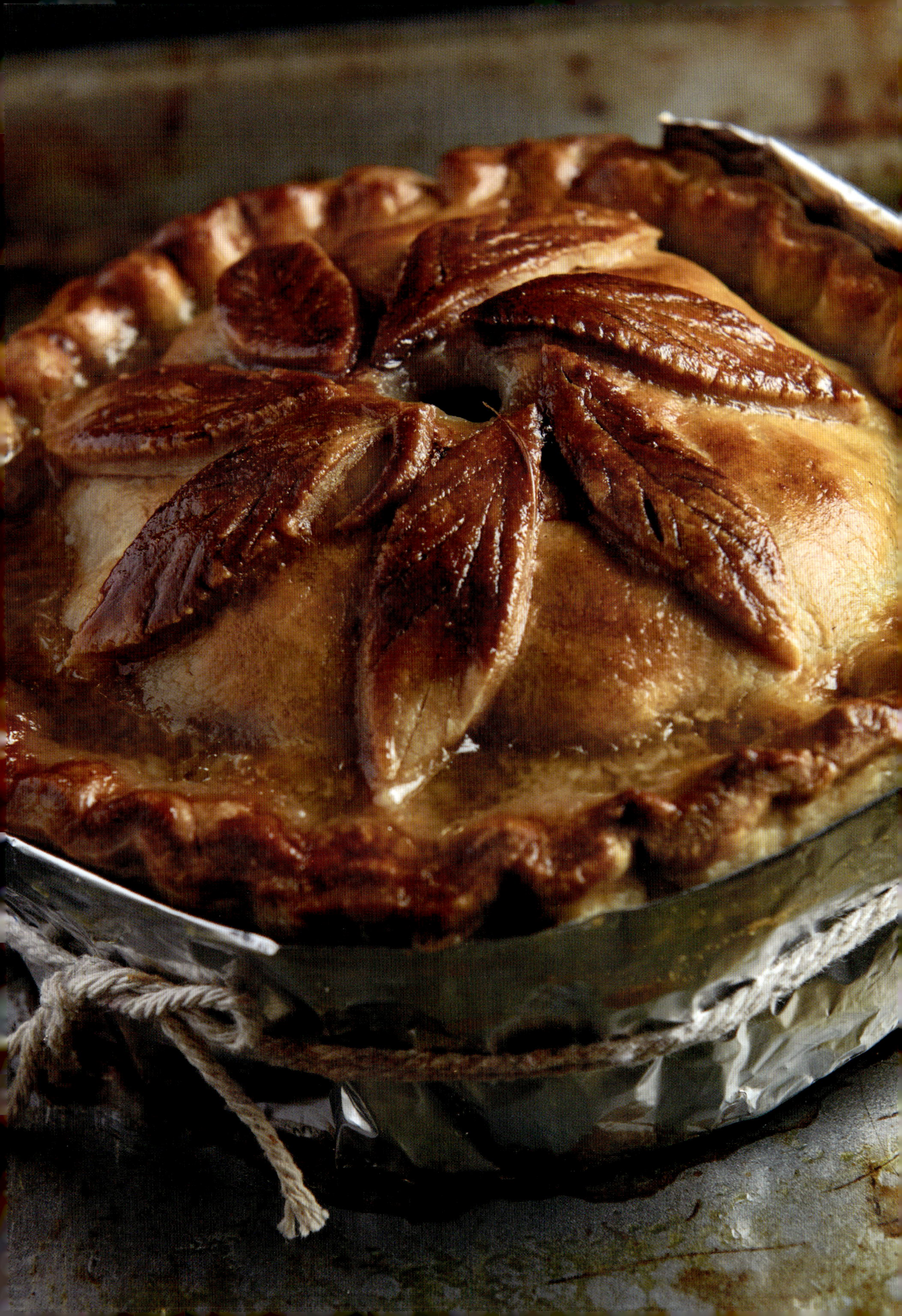

Puff Pastry

INGREDIENTS:
Makes 500g

225g plain flour, sieved
pinch of salt or pinch of caster sugar (depending on whether the pastry is wanted for a sweet or savoury recipe)
30g lard
150ml iced cold water
150g salted butter

METHOD:

Place the flour and salt or sugar into a large bowl and rub in the lard until it all comes together.

Using a butter knife, add the water into the mixture until a firm pastry texture is developed.

Cover the bowl with cling film and leave to rest for 5 minutes.

While the pastry is resting, in a separate bowl soften the butter until pliable.

Roll out the pastry to roughly the size of A4 paper. Dot all the butter on the top two-thirds then fold the bottom third up onto the middle third, then up again onto the top third.

Turn your pastry and butter sandwich a quarter turn then roll out again to half its thickness and fold again as previously. Cover with cling film and place in the fridge for at least an hour.

Repeat the process of rolling, folding and chilling 6 times. The pastry is now ready to use or can be frozen until required.

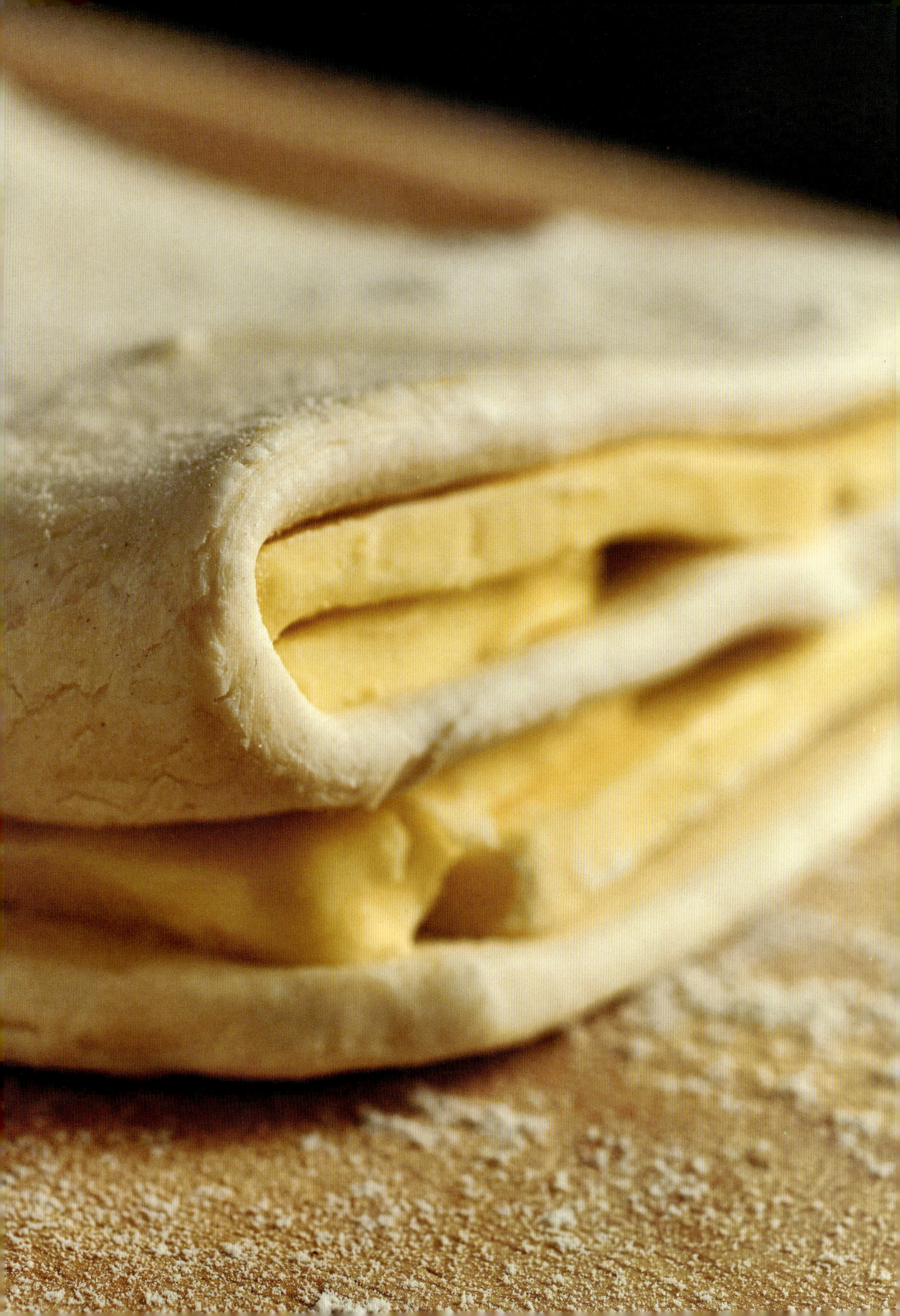

Shortcrust Pastry

INGREDIENTS:
Makes 450g

250g self-raising flour
55g salted butter, diced
55g lard, diced
1 whole free range egg
30-50ml cold water

METHOD:

Sieve the flour into a large mixing bowl. Add the butter and lard and rub into the flour until you achieve a breadcrumb texture.

Make a well in the centre, and pour in the egg and half of the cold water.

Using a butter knife, bind the ingredients together adding the remaining water if necessary.

Wrap in cling film and refrigerate until needed.

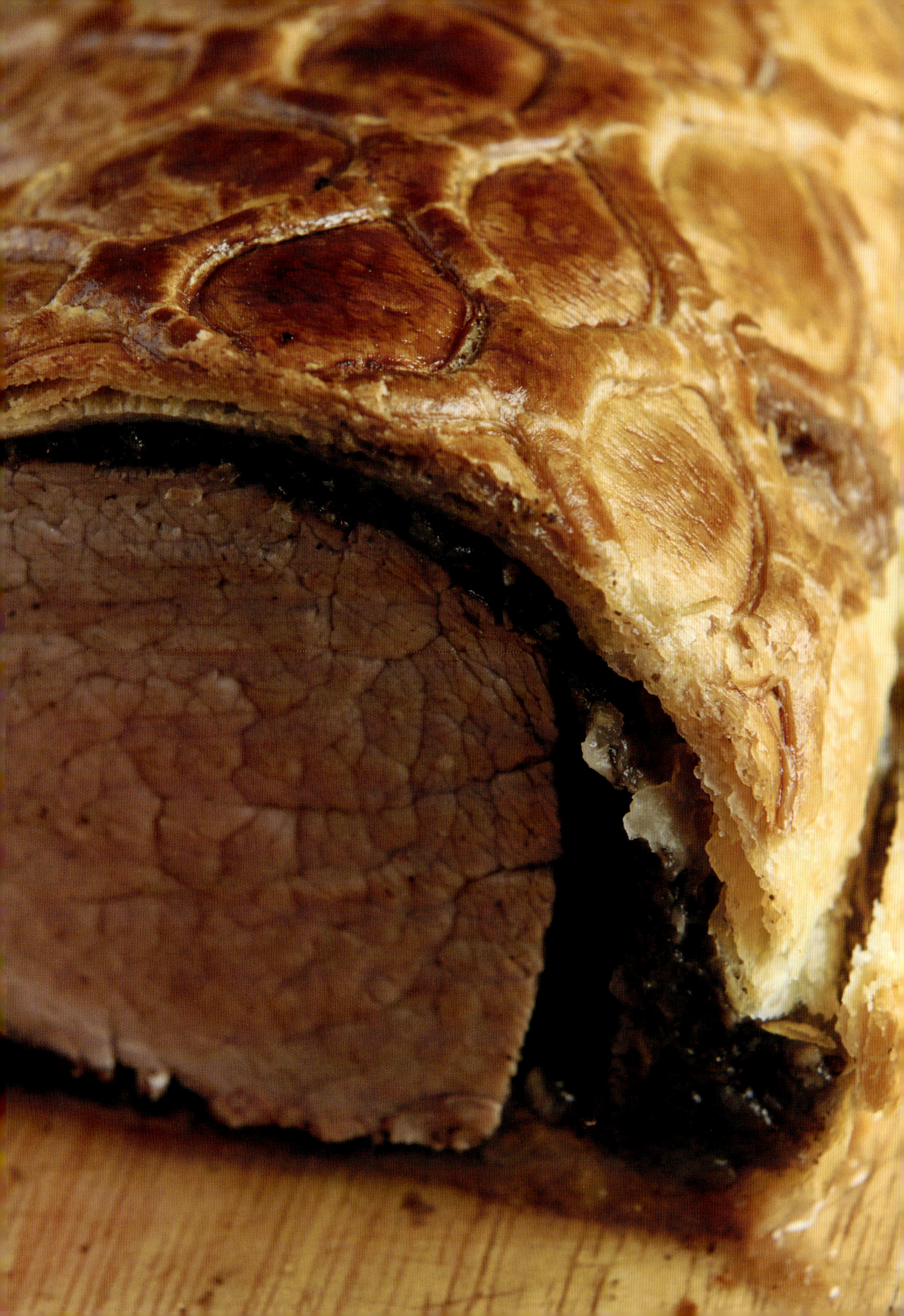

Suet Pastry

INGREDIENTS:
Makes 550g

350g self-raising flour
pinch of salt
110g beef suet
water to bind

METHOD:

Sieve the flour into a large bowl and add the salt and beef suet.

Using a butter knife gradually incorporate the water until a firm pastry is achieved.

Roll in flour, place in a bowl and cover with cling film. Refrigerate until needed.

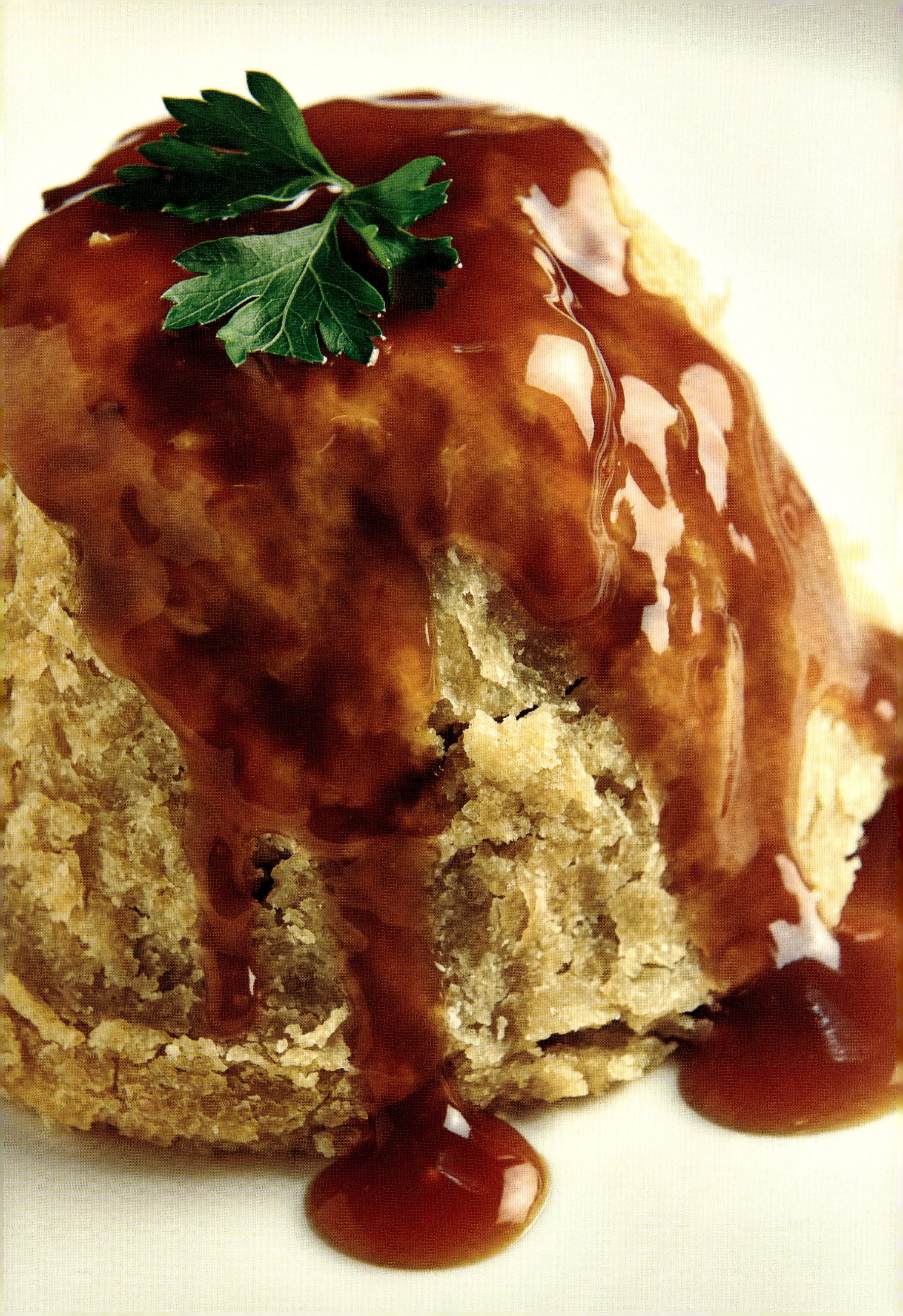

Sweet Pastry

INGREDIENTS:
Makes 400g

225g plain flour
110g butter, softened
55g caster sugar
a few drops of vanilla essence
3 free range egg yolks

METHOD:

Sieve the flour into a bowl.

In a separate bowl, cream the butter and sugar with the vanilla essence until it becomes light and fluffy. Blend the egg yolks into the mixture, one at a time.

Stir the flour into the mixture until a sticky dough is formed.

Wrap in cling film and refrigerate until needed.

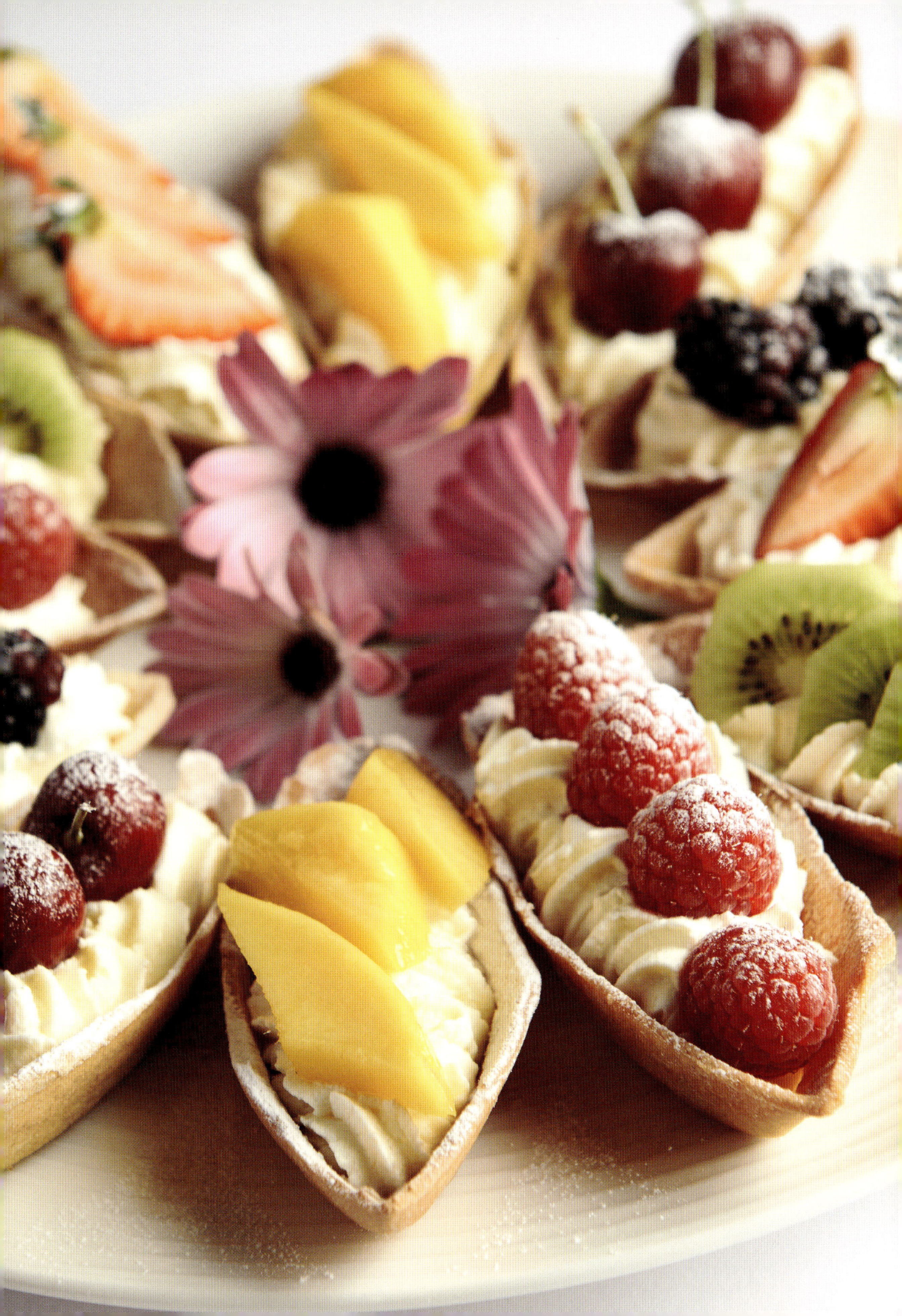

Béchamel Sauce

INGREDIENTS:
Makes 600ml

500ml whole milk
1 onion studded with 2 bay leaves
　　and 2 cloves
50g butter
80g plain flour
pinch of salt and ground white pepper

METHOD:

Place the milk and the studded onion into a thick-bottomed pan and bring to the boil, then remove from the heat.

In a separate pan, melt the butter and add the flour, stirring to create a paste. Reduce the heat and cook for 1 minute.

Gradually add the warm milk to the paste stirring continuously until the sauce coats the back of a spoon. Reduce the heat to low and continue cooking and stirring for a further 2 minutes.

Season with salt and pepper.

The sauce is now ready to use or can be refrigerated until required.

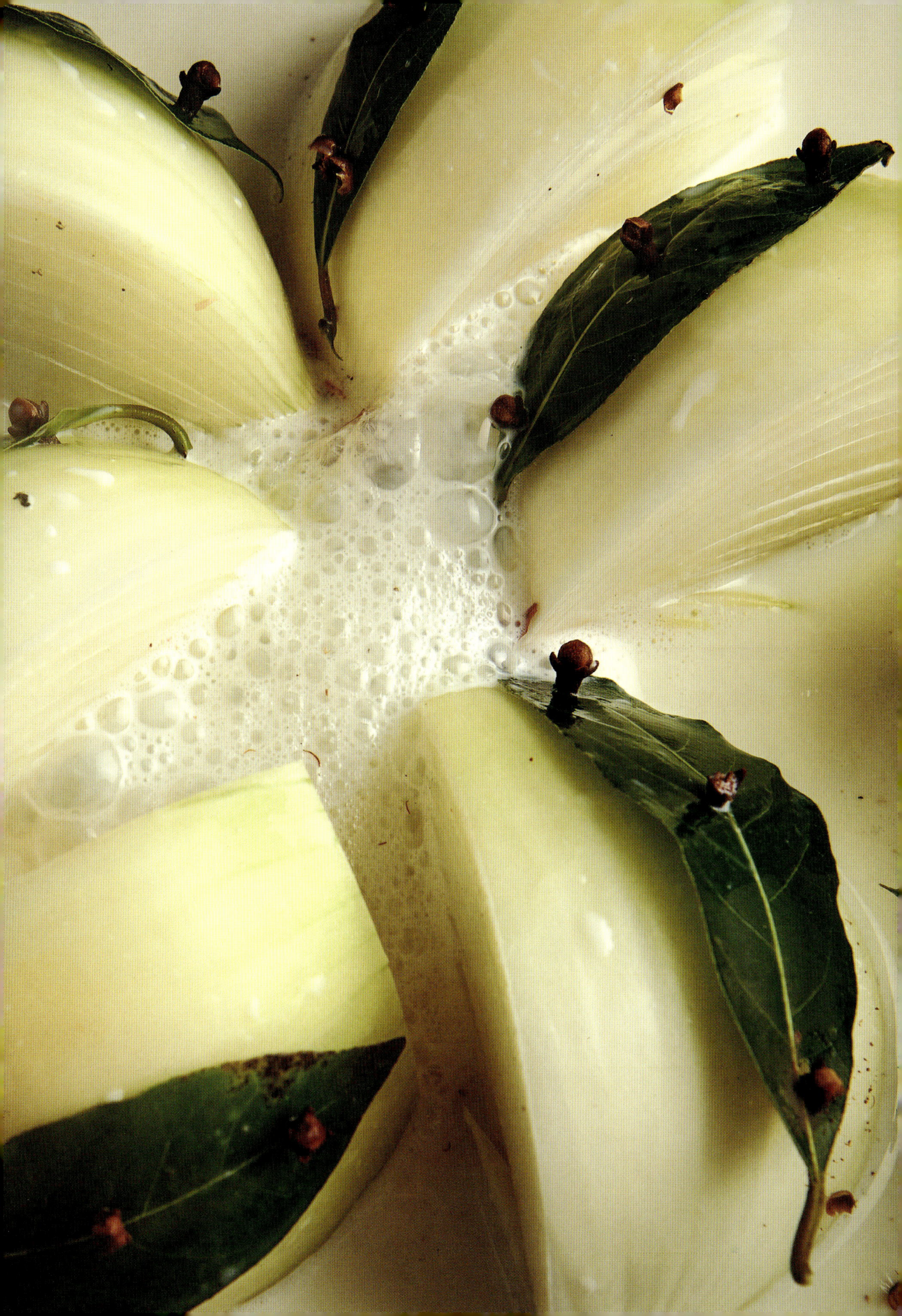

Chicken Velouté Sauce

INGREDIENTS:
Makes 600ml

50g butter
80g plain flour
500ml chicken stock, see page 218
pinch of salt and ground white pepper

METHOD:

Melt the butter in a thick-bottomed pan and stir in the plain flour to make a paste.

Turn the heat down and keep stirring for one minute.

Gradually add the chicken stock while stirring continuously until the sauce coats the back of a spoon. Reduce the heat and continue stirring for a further 2 minutes. Season with salt and pepper.

The sauce is now ready to use or can be refrigerated until required.

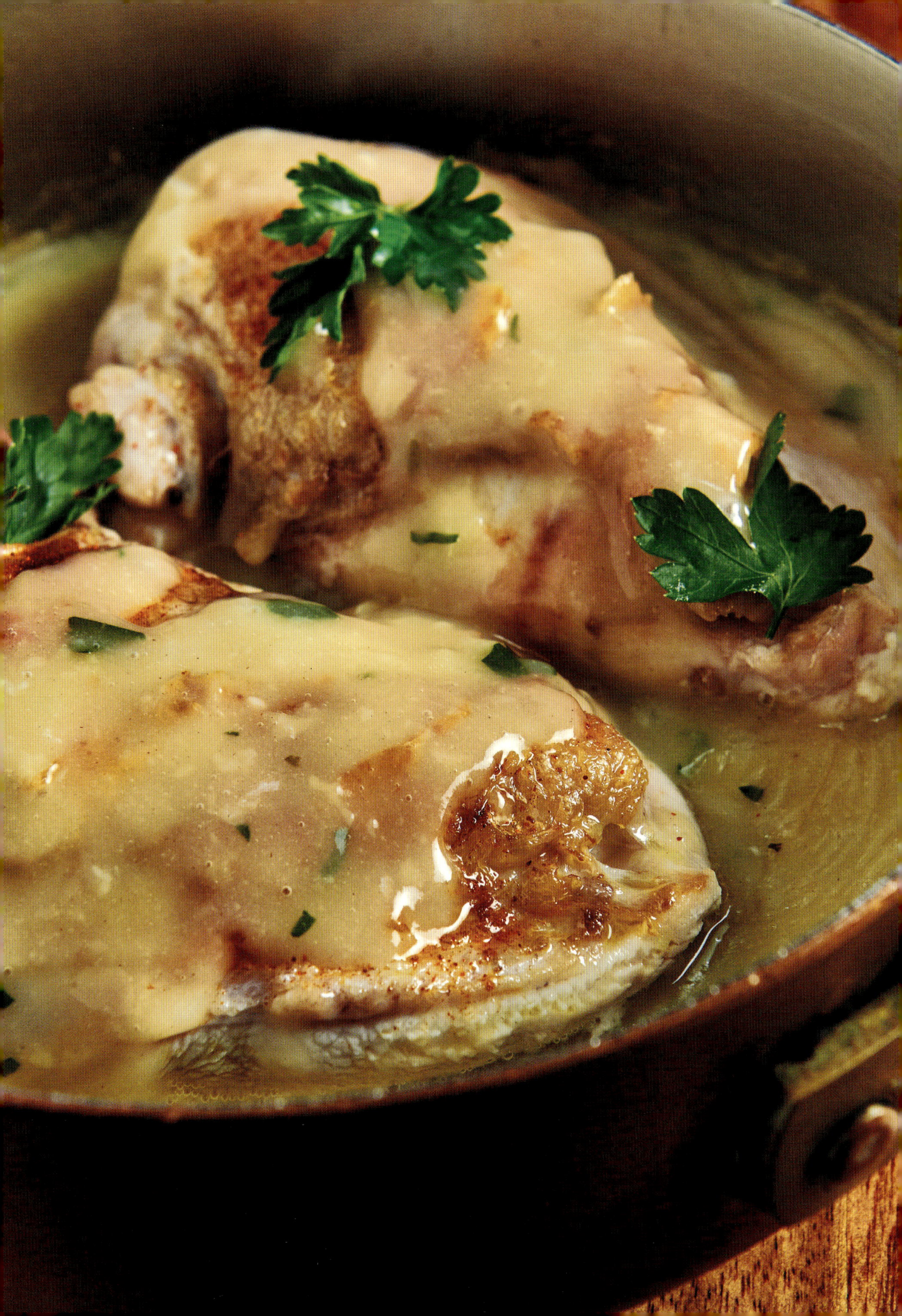

Española Sauce

INGREDIENTS:
Makes 600ml

50g butter
1 diced carrot
1 stick chopped celery
1 large diced onion
80g flour
500ml beef stock, see page 216
bouquet garni (1 leek leaf, washed,
　　2 bay leaves and a small bunch
　　of parsley and thyme tied together)

METHOD:

Place the butter into a thick-bottomed pan and melt. Add the carrot, celery and onion and cook for 3 minutes.

Add the flour to the pan and stir in to absorb the butter and vegetable juices.

Gradually pour in the beef stock whilst stirring and finally add the bouquet garni. Bring the sauce to a boil and simmer for 10 minutes.

Strain the sauce through a sieve into a bowl, cool and refrigerate until needed.

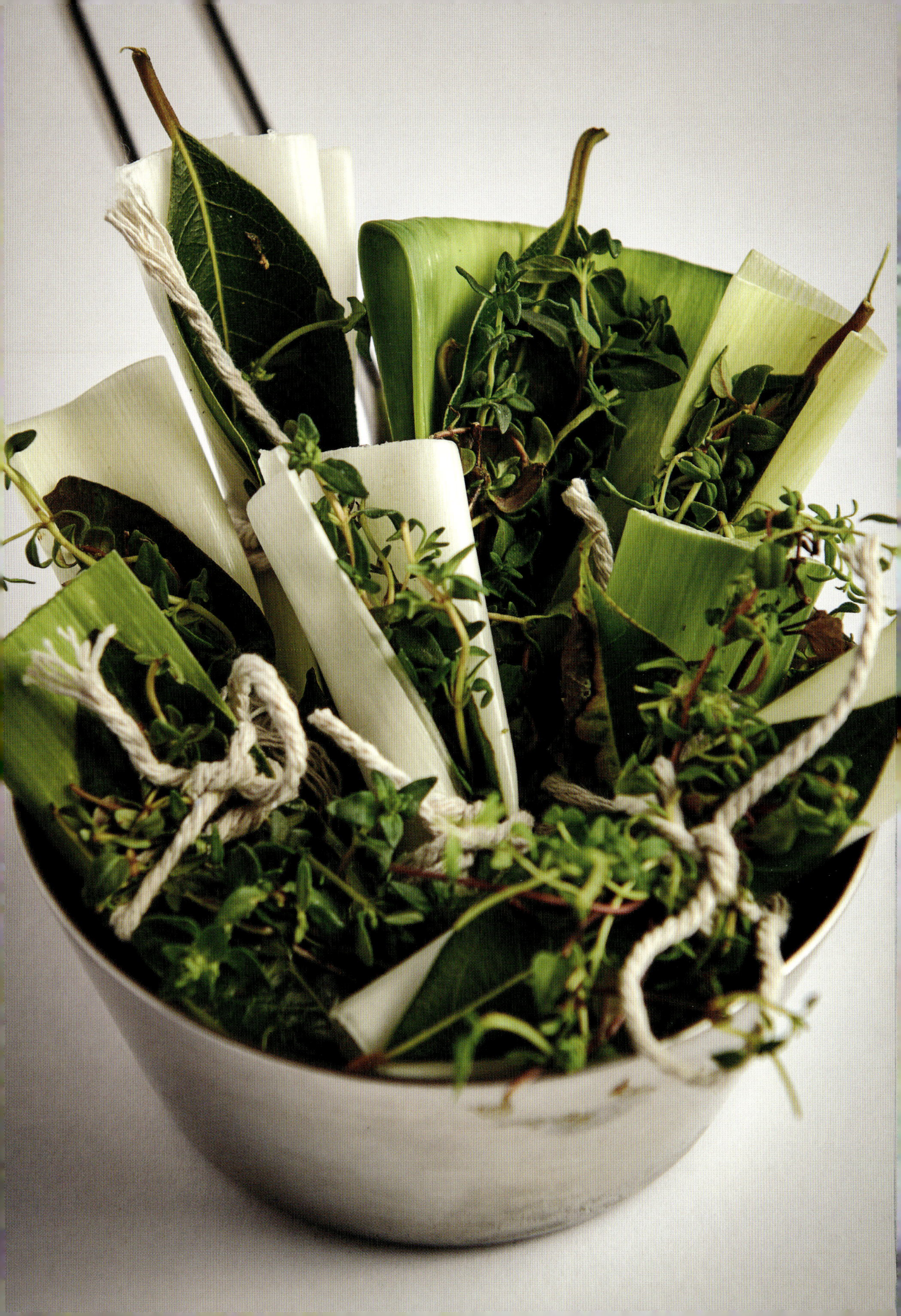

Hollandaise Sauce

INGREDIENTS:
Makes 300ml

50ml white wine vinegar
6 crushed peppercorns
125g unsalted butter
3 large free range egg yolks

METHOD:

Place the vinegar and crushed peppercorns into a pan and simmer until reduced by a half. Pass the liquid through a sieve into a bowl.

In a separate pan, melt the butter until it becomes a warm (but not boiling) liquid. Place the egg yolks into the white wine vinegar mixture and whisk over heat for one minute. Remove the bowl from the heat and and whisk continuously, while drizzling the warm butter into the mixture.

The sauce is now ready to use served warm or can be cooled and refrigerated until required.

To reheat, gently warm the sauce in a heatproof bowl over a pan of hot water, whisking occasionally. Do not boil.

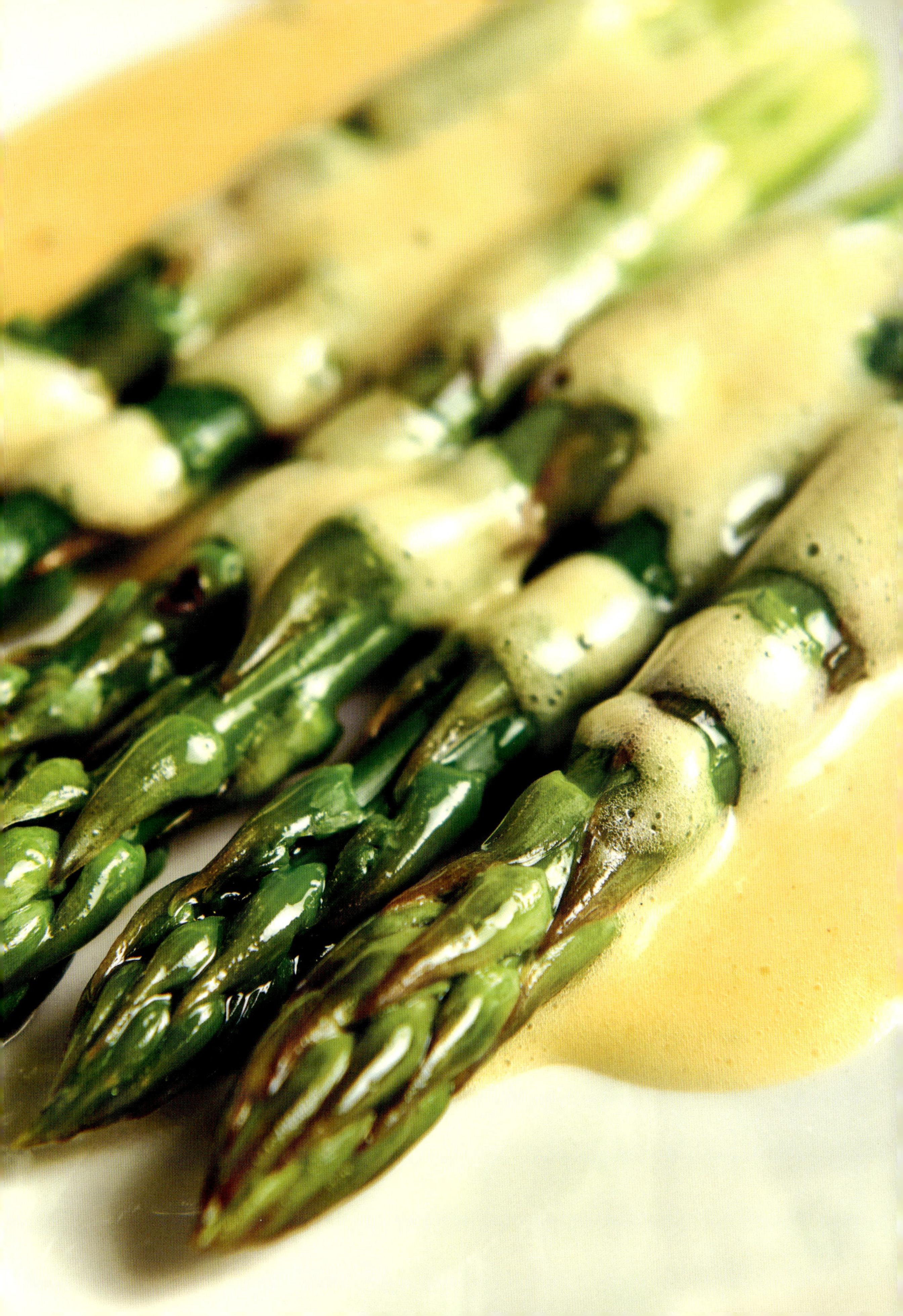

Mayonnaise

INGREDIENTS:
Makes 300ml

3 large free range egg yolks
pinch of salt
15g English mustard
20ml white wine vinegar
225ml rapeseed oil

METHOD:

Place the egg yolks, salt, mustard and white wine vinegar into a large mixing bowl and whisk together.

While whisking, slowly drizzle the rapeseed oil into the mixture until you have a mayonnaise consistency.

Cover the bowl with cling film and refrigerate until needed.

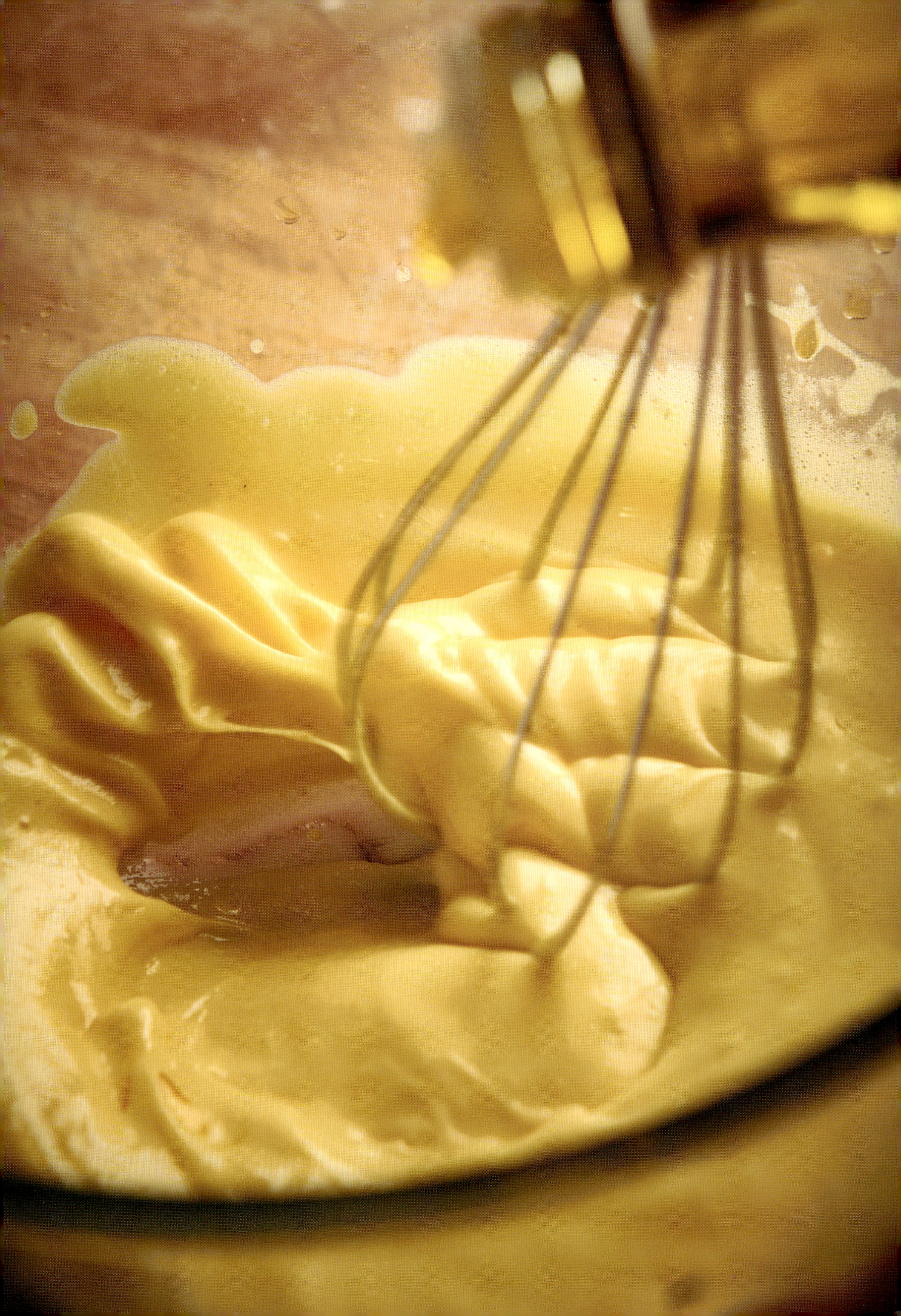

Pastry Cream

INGREDIENTS:
Makes 500ml

350ml whole milk
1 vanilla pod, or 5g vanilla paste
4 large free range egg yolks
65g caster sugar
40g plain flour

METHOD:

Place the milk and the vanilla pod or paste into a pan and bring to the boil.

Place the egg yolks, sugar and flour into a bowl and whisk to a paste consistency.

Strain the milk through a sieve into a pouring jug.

Whisk the hot milk into the paste and return to the pan, stirring continuously until the pastry cream has thickened.

Remove the pastry cream from the pan and place in a bowl. Cool, cover with cling film, and refrigerate until needed.

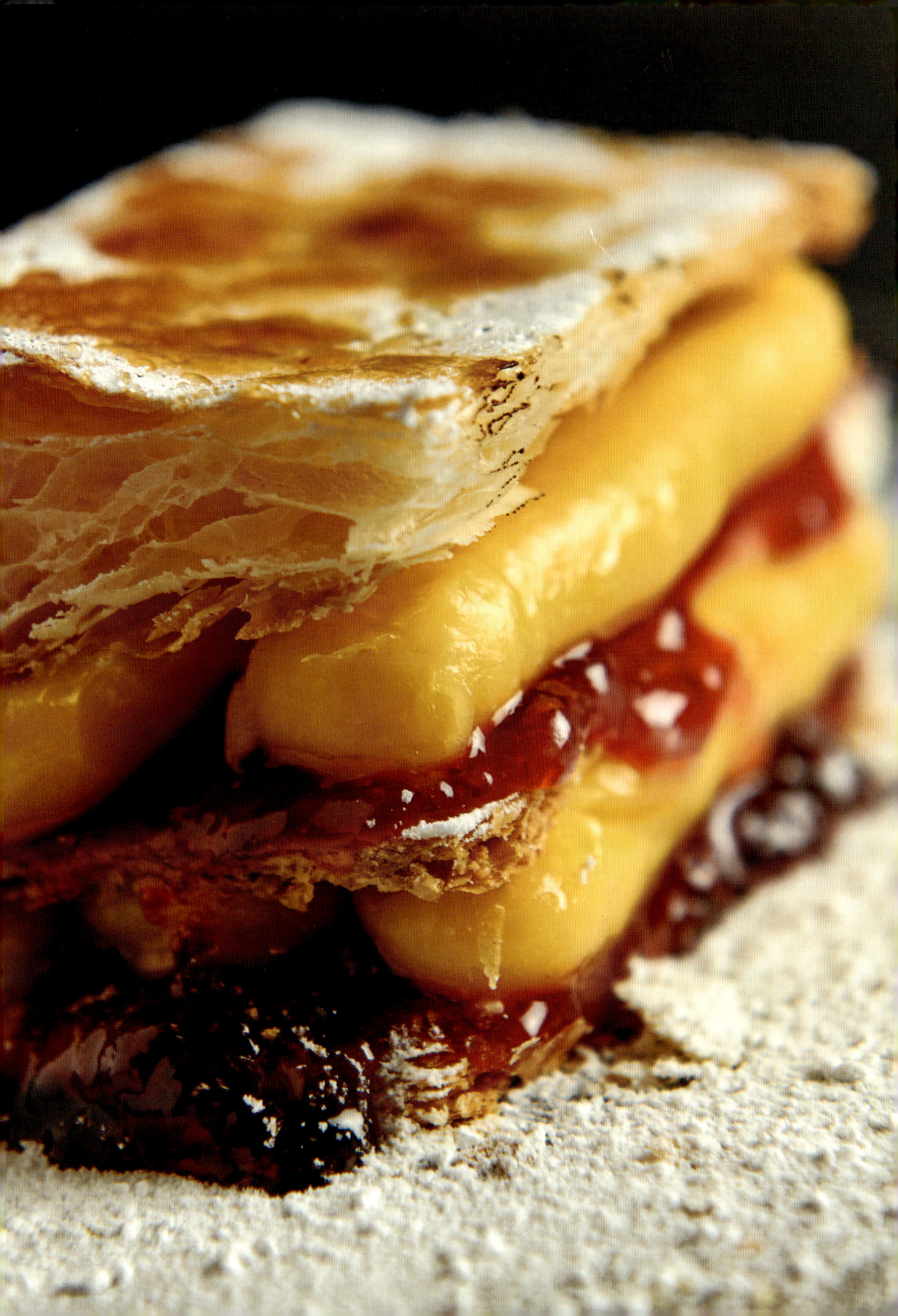

Vanilla Custard

INGREDIENTS:
Makes 600ml

500ml whole milk
1 vanilla pod and seeds, or 5g vanilla paste
6 free range egg yolks
30g caster sugar
30g cornflour

METHOD:

Place the milk in a thick-bottomed pan with the vanilla pod or paste and warm gently until almost boiling.

Place the egg yolks, caster sugar and cornflour in a bowl and whisk to create a paste.

Strain the hot milk through a sieve into a pouring jug. Pour the milk onto the egg paste, whisking continuously.

Place everything into a clean pan, re-heat (don't let it boil) and serve.

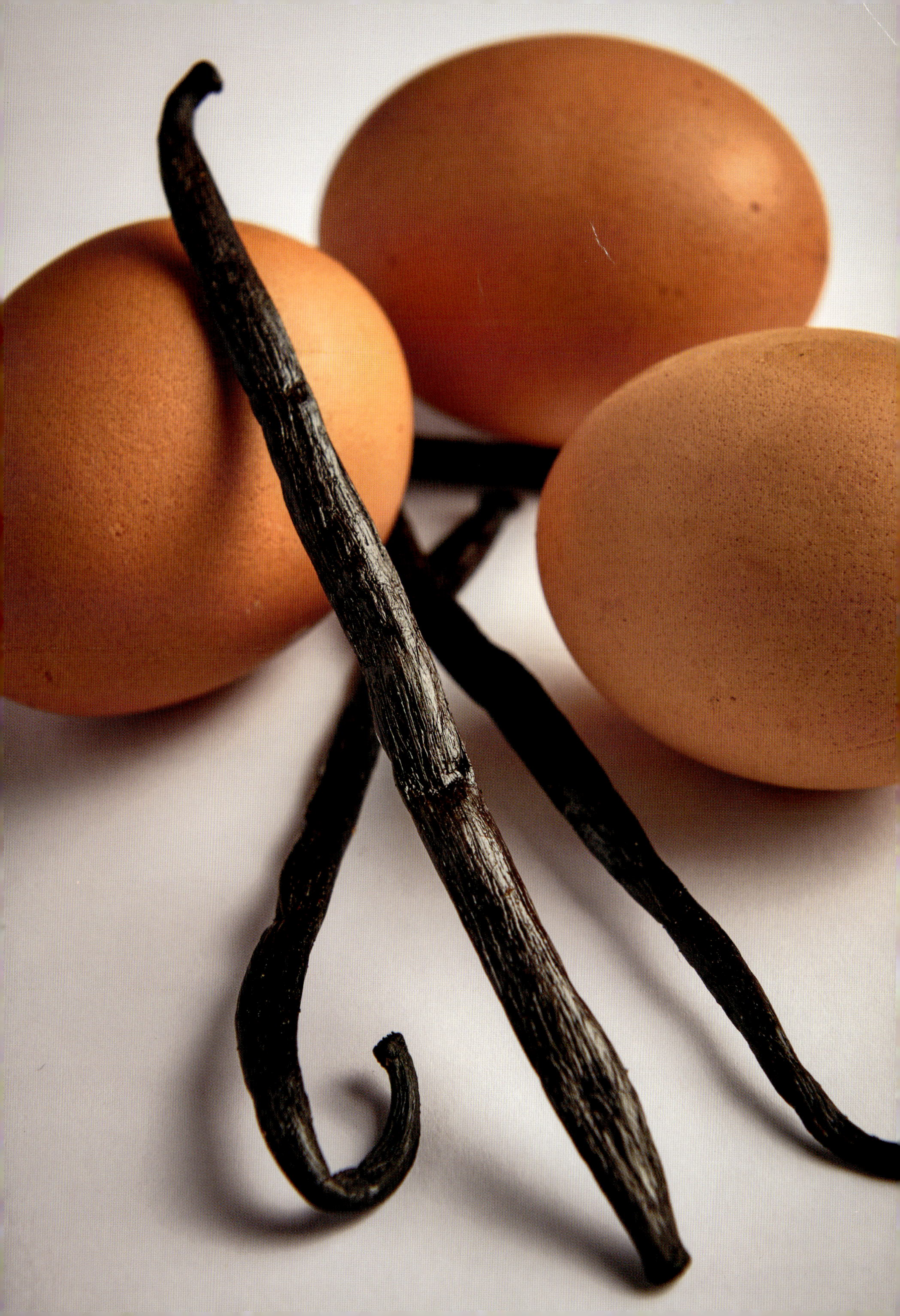

Italian Meringue

INGREDIENTS:
Makes 500g

300g caster sugar
25g glucose
65ml water
10 free range egg whites

METHOD:

Place the caster sugar, glucose and water into a thick-bottomed pan bring to the boil. Using a sugar thermometer allow the syrup to reach 115°C (no higher).

Place the egg whites in a large bowl and whisk until light and fluffy. Continue whisking for 3 minutes.

Slowly and carefully drizzle the hot sugar syrup into the egg whites, whisking continuously. Continue whisking until the meringue is cold. This is now ready to be used.

To finish, bake in the oven at 200°C for 2 minutes or until the meringue is light golden brown.

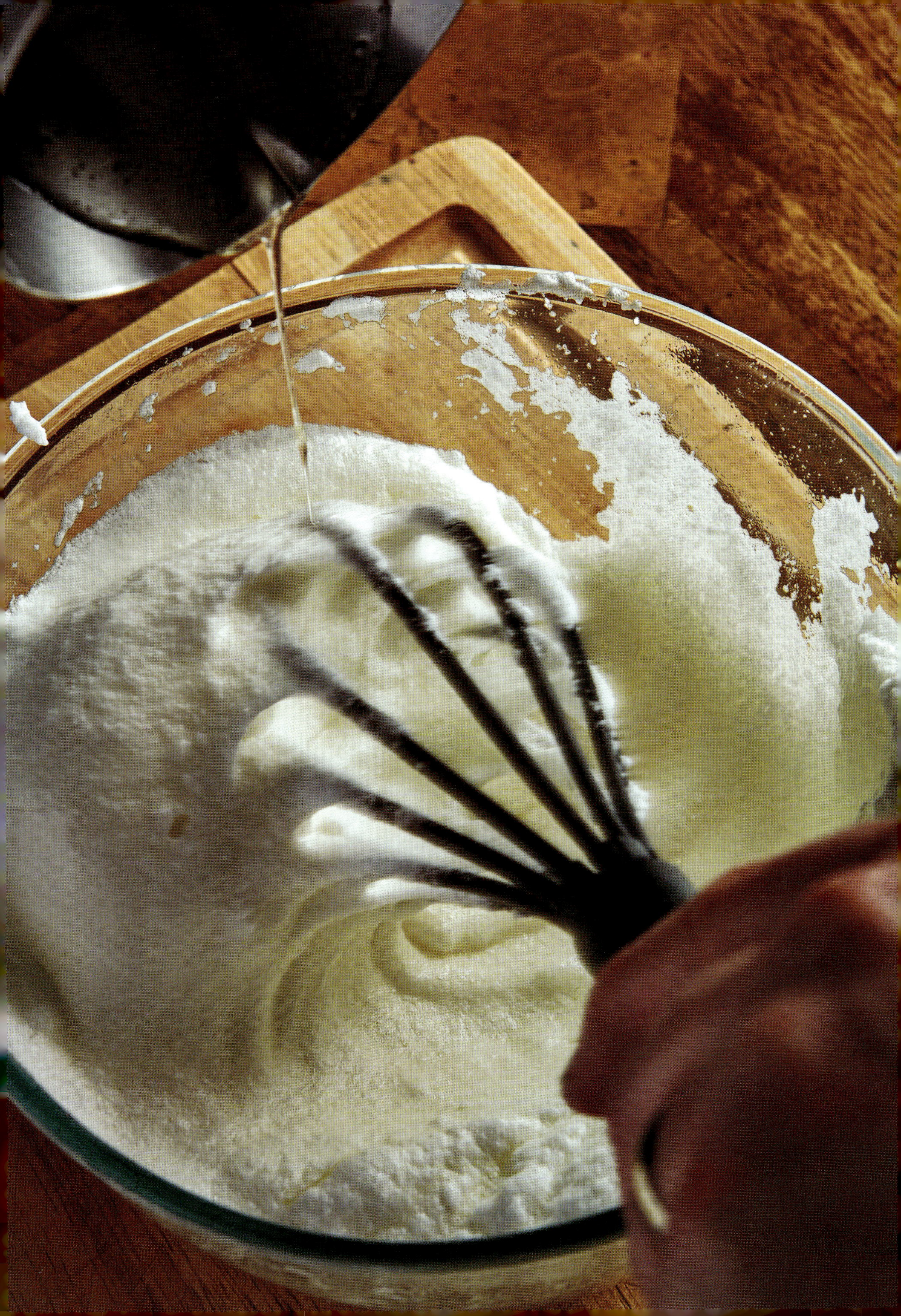

White Bread Rolls

INGREDIENTS:
Makes 12 bread rolls

500g strong white bread flour
3g salt
7g yeast
1g caster sugar
325ml water

METHOD:

Sieve the flour into a large bowl with the salt.

Place the yeast and caster sugar into the water and dissolve.

Make a well in the centre of the flour and pour the yeast liquid into the well. Stir with a butter knife until a firm dough is formed.

Tip the dough onto a floured surface and knead for 3 minutes. Rest until doubled in size (approximately 40 minutes) in a warm room.

Divide the dough into 12 even portions, roll each one by hand to form a round dough ball and place onto a greased baking tray. Leave to double in size again for approximately 30 minutes. Egg wash and sprinkle with seeds if desired.

Bake in the oven at 180°C until the rolls are golden brown and sound hollow when tapped on the bottom.

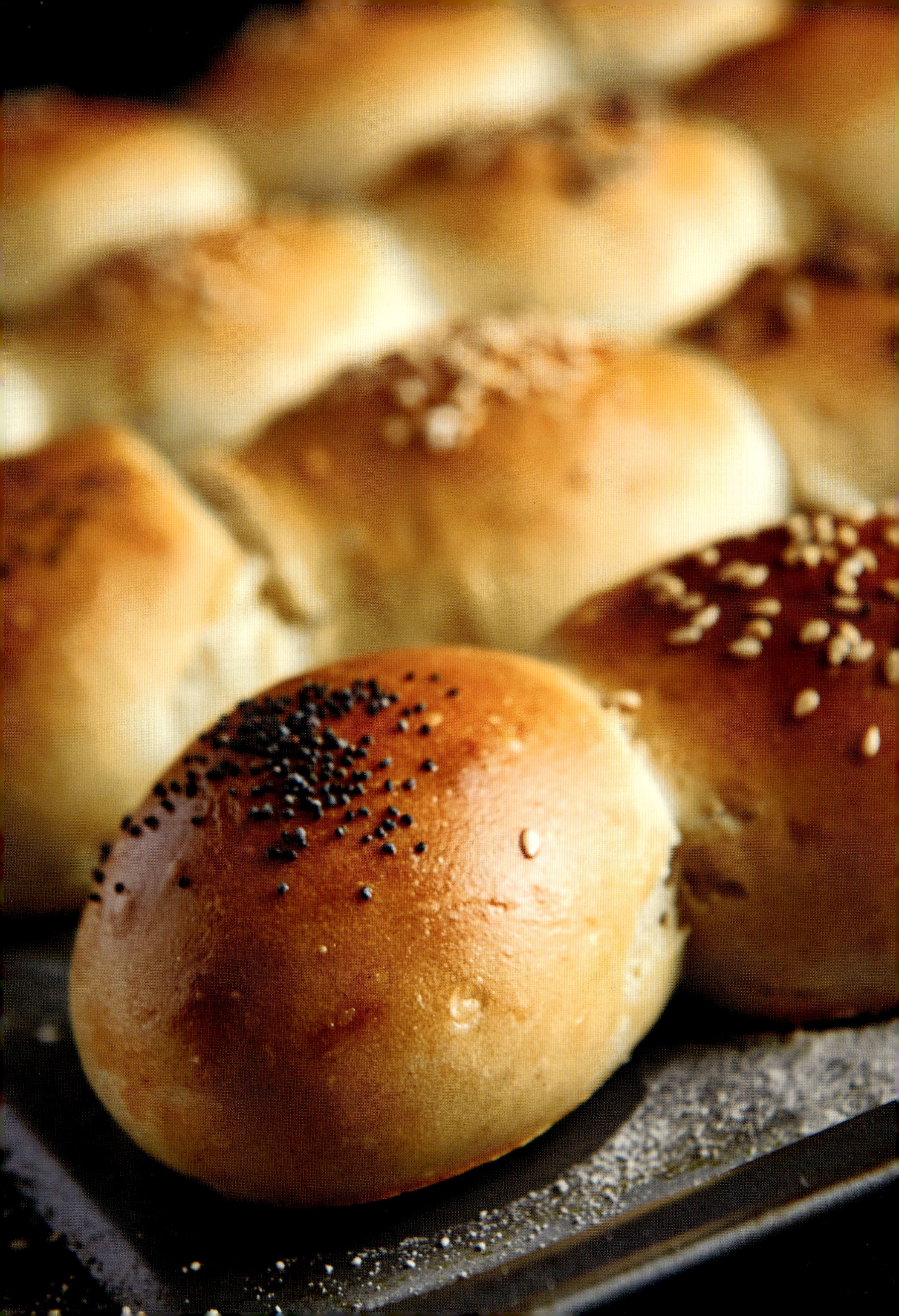

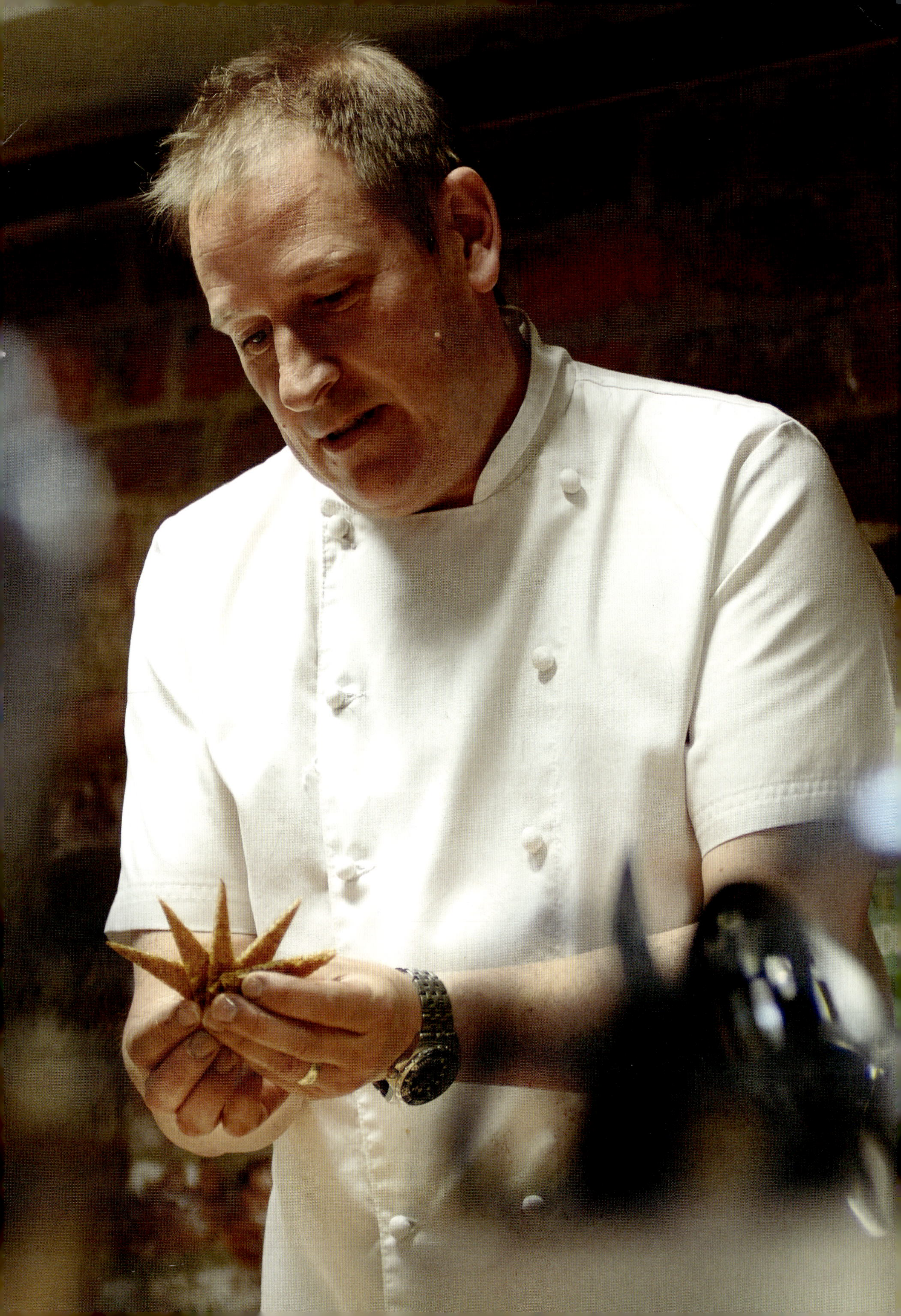

I HOPE YOU'VE ENJOYED SHARING AND COOKING SOME OF MY FAVOURITE RECIPES. WE HAD A BLAST CREATING THE BOOK. TIM, YOU REALLY WORKED YOUR MAGIC WITH YOUR CAMERA!

IT'S ALWAYS GOOD TO HAVE SOMEWHERE TO ADD A FEW EXTRA NOTES IF YOU LIKE TWEAKING THE ODD RECIPE, SO I'VE LEFT YOU A COUPLE OF PAGES TO JOT THEM DOWN, ADD YOUR OWN RECIPES, OR HIDE THE EMERGENCY £20 NOTE FOR A NIGHT OFF FROM THE KITCHEN AND A CHEEKY TAKEAWAY! THERE'S ALSO A QUICK GUIDE TO WEIGHT, TEMPERATURE AND MEASUREMENT CONVERSIONS.

NB.
KITCHEN NOTES

HOW TO COOK

Weights, Temperatures and Measures

WEIGHT CONVERSIONS

1oz	30g
4oz	110g
1lb	450g

FLUID CONVERSIONS

1fl.oz		30ml
5fl.oz	1/4 pint	150ml
20fl.oz	1 pint	600ml

TEMPERATURE CONVERSIONS

130°C	250°F	Gas mark 1
150°C	300°F	Gas mark 2
170°C	325°F	Gas mark 3
180°C	135°F	Gas mark 4
190°C	375°F	Gas mark 5
200°C	400°F	Gas mark 6
220°C	425°F	Gas mark 7
230°C	450°F	Gas mark 8
240°C	475°F	Gas mark 9

SUGAR BOILING GUIDE

EVAPORATION OF WATER — 100°C
Usage: Sugar is dissolved

SMALL THREAD — 102°C
Usage: Used in glazes

LARGE THREAD — 104°C
Usage: Used in preserves

SMALL BALL — 110 - 115°C
Usage: Used for Italian meringue

LARGE BALL — 119 – 122°C
Usage: Used in filled chocolates

LIGHT CRACK — 129°C
Usage: Used in semi-hard boiled sweets

HARD CRACK — 165 –166°C
Usage: Used for butterscotch

LIGHT CARAMEL — 180°C
Usage: Used for cinder toffee

MEDIUM CARAMEL — 180 – 188°C
Usage: Used for caramel creations

STEAK COOKING GUIDE

RARE	52°C
MEDIUM RARE	54°C
MEDIUM	60°C
MEDIUM WELL	65°C
WELL DONE	70°C

Kitchen notes

ON THE NEXT COUPLE OF PAGES YOU'LL FIND SEASONAL PRODUCE FROM FRUITS, VEGETABLES, FISH AND SHELLFISH, MEAT, POULTRY AND GAME TO HELP YOU CREATE THE RECIPES IN THIS BOOK IN THE PERFECT SEASON.

NB.
SEASONAL INGREDIENTS

HOW TO COOK

Spring

FRUIT
Apricot	Rhubarb
Gooseberry	Strawberry
Lemon	

VEGETABLES
Asparagus	Parsnip
Cauliflower	Pepper
Carrot	Peas
Celeriac	Purple sprouting broccoli
Chicory	Radish
Jerusalem artichoke	Sorrel
Lambs lettuce	Spinach
Leek	Spring greens
Lettuce	Watercress
New potatoes	

FISH & SHELLFISH
Cod	Oysters
Crab	Salmon
Halibut	Sea bass
Mussels	

MEAT & POULTRY & GAME
Beef	Pork
Chicken	Veal
Lamb	

Summer

FRUIT
Apricot	Raspberry
Blackberry	Redcurrant
Blueberry	Rhubarb
Gooseberry	Strawberry
Plum	Watermelon

VEGETABLES
Artichoke	New potatoes
Asparagus	Pea
Aubergine	Pepper
Basil	Radish
Beetroot	Samphire
Broad beans	Sorrel
Carrot	Spinach
Cherry	Spring greens
Courgette	Sweetcorn
Fennel	Swiss chard
Garlic	Tomato
Lamb's lettuce	Watercress
Lettuce	Lettuce

FISH & SHELLFISH
Crab	Plaice
Halibut	Salmon
Lobster	Tuna

MEAT & POULTRY & GAME
Beef	Lamb
Chicken	Pork

Autumn

FRUIT
Apple
Apricot
Blackcurrant
Blueberry
Damson
Fig
Gooseberry
Peach
Pear
Plum
Raspberry
Redcurrant
Strawberry
Watermelon

VEGETABLES
Artichoke
Aubergine
Basil
Beetroot
Broadbean
Broccoli
Brussels sprouts
Cabbage
Carrot
Celeriac
Celery
Courgette
Cranberry
Garlic
Fennel
Kale
Lamb's lettuce
Leek
Lettuce
Parsnip
Pea
Pepper
Potato
Pumpkin
Quince
Radish
Salsify
Samphire
Sorrel
Spinach
Sweetcorn
Sweet potatoes
Swede
Swiss chard
Tomato
Turnip
Watercress

FISH & SHELLFISH
Crab
Lobster
Halibut
Mussels
Oysters
Salmon
Scallops
Tuna

MEAT, POULTRY & GAME
Beef
Duck
Goose
Grouse
Guinea Fowl
Lamb
Mutton
Pork
Rabbit

Winter

FRUIT
Apple
Date
Lemon
Pear
Rhubarb

VEGETABLES
Broccoli
Brussels Sprouts
Carrot
Cauliflower
Celeriac
Celery
Chestnut
Chicory
Jerusalem artichoke
Kale
Leek
Salsify
Swede
Sweet Potatoes
Turnip
Parsnip
Pepper
Potato
Purple sprouting broccoli

FISH & SHELLFISH
Cod
Halibut
Mussels
Oysters
Salmon
Sea bass

MEAT, POULTRY & GAME
Duck
Goose
Hare
Partridge
Pheasant
Turkey
Venison
Woodcock

NB.
RECIPE INDEX
HOW TO COOK

PÂTÉS & TERRINES
CHAPTER 1.24

Pâtés

CHICKEN LIVER PÂTÉ.26
DUCK LIVER PÂTÉ.28
MUSHROOM PÂTÉ.30

Terrines

CHICKEN AND HAM TERRINE.32
GAME TERRINE.34
SMOKED SALMON, CRAB AND WATERCRESS TERRINE.36

FISH & SHELLFISH
CHAPTER 2.38

Fish

OMELETTE ARNOLD BENNETT.40
PAN-FRIED SEA BASS WITH BEURRE NOISETTE.42
POACHED FILLET OF PLAICE VERONIQUE.44
POACHED FILLET OF SALMON WITH MUSHROOM REDUCTION SAUCE.46
SMOKED MACKEREL FISHCAKES.48

Shellfish

BROWN CRAB ON TOAST.50
BRIDLINGTON BAY DRESSED BROWN CRAB.52
HOT LOBSTER SALAD.54
LOBSTER THERMIDOR.56
SEARED SCALLOPS WITH ASPARAGUS SPEARS AND SAFFRON SAUCE.58

MEAT, POULTRY & GAME
CHAPTER 3.60

Meat

BEEF STROGANOFF.62
BRAISED LAMB SHANKS IN RED WINE.64
BRAISED STEAK IN BEER.66
PORK AND LEEK SAUSAGES.68
SLOW-ROASTED BELLY PORK WITH SAGE, ONION AND APPLE TART.70
SLOW-ROASTED LEG OF LAMB.72

Poultry

CHICKEN CHASSEUR.74
WHOLE ROAST CHICKEN.76

Game

POT ROAST PHEASANT WITH BEETROOT AND CORN FRITTERS.78
VENISON STEAK WITH STILTON AND PEAS.80

SAVOURY PUDDINGS, PIES & CASSEROLES
CHAPTER 4.82

Savoury Puddings

STEAK AND KIDNEY PUDDING.84
YORKSHIRE PUDDING.86

Pies

CHICKEN AND LEEK PIE.88
PORK PIE.90

Casseroles

BEEF BOURGUIGNON.92
LAMB HOTPOT.94

NICELY SPICY
CHAPTER 5.96

EGG FRIED RICE.98
JALFREZI CHICKEN.100
NAAN BREAD.102
STIR FRIED GINGER BEEF.104
SWEET AND SOUR PORK.106

PIZZA & PASTA
CHAPTER 6.108

Pizza

PIZZA DOUGH.110
MOZZARELLA, PARMA HAM AND OLIVE PIZZA.112

Pasta

PASTA DOUGH.114
SALMON RAVIOLI WITH TOMATO AND DILL DRESSING.116
SMOKED HAM AND MUSHROOM TAGLIATELLE.118

JUST DESSERTS
CHAPTER 7.120

BREAD AND BUTTER PUDDING.122
CHOCOLATE FONDANT PUDDING.124
CRÈME CARAMEL WITH CARAMELISED ORANGES.126
PASSION FRUIT SOUFFLÉ.128
STICKY TOFFEE PUDDING WITH SALTED CARAMEL SAUCE.130

CHOCOLATE & SUGAR WORK
CHAPTER 8.132

Chocolate

23CT GOLD CHOCOLATE CHAMPAGNE TRUFFLES.134
CHOCOLATE MACAROONS.136
FLORENTINES.138
HAZELNUT PRALINES.140

Sugar Work

CARAMEL CREATIONS.142
RICH BUTTER FUDGE.144

BREADS & SWEET DOUGHS
CHAPTER 9.146

Breads

BRIOCHE.148
TOMATO AND PARMESAN CIABATTA.150

Sweet Doughs

DEVONSHIRE SPLITS.152
DOUGHNUTS.154
HOT CROSS BUNS.156

SOMETHING FOR THE WEEKEND
CHAPTER 10.158

BLINIS AND BELUGA CAVIAR.160
CROQUE MONSIEUR.162
EGGS BENEDICT.164
FILLET STEAK WITH QUAIL EGGS AND BLACK SUMMER TRUFFLES.166
WELSH RAREBIT.168

SEASONAL FAVOURITES
CHAPTER 11.170

Spring

ASPARAGUS TART WITH HOLLANDAISE SAUCE.172
RHUBARB, GINGER AND TEA TIRAMISU.174

Summer

CHICKEN AND BACON CLUB SANDWICH.176
SPICED SUMMER BERRY PUDDING.178

Autumn

BAKED SALMON COULIBIAC.180
PEAR BELLE HÉLÈNE.182

Winter

BEEF STEW AND DUMPLINGS.184
BAKED APPLE AND ALMOND TART.186

AFTERNOON TEA
CHAPTER 12.188

CHOCOLATE ÉCLAIRS.190
FRUIT BARQUETTES.192
LEMON TART.194
RICH PORT FRUIT CAKE.196
SCONES.198
STRAWBERRY CHOUX SWANS.200

ULTIMATE DINNER
CHAPTER 13.202

SMOKED HADDOCK & GRUYÈRE CHEESE TARTS.204
HAM HOCK TERRINE.206
LOBSTER BISQUE WITH STEAMED MUSSELS.208
BEEF WELLINGTON.210
CRÈME BRÛLÉE.212

THE BASICS
CHAPTER 14.214

Stocks

BEEF STOCK.216
CHICKEN STOCK.218
FISH STOCK.220

Pastry

CHOUX PASTRY.222
HOT WATER PASTRY.224
PUFF PASTRY.226
SHORTCRUST PASTRY.228
SUET PASTRY.230
SWEET PASTRY.232

Sauces

BÉCHAMEL SAUCE.234
CHICKEN VELOUTÉ SAUCE.236
ESPAÑOLA SAUCE.238
HOLLANDAISE SAUCE.240
MAYONNAISE.242
PASTRY CREAM.244
VANILLA CUSTARD.246

Bakery

ITALIAN MERINGUE.248
WHITE BREAD ROLLS.250

NIGEL BROWN

Nigel was born in Bridlington, the youngest son of parents who have spent a lifetime in the hotel and catering industry. It is not surprising that Nigel, having grown up in this environment, should follow in their footsteps.

During his career Nigel has worked at some of the UK's biggest and busiest hotels, and competed in national competitions including the London Hotelympia Salon Culinaire and Forte's Chef of the Year. He's spent time at the highly acclaimed French cookery school Ecole Lenôtre where he picked up a wealth of experience and knowledge in areas of specialist patisserie work.

As well as running his own cookery school, Nigel has been a guest chef at the world famous Novelli Academy, and regularly demonstrates at food festivals and events throughout the UK.

This book brings together 100 classic recipes from the renowned cookery school. Nigel's style, and ability to create recipes from the most basic to the very complex and demanding, is unique.

Nigel's written the recipes so that they can be recreated by everybody from novice cooks to accomplished chefs, stripping them of all the professional terminology that can often put people off.

This is a truly unique and very accessible book for all to read and cook from with confidence.

TIM GREEN

After studying photography at Batley School of Art and Design, West Yorkshire-based photographer Tim Green's journey took him to work in one of Leed's biggest photographic studios working for a range of commercial clients from Asda to British Gas.

Many years later, whilst working for himself, he met Tim Bilton of The Spiced Pear, who asked him to do the photography for his first cookbook, his road to becoming a specialist editorial and cookbook photographer began.

Tim has worked with a host of culinary greats, such as Jean-Christophe Novelli, Stephen Terry, Will Holland and Adam Handling. He is currently working on books with Daniel Clifford and Colin McGurran.

Tim is proud to add Nigel to that list: his attention to detail in his recipes is second to none, making this a book to reach for when you need culinary inspiration.